i

THE
MARTIN FAMILY HISTORY
VOLUME I

HUGH MARTIN

(1698 – 1761)

Of
County Tyrone, Northern Ireland
&
Hunterdon County, New Jersey

His parents, siblings and descendants

"Go traveler, and imitate his virtues"

Francie Lane
392 Gabriel Avenue
Yuba City, CA 95993

ISBN# 978-1-304-80264-4

Copyright © 2014 Francie Lane. All rights reserved.

No part of this book may be reproduced or transmitted in any form or by any means, electronic or mechanical, microfilming and recording, or by any information storage and retrieval systems without permission in writing from the author.

Dedicated to my dear husband Pat

for his many years of love, patience and understanding ~

Here lies the remains of
Hugh Martin
who lived in this vicinity many years during which
possessing the confidence of his government
and his fellow-citizens
he discharged the duties of several offices
of profit and trust with integrity and honesty.
In the practice of the private and
public virtues, eminent;
as husband, father, relative, and friend, beloved;
as a magistrate, revered.
To religion a support, to science a patron,
and
to the poor, a friend.
He was born in Ireland, County Tyrone,
and
died March 7th, Anno Dom. 1761, aged 63 years.

Let sculptured marble vainly boast,
And birth and titles scan;
God's noblest work, of value most,
Here lies an honest man.
'His weeping sons in North Carolina
pay this tribute to his memory.

Go, traveler, and imitate his virtues.

[Transcription of Hugh Martin's gravestone, Hunterdon Co., NJ]

CONTENTS

	Page
Preface	x
Prologue	xiii

Chapter 1   **ALEXANDER MARTIN** (c1670 – c1723) 1

Chapter 2   **WILLIAM MARTIN** (c1695 – c1776) 11

Chapter 3   **JAMES MARTIN** (c1696 – 1761) 14
　　　　　　His children: James Martin, Jr., Lt. William Martin,
　　　　　　　　Martha Martin, Mary Martin and
　　　　　　　　Rachel [Martin] Johnston

Chapter 4   **HUGH MARTIN** (1698 – 1761) 26
　　　　　　His child: Rev. Thomas Martin (Chapter 10)
　　　　　　(The following children will be featured in
　　　　　　subsequent volumes):
　　　　　　North Carolina Governor Alexander Martin
　　　　　　Col. James Martin
　　　　　　Martha [Martin] Rogers (Mrs. Samuel Rogers)
　　　　　　Col. Samuel Martin
　　　　　　Robert Martin, Sr.
　　　　　　Jane [Martin] Henderson (Mrs. Thomas Henderson)

Chapter 5   **THOMAS MARTIN** (1708 – 1760) 69
　　　　　　His child: Daniel Martin (1753-1801)
　　　　　　　　Daniel's children: Mary Martin, Frances Martin,
　　　　　　　　　　Thomas Martin, Ann [Martin] Mitchel,
　　　　　　　　　　William Murray Martin, Daniel Martin, Jr.
　　　　　　　　　　and Charles Alexander Martin

Chapter 6   **ROBERT MARTIN** (1710 – 1776) 132

Chapter 7	**AGNES [MARTIN] DAWSON** (1712-1787).... 141	

Her children: Esther [Dawson] Blackfan,
    Rachel Dawson, and Sarah [Dawson] Smith.

Chapter 8   **ESTHER [MARTIN] MASON** (1718-c1791) ... 156

Her children: Thomas Mason, Lydia Mason,
    Henry Mason, Mary [Mason] Middaugh,
    Martha [Mason] White, and William Mason.

Chapter 9   **Rev. HENRY MARTIN** (1720 – 1764) 169

Chapter 10   **Rev. THOMAS MARTIN** (1743 – 1770).........185

Index 202

Preface and Acknowledgement

I began the search for my Martin family ancestry in 1991, having only my Mother's copy of the original Last Will & Testament of Alexander S. Martin, written in Holmes Co., Mississippi, on March 8, 1860. I knew that my maternal Grandfather, Boyd Kelley Andrews had been born in 1884, Holmes Co., MS; his father had been Alexander Samuel Andrews; and his grandparents had been Calvin J. Andrews and wife Mary S. [Martin]. Mary S. Andrews was named as a daughter in the 1860 Will of Alexander S. Martin. The only bit of family lore concerning the Martins was that someone in this lineage had been "a Governor of some state". With nothing more to go on, I followed up on a clue in the Will, which named two married daughters as 1860 residents of Rockingham Co., NC. I resolved to visit a Family History Center Library to see what I could find on these two daughters, Mrs. Sarah F. Cardwell and Mrs. Elizabeth Allen – as well as any other Martins in Rockingham Co. Reading through the microfilmed Rockingham Co. Will Book, I found the 1807 Will for Governor Alexander Martin, and the bequests to his son, Alexander Strong Martin. Indeed, I had found my "roots", and commenced a twenty-year-long search for my Martin family.

I rarely enjoy reading a genealogy book filled with merely names and dates. I want to know who my ancestors were, how they lived their lives through love and grief, set in the historical context of their era. Yes, detail, detail, detail ... and I readily confess to being overly consumed with minutia.

I cannot begin to acknowledge all the assistance I've had along the way from friends and cousins, such as Linda Vernon, Jeanie Zadach, James R. Rolff and Josiah Mason. My early encouragement came from my Mother and sister Donna Taylor, who both enthusiastically read about my discoveries. About twelve years ago, I made the acquaintance of Charles D. Rodenbough, who was in the process of writing a book on the public life of Gov. Martin, *"Governor Alexander Martin – Biography of a North Carolina Revolutionary War Statesman"*. I was thrilled that at long last there would be a biography on Gov. Martin; however, I knew Mr. Rodenbough's book could not realistically extend to include Gov. Martin's personal life, nor his siblings, parents, aunts and uncles, who were, incredibly, as complex and interesting as Gov. Martin, himself. When I met brothers Thomas and Robert Upshur, descendants of Col. James Martin, who shared with me copies of Martin family treasures saved by generations of their direct ancestors, I came to the realization that I had accumulated more Martin family information than any one person has ever seen, and that I had a responsibility to compile all into a book. In December, 2010, I was contacted by Dr. Linda Peacock, a descendant of Jane [Martin] Henderson, who convinced me I should expand my research on the Henderson branch. With Linda's able assistance, I soon realized that little factual information had previously been known of Jane [Martin] & Thomas Henderson. I feel Martin descendants will become as absorbed with the Henderson family as the Martin family history.

This book will not be the most scholarly book you will ever read. Certainly, I've never envisioned a New York Times "Top Ten". I research for the enjoyment of discovering a new facet of my family's past. Publishing a book on the family was actually an afterthought. I would hope the readers will find the Martin family as fascinating as I have – whether the readers be Martin descendants or people interested in the history of the various locales.

This book will soon be available for purchase in paperback and an e-book version, but for those interested in having a more permanent edition for their library, I have arranged for this hardcover edition. Please contact me directly for further information. I shall soon publish Volume II, which will comprise two of Hugh & Jane [Hunter] Martin children; i.e., Col. James Martin, his known descendants; and Martha [Martin] Rogers with her known descendants.

Col. James Martin penned the following "family history" in the latter years of his life, c1830, which served as an outline for my research. Without Col. James' narrative, there would be no way to know, for instance, that his grandfather had been Alexander Martin, who immigrated to America from Co. Tyrone, N. Ireland, or that his aunt had been Agnes [Martin] Dawson of Bucks Co., PA. Thus with profound gratitude to all my family and friends – as well as my Martin ancestors - this first volume in my series of five, will begin with Col. James' narrative:

Prologue

A HISTORY OF THE MARTIN FAMILIES

AS RELATED BY TRADITION FROM ONE GENERATION TO ANOTHER

By
JAMES MARTIN OF SNOW CREEK

My father, Hugh Martin, was born in the Kingdom of Ireland, and County of Tyrone, near a small town called Inniskilling, about the year of 1700. He was the eldest of a second marriage. His father's name was Alexander. My grandfather, the latter, was a leading Elder in the Presbyterian Church near where he lived, and was very much respected. Though not rich, he lived far from want. He married my grandmother, whose name was Coughran of a family of equal respectability with his own, and was said to be very comely and handsome featured, as the most of her descendants have been since they have come to maturity.

When my father came to years of discretion, my grandfather sent him to explore America and inform him if it would suit to move there with his family. My father accordingly visited this country and landed at New Castle about two year after, <there seems to be a sentence missing here referencing the arrival of the grandfather> but the poor man took sick and died soon after he landed. His family then consisted of my grandmother (whose name was Martha) two daughters, named Agnes and Esther, and four sons. After the death of my grandfather, my grandmother moved where my father and his three brothers, Thomas, Robert and Henry then lived.

My father said he kept an English school for a year or two before he married. My mother's family, the Hunters, had not come to this country. My father's and mother's families had never seen or heard of each other in Ireland.

My Uncle Robert kept a school for several years, and my Uncle Thomas had learned the stone-mason's trade, and they both by their industry made a considerable property. My Aunt Agnes married a Quaker by the name of Dawson, a respectable farmer who lived near Carroll's Ferry on the Delaware in Pennsylvania, and their descendants may be living there still. They had no sons. My Aunt Esther married Francis Mason, a farmer who lived in the forks of the Delaware. They reared three or four strong athletic sons as any to be found anywhere. My grandmother, Martha, went to live and died with my Aunt Mason, aged upwards of seventy years.

Now to say something of my mother's family. They came to Ireland two or three years after my father's family. They lived in the County of Antrim, the principal town of which is Belfast. They, too, after landing at New Castle on the Delaware, came up to New Jersey, where my father first saw my mother. He, by this time (as I have heard him say) had got to be a pretty old bachelor about forty. My mother was then about eighteen. They soon made a match. She was very handsome. My father had bought a plantation in the township of Amwell in Hunterdon County, where my brother, Alexander, was born. I have heard my mother say he never spoke a word until he was four years old; but he learned to speak well enough afterwards.

I forgot to say that my Uncle Henry, after he came to my father's, signified he wished to have some college education, that he might study divinity and fit himself for the University. Not having funds of his own, my father and his other brothers, Thomas and Robert, contributed each their share, and sent him to Newark College. He learned very well and was soon prepared to take Holy Orders. He got a congregation in Harvey's, Pennsylvania, and was doing very well. Previous to this, he was the cause of father's sending my brother, Alexander, to the same college, which was before it was moved to

Princeton, where he learned very well, and in due time, graduated.

But to account more of my Uncle Henry. He married a respectable and much beloved lady about two years afterwards. He was in health when he went to bed, and lying long in the morning, his servant went to call him to breakfast, and found him dead. His wife had died some time before so he was alone when it happened. He was well proportioned and handsome featured. He was to go frequently to preach in Philadelphia, where the ladies used to call him the handsome minister.

Now to say more of my mother's family. They emigrated from Scotland to the north of Ireland and lived in the county of Antrim. My two uncles, John and Alexander Hunter, with my mother, were all that came to this country. John Hunter, the eldest, moved to Buckingham County, Virginia and after a few years, acquired considerable property. He then moved to Dan River near Eagle Falls in Rockingham County, North Carolina, where he died.

My Uncle Alexander Hunter moved and settled in the forks of the Delaware, six miles above Easton. The Indians were then thickly planted with their wigwams over the country, and were very troublesome though not at open war. My Uncle Alexander being a very strong, stout, athletic man, was the only one in that part, who could keep them in order. As to ability of body, he was said to have excelled all others anywhere to be found in the country, for the Indians went all over the nation and country to get someone who would be able to foil him in wrestling. Several trials of strength were made, but they all proved abortive. At length the Indians gave up, and always behaved in a very submissive manner when he was in their company, and would have no more to do with him. He afterwards, moved to Bedford or Buckingham County, Virginia, where he died. He was the father of Colonel James Hunter of Beaver Island, Rockingham County.

My Uncle left a sister in Scotland, when he emigrated to Ireland. I have forgotten her name. She married a man named

Lunman. I have not heard from her in a long time. This is all I can recollect from my Mother's family.

Now I must recount more of my grandmother's family in Ireland, as related to me by my half-uncle, James Martin, for whom I am named. He lived in two miles of my father in Jersey on the South Branch of the Raritan River. He said that my grandfather had another son by his first marriage, whose name was William. He emigrated to South Carolina to a place called Pou Pou, on the Edisto River. My brother, Alexander, at the beginning of the Revolutionary War, having command of a regiment, was ordered to South Carolina to suppress a number of Tories, who were headed by one of their leaders called Scofield. They were called Scofieldites. On his route he came to the neighborhood of Pou Pou, and enquired if anyone of the name Martin lived there. They told him that there had, but they had all died but the daughters, and they had married, so the name of Martin was lost as far as that branch of the family was concerned. I have heard nothing since.

My half-uncle, James Martin, who lived near us was married to Annie Drummond, daughter of James Drummond, Governor of New Jersey. He kept a large shoemaker shop. He had a great many apprentices, and it is said, made a good deal of profit by it. He had two sons, James and William and several daughters, Patsy, Polly, and Rachel. All married before I left New Jersey. James and William lived at home in 1774, and William got a Lieutenancy in the army, and being ordered to go in advance guard against a part of the British army, he and his party were beaten, and he was cruelly murdered in a shocking manner, was pierced by a number of bayonets which drew the attention of General Washington, who sent his body to the British commander under a flag of truce, but he had the excuse to say that he was obstinate, and would not give or ask for quarter. The old man and his wife died before I left New Jersey.

(By tradition as my grandfather told my Uncle James Martin.)"

[Note: Col. James Martin was indicating that his Grandfather, Alexander Martin told this family history to Col. James' Uncle, James Martin, Sr.]

I received a copy of Col. James' narrative from Robert I. Upshur, whose copy included the following notation: "This History of His Martin and Hunter Families was written by Col. James Martin of Snow Creek, Stokes Co., North Carolina .... passed to his son, Edmund Loftin Martin, I, whose wife was Hartie Williams, passed by him to his son, Edmund Loftin Martin and whose wife was Mrs. Martha D. Foy Martin, passed by him to their only child (to live) Sadie Estes Martin who married Benj. Robert Wall, passed by her April 1931 to Nancy Goodburn Watkins to be copied and returned to said Sadie Martin Wall.

I also received a copy of the narrative from Charles Rodenbough January 16, 1999, in which he noted:

"Francie, I was given this copy by Lenora Wall Sutton."

CHAPTER ONE

ALEXANDER MARTIN
(c1670-c1723)

Alexander Martin was born in either Scotland or Northern Ireland about 1670. It has been speculated that he was the son of a William Martin, and grandson of John Martin, although no actual proof of Alexander's lineage is known to exist. Alexander's grandson, Col. James Martin, b. 1742, of Stokes Co., NC, wrote a brief family history prior to 1834. Col. Martin recalled that his grandfather Alexander Martin had resided near a small town called "Inniskilling", County Tyrone, in the Kingdom of Ireland.

There has never been a town named "Inniskilling" in Co. Tyrone; however, Enniskillen is an ancient fortress town and county seat of Co. Fermanagh. Enniskillen has never been within the border of Co. Tyrone. Col. Martin's recollection, if taken literally, probably means that the family's farm was located in Co. Tyrone, near the border of County Fermanagh, with the nearest market/trading center being Enniskillen.

During a vacation to Ireland in 1998, my husband & I spent three days in Dungannon, Co. Tyrone, attempting to find records of the Martin family, to no avail. All of the civil records and church registers of Co. Tyrone are held under the auspices of the family research center, called "Irish World Heritage Center", located at the "top end" of the charming town square in Dungannon. The following are my notes:

The consultant was very helpful and patient, but unfortunately, the years during which my Martins would have resided in Co. Tyrone, were the period when records are extremely scarce. The absentee landowners would generally remain in England or Scotland; would lease property to settlers willing to come to Co. Tyrone or Fermanagh to farm and establish plantations, beginning in 1612-1613. Some settlers, of course, could have owned their property, but no property records exist in Tyrone. There are possibly records existing in Great Britain, kept of renters that might indicate where the renter originated. There is no particular area of Scotland or England that would narrow one's search for such records. England did not permit the Catholic Church or Presbyterian Church to keep records for births or burials until the 1800's. The Church of Ireland has been reluctant in making their records available, but may begin computerizing them in Belfast in a few years. Out of 42 "known" parishes in Co. Tyrone, only one remains, and likewise, only one in Co. Fermanagh, which would be Enniskillen. Co. Tyrone's borders were established in early 1600's, and have remained firm to the present day. Irish World has computerized gravestones, but if searching for early 1700's, the stones would no longer have been legible to transcribe. Most of the early records were burned in an 1822 fire, and parishes rarely had kept a local copy. Usually those families who settled from Scotland were given very low rents to attract them. The younger generation, who moved away, left their elders behind. When these elders died, there were no family members left to erect a tombstone; therefore, many graves were never marked with headstones.

The only two "Martin" records that exist for the region are:

William Martin, age 14, who died in mid 1700's.
John Martin, age <illegible>, died 12 February 1729 in Co.
    Fermanagh – Derryvaulm.

I inquired about a record I had found in the Kilmore Diocesan Wills; i.e., James Coughran – Will date: 1764; died / probate: 1768, a farmer of "Lisnageer".

The consultant stated Kilmore Diocese extended to Counties Armagh, Tyrone, and Fermanagh, and said Lisnageer was no doubt in Co. Cavan. When I returned to the hotel, reception said "Lisnagleer" was north of Dungannon and south of Cookstown, and thus, in Co. Tyrone. I did not think it worthwhile to visit Lisnagleer, because if there had been records – they would have been available at the Irish Heritage center. We left Co. Tyrone after having spent three days, coming no closer to finding the Martin's Scottish origins. The suggestion given me by the consultant was to commence a study of the landlords, who resided in England or Scotland, in hopes of finding business records that might mention a lease or payment of rent by Alexander Martin. That seems a daunting task, not having a clue regarding the landlord's name or location. Even if successful, a mere mention of a lease to Alexander Martin would hardly include the names of his siblings, parents, etc.

Without benefit of baptismal, marriage or death records from an Irish church, it would seem we must be content with Alexander Martin, being our earliest known Martin ancestor. Undoubtedly, Alexander was the first of this line to immigrate to America. The side trip to Co. Tyrone was not in vain, however, as we thoroughly enjoyed the beauty of the countryside dotted with prosperous farms and town homes. Dungannon, itself, was a lovely town and all the people we met were friendly – as opposed to the negative feelings we had while driving through nearby Cookstown.

Since my trip to Ireland, I was fortunate to make the acquaintance of Josiah L. Mason of Ashland, OH, a descendant of Esther [Martin] Mason, b. c1718, the daughter of Alexander. Mr. Mason had read Mrs. Lucy Henderson Horton's rendition[1] of Col. James Martin's family history; namely, [p. 185] *"Mrs. Ingles says from early records handed down in a paper written by one James Martin, who was a son of the immigrant, is given the name of Hugh Martin, who came to America at the age of 21. He was born in the county of Tyrone, Ireland, near the town of Tuskilling, about 1700. He was the eldest son by a second marriage of Alexander Martin to Martha Coghran, of Coughran, who came over about 1723, landing at Newcastle, on the Delaware."*

In 1989, Josiah Mason contacted "Ullster Pedigrees"[2], a genealogical research firm in Belfast, N.I., for assistance in finding a freehold/leasehold document in which Alexander Martin had sold his land before departing for the Colonies, etc. Josiah was informed that there was "no town/village/townland anywhere in Ireland

---

[1] "Family History Compiled by Lucy Henderson Horton", 1922
[2] Andrew Davison, Ullster Pedigrees, 14 Hampton Place, King's Bridge, Belfast BT7 3BZ, N.I. Tel: (0232) 642817

named "Tuskilling" or "Coughran". However, there were "sub-denominational proper names" (areas smaller than townlands), which are unlisted by any authority, and even a single field in Ireland could have had its own name. The Belfast genealogist, Andrew Davison, recommended that no further "Martin" research be undertaken, because he believed the chances of success were very limited.

Mr. Davison further opined that because our Martins enjoyed social position and education in the Colonies that it is "indeed suggestive of the fact that they must have been 'of rank' in Ireland, too". The only lead offered was that Mr. Davison had researched Lord Charlemont, discovering in the process, a reference to George Martin of Wiche, Worcestershire, England, who married Alice Caulfield, sister of the 2nd Lord Charlemont, in the early 1600's. George & Alice [Caulfield] Martin's son, John Martin settled in Lurgan, Co. Armagh by the mid 1650's. The town of Lurgan is about 12 miles from the border of Co. Tyrone. Additionally, John Martin's uncle, Lord Charlemont owned lands in both Armagh and Co. Tyrone.

On the premise that Alexander was born c1670, his father must have been an adult in 1666. Whether our family had settled in Ireland as early as 1666 is, of course, debatable. In 1666, the Crown levied a tax on householders on the basis of 2 shillings per hearth.

Mr. Davison stated, "[The 1666 County Tyrone Hearth Money Roll] lists the following Martins: John Martin, p158; John Martin, p263; Paul Martin, p239; John Martine, p260; Thomas Martine, p226."

The County Tyrone Hearth Money Roll from LDS microfilm has been searched, which shows fewer Martins than Mr. Davison had found; however, some pages of the film are not legible, and marked "faded document":

LDS British Film #1279356 – Item 18: Co. Tyrone Hearth Money Roll c1670, poll book 1660, subsidy roll 1665[3]. Undated Hearth Money Roll skin 4:

DUNGANNON BARONY – TYRONE COUNTY:

Belleclog & Artrea Parishes: p. 1
    Mullaghterory: Thomas Dawson
Drumglass Parish: p. 4 - 5
    Duvaheduan: Hugh m'Ilmartin <McIllmartin>
                           James m'Ilmartin
    Crevagh: Willm m'Ilmartin
Derriloran Parish: p. 6 - 7
    Tatnegiltah: Paul Martine
    Dunmor: Hugh oge o'Martian

From the Pool Book of the P'rish of **Doneghkidy: p. 1 - 2
    Gortmeslane: John Martine & wife, servants– 2s 6s
    Lisdoovan: Robert Mortan & wife, yeoman 4s 9s

[Note: **Andrew Davison stated, "….we know that the Donaghedy family, for example, used Christian names later found in use among the North Carolina Martins"].

As they say, "Hope springs eternal", and perhaps a diligent researcher will be able to discover the proof necessary to link our Alexander Martin to the speculative "William Martin, son of John Martin", who might possibly have been "John Martin, the son of George Martin of Wiche, Worcestershire, England".

Col. James related that his Grandfather Alexander Martin was a leading Elder in the Presbyterian Church near where he lived, and was well respected. Alexander was not wealthy, but lived comfortably. The name of Alexander's first wife is unknown, but there were two sons born of that marriage; namely, William Martin and James Martin.

---

[3] LDS British Film #1279356 – Item 18: Microfilm from typescript copy of originals: [19--]. 1 v. Typescript is at the Armagh County Museum, Armagh, N.I.

After the death of his first wife, Alexander remarried to Martha Coughran, said to be from a respectable family, and very "comely and handsome featured". Martha was born in 1679.

I tend to feel that the 1768 Coughran record I found is pertinent to our Martin family. Surely, James Coughran who died in 1768, would not be Martha's father, but it's conceivable that he was her brother. Kilmore was one of 10 dioceses, which constituted the ecclesiastical province of Armagh, and comprehends part of Co. Meath (Leinster), part of Leitrim (Connaught) and part of Fermanagh and the greater part of Cavan (Ulster). The Index to Co. Fermanagh's Kilmore Diocesan Wills: 1682-1838, lists the only "Coughran" I've found in early Irish records of the region:

James Coughran, Farmer of Lisnageer <sic: Lisnagler>, *wrote his will in 1764, and it was probated in 1768.*

In customary Scots-Irish naming patterns, the first son is named for the paternal Grandfather; the second son is named for the maternal Grandfather. If these naming patterns were applicable to Alexander's children, one would expect that Alexander's father was William Martin. Alexander's first "unknown" wife's father would have been "James". Martha [Coughran] Martin's father then may have been Hugh Coughran.

Col. James' narrative tells us that his father, Hugh Martin, the eldest child of Alexander & Martha, was sent by Alexander to explore the feasibility of relocating the entire family to America. The closest hint of this date is from Col. James' statement that Hugh had come to his "years of discretion". This would probably mean that Hugh visited America at the age of 21, or about 1719, scouted the area, and returned to Co. Tyrone to assist with his parents' move. It was undoubtedly near 1720 when the Martin family embarked on their immigration to America. The family first landed at New Castle, Delaware, traveled up the Delaware River, and settled in Bucks County, Pennsylvania, in what is now Northampton Co., Pennsylvania.

It is not known whether Alexander's eldest son William Martin had married in Ireland. It is clear that the younger son James did not marry until after he settled in America. Col. James may have merely failed to fully detail that one or both of the older half-brothers accompanied Hugh on the exploration voyage. It would seem that Alexander had the financial ability to purchase more than one passage, and would surely have worried about the safety of sending his third son alone on a trans-Atlantic trip.

It is a fact that both William and James came to America, and probably in the company of their father, stepmother, and half-siblings; i.e., Hugh, Thomas, Robert, Agnes, Esther, and infant Henry.

Soon after the family settled near the Forks of the Delaware, then Bucks Co., PA, Alexander became ill and died. The date of Alexander's death is unknown; there are no Pennsylvania Presbyterian Church records existing for that time period, there are no mentions of Alexander's death in the Bucks Co., PA Orphans Court records, and he has no known gravesite.

According to Col. James, "After the death of my grandfather, my grandmother moved where my father and his three brothers, Thomas, Robert and Henry then lived." Henry Martin was not born until 1720, and although he was known to have later lived in Hunterdon Co., I think Col. James should have more accurately written that widow Martha with her young son Henry moved over to Hunterdon Co., NJ under the care and protection of the older sons Hugh, Thomas and Robert.

Sometime after the marriage of daughter Esther [Martin] to Francis Mason, Martha resided with Esther, where she died on May 11, 1753, Hunterdon Co., NJ.

In 1881, historian, James P. Snell, wrote that Martha's grave was near Annandale on the John Fulkerson place, but incorrectly identified Martha as Hugh Martin's sister-in-law:

"There is an old burial-place on the John Fulkerson place, near Annandale, but, save in the cases of two graves that have been especially cared for, the resting-places of the dead in that spot are unmarked except by here and there a fragment of a headstone. The two graves alluded to are

those of Hugh Martin and Martha, his brother's wife. About these graves David Fraser years ago built a stone wall, which fronts the highway." [4]

Judge Walter M. Hunter wrote a letter to a Martin descendant in 1956, stating Hugh Martin & his mother Martha were buried "at Lebanon, a few miles east of Annandale". Charles Martin, a descendant of Col. James Martin, advised me that the graves have been moved twice – once in 1946 due to the widening of a Federal highway; then again in 1975 due to construction of the Interstate Highway.[5] I found both graves and stones located in Clinton, N.J. in the Evergreen Cemetery, on Halstead Street, amongst contemporary burial sites.

Martha Martin's grave is designated by a scallop-topped stone marker. In 2002, the inscription was barely legible. The first five lines are still fairly clear. The last line is obviously in Latin, and would seem to be Era = Mistress of the house; Eratis = lived; next word is not decipherable; then 74 = meaning she died at age 74.

'Here lyeth the Body of
Martha Martin
Widow of Alexander Martin
who departed this Life
May the 11th Anno Dom. 1753
Era Eratis _hife 74'

---

[4] History of Hunterdon and Somerset Counties, New Jersey, compiled by James P. Snell (Philadelphia: Everts & Peck, 1881), 538-539.
[5] Letter from Charles M. Martin of Indialantic, Fl, dated November 11, 1999.

I commissioned photographs of the Martin gravestones in July, 2002, at the Evergreen Cemetery, Clinton, Hunterdon Co., New Jersey.

The gravestone of Martha [Coughran] Martin (in the background) beside the gravestone of her son, Hugh Martin

The sons born to Alexander Martin and his first unknown wife were:

William Martin, born about 1695 – Chapter Two
James Martin, born about 1696 – Chapter Three

The children born to Alexander and Martha [Coughran] Martin in Co. Tyrone were:

Hugh Martin, born 1698 – Chapter Four
Thomas Martin, born about 1708 – Chapter Five
Robert Martin, born about 1710 – Chapter Six
Agnes Martin born about 1712 – Chapter Seven
Esther Martin, born about 1718 – Chapter Eight
Henry Martin, born about 1720 – Chapter Nine

CHAPTER TWO

WILLIAM MARTIN
(b. c1695 – d. before 1776)

William Martin, the eldest son of Alexander Martin and his unknown first wife, was probably born in Co. Tyrone, Northern Ireland, about 1695.

Col. James stated in his brief "family history" narrative: "Now I must recount more of my grandmother's family in Ireland, as related to me by my half-uncle, James Martin, for whom I am named. He lived in two miles of my father in Jersey on the South Branch of the Raritan River. He said that my grandfather had another son by his first marriage, whose name was William. He emigrated to South Carolina to a place called Pou Pou, on the Edisto River. My brother, Alexander, at the beginning of the Revolutionary War, having command of a regiment, was ordered to South Carolina to suppress a number of Tories, who were headed by one of their leaders called Scofield. They were called Scofieldites. <sic: Scovillites, a band of Tories led by Col. Scophol> On his route he came to the neighborhood of Pou Pou, and enquired if anyone of the name Martin lived there. They told him that there had, but they had all died but the daughters, and they had married, so the name of Martin was lost as far as that branch of the family was concerned. I have heard nothing since".

I presume that Col. James' handwriting was misread, or he, himself, was not familiar with the correct name. "Pou Pou" was actually "Pon Pon", which in Colonial days, was an Indian name given to the last twenty miles of the Edisto River, and is now known as Jacksonboro, Colleton Co., SC. Pon Pon was situated in St. Bartholomew's Parish.[6] A Revolutionary War Pension declaration

---

[6] http://www.oldplaces.org/Colleton/colhistory.html

made by a soldier[7] serving under Colonel Alexander Martin stated he was "stationed about forty miles west of Charleston (SC) at a place called the PonPon Roads".

From South Carolina land grants[8] discovered by Linda Peacock, William Martin was residing in Colleton Co., SC by at least April, 1723:

"83 - *South Carolina: Pursuant to a precept to me directed by James St. John, Esq., his Majesty's Surveyor General bearing date the 21st day of April 1723. I have admeasured and laid out unto Mr. William Martin a tract of land containing in the whole six hundred acres in Colleton County and on all sides on land not laid out, and hath such other forms, shapes and marks as are specified in the above delineated plat. Given under my hand this 8th day of January 1728. /s/ Thomas Gifford, D.S."* William's rectangular plat shows vacant land on all four sides.

A survey was directed on February 19, 1733, p. 284, on behalf of John Newton for 300 acres in Colleton Co. on the West side of Pon Pon River. The plat map shows Newton's survey as butting on the south and north of the lands of Mr. William Martin; on the west, the lands of Mr. Boon; to the north was also a part of Mr. Martin's land; and to the east, Mr. Gwin. The survey was certified on March 13, 1733.

William Martin is cited as previously laying claim to the lands on the southside of Thomas Bee's survey in April 1764, in Colleton County on the NE side of the NW Branch of Combahee or Saltcatcher River, also adjoining James Donnom and David Hixt. In August, 1765, a survey made for James Donnom, stated the southwest boundary line adjoined lands formerly laid out to William Martin, on the waters of Combee River.

In November, 1767, William was granted an additional 100 acres on Rocky Creek of the Edisto River:

42 – South Carolina: Pursuant to a precept to me directed by John Troup, Esq., Dep. Sur. Gl. And dated 28th May 1767, I have laid out for

---

[7] Nicholas McCubbin's Revolutionary War Pension File – W3574, National Archives & Records Administration
[8] South Carolina Department of Archives & History

William Martin** a tract of land containing one hundred acres,* ***situate in *Colleton County, on a Creek called Rocky Creek waters of Edisto, the sd. Creek being nine feet wide, Butting and bounding all sides on vacant land: And hath such shape, form and marks as the above plat represents. Given under my hand Nov. 14th 1767. /s/ George Strother".*

  I've found no wills, deeds or marriage records to ascertain William Martin's marriage, his death date or his daughters' marriages.

CHAPTER THREE

JAMES MARTIN
(c1696 – 1761)

James Martin, the son of Alexander Martin and his unknown first wife, was born in Co. Tyrone about 1696. He may have immigrated to America with his father about 1720.

Col. James Martin well remembered his half-Uncle James, and was his namesake. James Martin made his home in Hunterdon Co., New Jersey, on the South Branch of the Raritan River. His home was within two miles of half-brother Hugh Martin. Col. James' narrative states that James married Annie Drummond, daughter of James Drummond, Governor of New Jersey. I have never found the name "Drummond" among the names of the Royal Governors of colonial New Jersey. The only Governor Drummond in the American Colonies was William Drummond, but he was appointed Governor of North Carolina for the period 1664-1667, and was not near New Jersey. There had been a James Drummond, 4th Earl of Perth, who started a Scottish settlement in E. NJ in c1680's, but he went on to become a Governor of Gibraltar and died in France. I can't find that he left behind a daughter in NJ, as he appears to have been an absentee NJ Proprietor.

It would be a fair guess that if Anne had been from such a prestigious family, James would have needed to financially establish himself in New Jersey to be considered a worthy prospect for such a marriage. I suspect that a misunderstanding or transcription error occurred concerning "Gov." Drummond, and that Anne's father might have been "Gav." Drummond. Gavin Drummond was prominent in many records in early 1700's NJ, though principally in Monmouth Co. Although "Gavin" has only 5 letters, he usually signed his name abbreviated as "Gav. Drummond". Another strong possibility I derived solely from names of landowners on the Hunterdon Co. "Manuscript Maps" by

D. Stanton Hammond, JD, published by the Genealogical Society of NJ. The Index Map – 1963, shows a John Drummond, whose 1,000 acres, Lot #217, granted on November 9, 1685, borders on the west side of the South Branch of the Raritan River. Drummond's land adjoined on the north and the south, tracts of land owned by "Capt. Andrew Hamilton"; the subset maps, Sheet E, shows Drummond's name as "Dromon". Perhaps the family lore became confused by the fact that John Drummond's land adjoined Andrew Hamilton, who was, indeed, a Royal Governor of both East Jersey and West Jersey. As an interesting historical aside, Hamilton was removed from office in New Jersey because he had been born in Scotland and "no other than a natural-born subject of England could serve in any public post of trust or profit". He was later appointed by William Penn to serve as the Deputy Governor of Pennsylvania, and Hamilton died in 1703.

James & Anne's children, with the exception of James, Jr., were all under the age of twenty-one at the time of James' death in 1761. Thus, I feel James' marriage did not take place until about 1738, with the children's births beginning c1739.

Col. James recalled that Uncle James Martin kept a large shoemaker's shop, had many indentured apprentices, and maintained a profitable business.

There are few records that assist in detailing James Martin's life. I've searched the early Hunterdon Co. Deed Books, and found nothing. The records of Bucks / Northampton Co., PA as well as Hunterdon Co., NJ are very scarce during this period of time. James Martin was not listed as a Hunterdon Co. Voter in the election held in 1738[9]; nor was he listed as a Freeholder of Hunterdon Co. in 1741. The Freeholders' List includes "every Planter and Inhabitant dwelling and residing within the Province, who has acquired rights to and is in possession of Fifty Acres of Ground, and hath cultivated ten Acres of it; or in Boroughs, who have a house and three Acres; or have a house and Land only hired, if he can prove he have Fifty Pounds <£50> in Stock of his own". Freeholder lists were used to

---

[9] "1738 Voter List for Hunterdon County" – Hunterdon Co. Historical Newsletter – Winter 1993, p. 658-660

select jurors, being "Freemen above five and Twenty Years of Age".[10]

Although it's very difficult for me to coordinate locations from the Genealogical Society of NJ historical "Index Map – 1688-1765" covering the whole of Hunterdon Co., which mainly denotes the original massive pre-1700's land grants, to the subset map series of the subsequently subdivided tracts, I feel I've been able to determine that James Martin's plantation had been a portion of the 5,000 acre tract granted to Daniel Coxe, which was split in half north to south by the South Branch of the Raritan River, and located to the west of "Kingtown" and about three miles southwest of Annandale. On the subset Map Series #4, published in 1978, James Martin is shown as the landowner of what looks to be over 1,000 acres on both sides of the South Branch of the Raritan River, adjoining Charles Stewart to the South, and William Coxe (who sold in 1764 to Samuel & Alexander Rogers and John F. Grandin).

A very important book was published at the end of 2010, and I was immediately in line to purchase "John Reading's Diary – The Daily Business Record of the First American-Born Governor of New Jersey", edited by David R. Reading (John Reading's 5th Great Grandson) from original transcriptions by Dorothy A. Stratford, published by The Mount Amwell Project, Alexandria, VA 22314. There are so few records available for the time period covered by the 1746-1767 diary, that any clue or mention of our Martin family is to be treasured. Although "James Martin" would be a fairly common name, it seems certain John Reading had financial dealings with our James, because of the association of other identifiable relatives. For instance, In January, 1746 (O.S.), John Reading received from <u>Alexander Hunter</u> money to be paid toward James Martin's account. Two months later, there was an entry stating that James Martin had paid his account in full. [Alexander Hunter was James' brother, Hugh Martin's brother-in-law.]

In September, 1748, John Reading agreed to sell 284 acres of his land lying on the Muskonetcong River (Morris Co., NJ) jointly to

---

[10] "Hunterdon County Freeholders 1741" – The Genealogical Magazine of NJ – Vol 37, No. 2 – May, 1962.

a James Martin and George Beatty for about £170, plus interest, in installments with final payment due April, 1751. Reading's entry in January, 1752, reads "James Martin by <u>Thomas Martin</u> paid for a Deed." There's no way of telling if the Martin-Beatty property pertained to our James Martin, but undoubtedly, a debt James owed to Reading was paid by his half-brother Thomas. In May, 1754, John Reading's diary entry is partially illegible, but mentions Thomas Martin's Plantation on the Muskonatcong River. Thomas' residence and 210 acre plantation was near Ringoes in Amwell Township at that time and far to the south of the Muskonatcong River. There's a possibility that James (a shoemaker) operated a tanyard on the Muskonatcong as slaughtering cattle and curing leather is not what one would particularly want at their residence; and/or that Thomas (a stone mason) had a quarry on the Muskonatcong River as a source for his stones. I've not done any research into Morris Co., NJ, to see whether there could be records for our James Martin during the early period where he is missing from Hunterdon Co. Freeholders' Lists.

On September 28, 1754, "James Martin of Hunterdon Co." was listed as having a letter remaining at the Post Office in Trenton[11].

James Martin became ill and wrote his Last Will & Testament on December 1, 1761. James' handwritten signature on the LWT is very shaky, and seems to portray his feeble physical condition. James died within the month, probably near December 27, 1761. An inventory was taken of his goods & chattels on December 28th, and his LWT was presented by his widow / Executrix Anne Martin, and Co-Executor, son James Martin, Jr. on December 31, 1761.

One witness to the LWT was William Rogers, who I believe was the son of Thomas Rogers; therefore, William would have been Hugh Martin's children Col. James Martin's and Martha [Martin] Roger's brother-in-law. The other witness was John Anderson, who

---

[11] "Genealogical & Personal Memorial of Mercer Co., NJ – Vol. I", edited by Francis Bazley Lee, Lewis Publishing Co., 1907.

was undoubtedly Hugh Martin's adjoining neighbor and a Hunterdon Co. magistrate. James Martin's LWT names as heirs: Wife Anne, sons James, Jr. & William (not yet 21); and daughters Martha, Mary, Ann & Rachel (all under the age of 21 and unmarried).

If it were not for Col. James' family history, it would be impossible to ascertain that James had been a successful shoemaker. His inventory lists "shoemaker's tools", but there is no tanning equipment or supply of leather on hand at the time of his death. This might be an indication that these goods were sold in anticipation of his death, even though it would be logical for James, Jr. to continue the business operation. James made provision for his children in the tradition of the times; i.e., the eldest son inherited the real estate. It is interesting to note that James left open the option of his younger son William choosing to go to college. Because James' half-nephews, Alexander, James, and Thomas (sons of Hugh Martin) had all attended Princeton, it was probably understood that if William should opt for college – it would be Princeton.

JAMES MARTIN, SR.
LAST WILL & TESTAMENT
WILL & INVENTORY[12]
Recorded in
Lib No. 11, Folio 144
Hunterdon Co., New Jersey
1761
Will #539J

In the name of God, Amen. I, James Martin of Lebanon in Hunterdon County & Province of New Jersey being Sick of body but of sound and Perfect Memory Calling to mind the Uncertainty of Human Life do Make and Ordain this my Last Will and Testament in Manner Following ~ First, I Bequeath my Soul to God that gave it hoping for

---

[12] Transcribed by Francie Lane from FHC film # 461817 – Hunterdon Co., NJ Will Book

forgiveness of my sins through the Mediation of Our Savior Jesus Christ and in regard to my Real & Personal Estate with which I have been blessed I Bequeath the same in Manner Following Viz ~

My Will is that all my just debts and funeral Charges be paid as soon as Conveniently may be after my Decease.

Item   I give and bequeath to my Loving Wife Anne the unlimited use of the East End of my dwelling house with Furniture for a Room a Bed just as she may choose Firewood to be Cutt and hauled for her, Pasture for two Cows on the Farm and the Sum of fifteen pounds proclam^n Money to be paid to her yearly if demanded during her Widowhood but if She marry the said Sum of fifteen pounds aforesaid shall not be paid her after marriage by my son James.

Item   I will and bequeath to my Son James all and singular my Plantation in Lebanon aforesaid and whereon I now Live According to the Boundaries thereof, with all my Stock of Horses Cows Sheep & Swine with my Desk and Cupboard to him his Heirs and Assigns for Ever the better to Enable him to pay the following Legacies and sums of Money Viz: To my Son William the Sum of Two hundred pounds when he arrives at the age of Twenty One years, to my Daughter Martha the Sum of fifty pounds on the day of her Marriage with Interest from this day. To my Daughter Mary the sum of fifty pounds on the Day of her Marriage with Interest from this day. To my Daughter Ann the sum of fifty pounds when she arrives at age. To my Daughter Rachael the like Sum of fifty pounds to be paid when she is of age and my said son James shall give Each of my said Daughters a Cow and Calf when they are married or Arrive at Age. And if my son William doth die before he is of Age my will is that his share shall be Equaly Divided Between my said four Daughters and if any of my Daughters die before they come to full Age, my will is that their share shall be Equaly divided between the Survivors of my said Daughters Provided always that if my son William Choose to go to Colledge then in Lieu of the said sum of Two hundred pounds my will is that my son James shall support my said son William in Cloaths and all necessaries while he is Learning at School & Colledge & pay all the Expenses that attends William's Education & when he Leaves Colledge give him a good Horse and saddle.

Item   My will is that all my Household Furniture be Equaly Divided between my said four Daughters Except what is already given to my Wife & the Desk & Cupboard to my son James ~

I Constitute and Appoint my Loving Wife Ann & My son James Executrix and Executor of this my Last Will and Testament and I hereby revoke & Disanull all and every other Will and Wills heretofore by me made & done Acknowledging this to be my Last Will and Testament.

In Wittness whereof I have hereunto sett my hand & Seal this first day of December in the Year of Our Lord One thousand Seven hundred and Sixty One   1761

T:

John Anderson   James Martin {Seal}
William Rogers

William Rogers and Charles Stewart Two of the Witnesses to the within Will being Sworn on the Holy Evangelists of Almighty God did Depose that they saw James Martin Deceased the Testator therein named Sign and Seal the Same and heard him publish pronounce and declare the within Instrument to be his last Will & Testament and that at the doing thereof the said Testr. was of sound and Disposeing Mind & Memory as farr as they know and as they verily believe and that John Anderson the other subscribing Witness was present at the same time and signed his name as a Witness to the said Will In the presence of the said Testr. & in the presence of each other.

William Rogers
Chas. Stewart

Sworn the 31 day
  of December 1761 before
Theo. Severns Juris.

Anne Martin Executrix and James Martin Junr. Executor in the Within Testament Named being Sworn on the Holy Evangelists of Almighty God do depose that the Within Instrument Contains the last Will & Testament of James Martin Decd the Testator therein Named So farr as they know and as they verily believe and that they will well and Truly perform the same by paying first the Debts of the said Deceased and then the Legacies in the said Testament Specified so farr as the Goods

Chattels and Credits of the said Deceased and thereunto Extend. And that they will make a True and perfect Inventory of all and Singular the said Goods Chattels and Credits of the said Decd wch. have or shall hereafter come to their knowledge or possession or to the possession of any other person or persons for their use and Exhibit the same into the prerogative office in Burlington & render a just & True Account when thereunto Lawfully required.

Sworn the 31 day of
December 1761
  Theo. Severns, Juris.

Anne (her "W" mark) Martin
James Martin

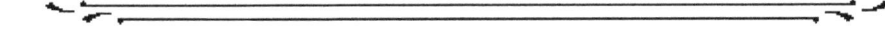

INVENTORY OF JAS. MARTIN, SENR.
GOODS & CHATTELLS

Charles Stewart One of the appraisers of the within Inventory being Sworn upon the Holy Evangellists of Allmighty God did depose that the Goods Chattells and Creditts set down and specified in the within Inventory were by him appraized According to their Just and True Exhutive Rates and Values as to the best of his Judgment and Understanding and that John Anderson the other Appraizer Consents in all things in the doing thereof and that they appraized all things that were brought to their View for appraizment.

Chas. Stewart

Sworn before me this thirty first day
  of December Anno Domini 1761
Theo. Severns, Juris.

Anne Martin Executrix & James Martin Junr Execr. of the Last Will and Testament of James Martin, being sworn on the Holy Evangelists of Allmighty God did depose that the within Writing contains a True and perfect Inventory of all and singular the Goods & Chattells of the said

Deceased which have come to their hands or possession or to the possession of any other person or persons for their use.

                        Anne (her W mark) Martin

Sworn before me this Thirty first   James Martin
  day of December 1761
  Theo. Severns Juris

INVENTORY OF THE GOODS & CHATTELLS OF JAMES MARTIN, SENR. OF LEBANON, DECEASED taken DECEMEBER 28th 1761 by JNO. ANDERSON & CHARLES STEWART APPRAISRS., VIZ ~

Item	£	S	P
Eight Cows @ 65/per	26	0	0
four Heiffers	7	0	0
Seven Calves	5	0	0
15 Swine	3	0	0
A roan Horse	9	0	0
Two Old bay Horses @ 3per	6	0	0
A Bay Mare	1	0	0
A Black Mare	6	0	0
A Sorrell Colt	4	0	0
Ten Sheep @ 8/per	4	0	0
A Parcel of Flax & Flaxseed	4	0	0
Four Stacks of Wheat	30	0	0
One ditto of Oats	1	10	0
One plow & a Harrow	1	5	0
A Waggon & Geers	6	0	0
A Parcell of Corn in the Cribb	2	0	0
A Bee Hive & bees	0	8	0
A Sled 5/ three Axes 12/ Two Grubbing hoes 7/6 Iron Widges & rings	1	12	0
three broad hoes 9/ Carpenters Tools 15/	1	4	0
Old Casks, Troughs, a Coopers bench & a Grind Stone	0	16	0
Wheat & rye in the Ground	35	0	0
Hay in a Barrack	8	0	0
Provisions, Cyder & Casks in the Cellar	13	10	0
A large Tubb 10/ Six small d° 9/ 2 pails 3/ 2 piggins & a churn 7/6	1	9	6
Pewter 40/ four Iron Potts & a kettle 30/ Smoothing Irons & hand Irons	4	10	0
Two Tramells Shovells & Tongs 20/ Two Tables 12/ three Chairs 7/6	1	19	6
A Looking Glass 3/ A Desk 25/ a Bed, bed Cloaths Curtains 15/	7	15	0
A Chest of Drawers 40/ a Case & Bottles & a Bed Sted 25/	3	5	0
A Bed & Bed Cloaths £8.0.0 A Chest 20/ Shoemakers Tools 20/	10	0	0

four Wheels 30/ a Tan. 7/6 Books 31/ Two basketts 2/6		3	11	0
A Bed £3.0.0 One ditto £5.0.0 A Cupboard 20/		9	0	0
A Table a Wheel & four Chairs 3/ Teapotts Cups &c 30/		3	0	0
3 Candle Sticks 2/6 Knives & Forks 5/		0	7	6
Wearing Apparell		<u>4</u>	<u>0</u>	<u>0</u>
		235	2	6

John Anderson } Appraizors
Chas. Stewart }

Col. James Martin stated that his 1st cousins were: James Martin, Jr., William Martin, Patsy Martin, Polly Martin and Rachel Martin – all having married prior to 1775. Col. James omits his cousin Ann Martin, which may indicate that she died young and before his move to North Carolina in 1774.

Col. James' remembrance of his Cousin William shows the bravery and resolve of the Patriot: *"James and William lived at home in 1774, and William got a Lieutenancy in the army, and being ordered to go in advance guard against a part of the British army, he and his party were beaten, and he was cruelly murdered in a shocking manner, was pierced by a number of bayonets which drew the attention of General Washington, who sent his body to the British commander under a flag of truce, but he had the excuse to say that he was obstinate, and would not give or ask for quarter."*

It is fascinating to note the accuracy of Col. James Martin's "family history", written in his eighties and at least fifty years after the death of his cousin William, in comparison to the actual 1777 newspaper report of his death:

Virginia Gazette – June 20, 1777, Page 2, Column 3[13]

"Extract of a letter from General Washington's headquarters, dated June 7, 1777. 'I think we shall have a movement about Tuesday or Wednesday next. – In the course of last week between 20 and 30 deserters came over to us. –A few days ago we sent out a scouting party, from which a lieut.

---

[13] Colonial Williamsburg web page: http://research.history.org/DigitalLibrary/BrowseVG.cfm

Martin, with 10 men, was detached as an advance scout, who soon fell in with and engaged a party of Hessians and British light horse, 15 in number. At the first fire he killed the commander of the gang; but they spurring up, our men gave way, and left the lieutenant on the field, who was soon surrounded, and (although calling out for quarter) was butchered with the greatest cruelty; 17 wounds were plain to be seen, most of which it is said, were mortal. The body, with a flag, was sent to the enemy, but they would not view it. The letter which accompanied it they did receive, and promised an answer in a few days.'

Col. James recalled that widow Anne [Drummond] Martin died prior to 1774.

The Hunterdon Co., NJ Tax Lists for 1778-1780 - Hunterdon Co., NJ, show James Martin, Jr. as living at Kingwood:[14]

In a letter to Col. James Martin from his former Hunterdon Co. neighbor, David Frazer, dated November 26, 1795, mention is made of "Red James" Martin having entered into a bond with Samuel Rogers. It would be a fair presumption that Red James Martin may have been the nickname of James, Jr. and an indication that he was red-headed. [See the Frazer letter in Col. James Martin's Chapter, Vol. II] If my assumption re Red James Martin is correct, David Frazer indicated that both James Martin, Jr. and his wife were deceased by November, 1795.

From a book on the graduates of Princeton, there is a reference to Philip Johnston, born August 27, 1741, Hunterdon Co., NJ, the son of Judge Samuel Johnston and second wife Mary Casier. *"As the chief Magistrate of his district, Judge Johnston was one of the wealthiest and most prominent citizens of West Jersey" and a contributor to the Bethlehem Presbyterian church. Son Philip Johnston remained at Princeton from 1755 to 1757, but left to serve in the French & Indian War, and later to assist Johnston was back in New Jersey to marry Rachel Martin. She bore him three daughters, one of whom was the mother of John Scudder (A.B. 1811)..... On his 35th birthday, August 27, 1776, Philip Johnston was mortally wounded by Hessian musket fire."*

---

[14] "Revolutionary Census of NJ, Based on Ratables During the Period of the Revolution" by Kenn Stryker-Rodda.

NJ Marriages - Hunterdon Co, p. 218
April 13, 1767: Rachel Martin & Philip Johnston

Judge Samuel Johnston served as a Justice with Hugh Martin on the Hunterdon County Court. A record of Hunterdon Co., NJ court summonses[15], gives a reference to: "James Martin of Lebanon 'lives near Sam'l Johnson Esq'r' – 1768 #33530". This summons implies that Philip Johnston had been a neighbor to Rachel Martin. It should be noted that Philip's brother-in-law, Col. Charles Stewart[16] [b. 1729, Co. Donegal, Ireland; m. Mary Oakley Johnston[17], b.1740; d.1771] also witnessed James Martin's Will and appraised his estate in 1761. Nothing more is known of James Martin's daughters Mary "Polly" and Martha "Patsy" Martin.

---

[15] "More Records of Old Hunterdon County" Vol. I, compiled by Phyllis B. D'Autrechy
[16] From Charles D. Rodenbough – cemetery records from Bethlehem Presbyterian Church at Grandin, Hunterdon Co., NJ
[17] Stewart Clan Magazine, April 1925, Vol. III, no. 10

CHAPTER FOUR

HUGH MARTIN
(1698 – 1761)

Hugh Martin was born in 1698, in County Tyrone, near the town of Enniskillen, in what is now Northern Ireland, the eldest son of Alexander and 2nd wife Martha [Coughran] Martin. Hugh undoubtedly received a good education as a lad in Ireland. His father showed a great deal of confidence in Hugh's ability and judgment, because Hugh was chosen at age 21 to set off to scout America as the family's future home. Hugh was apparently impressed with what he found, because his father, mother and all his siblings immigrated to America about 1720.

The Martin family first arrived at New Castle, Delaware, and made their way up the Delaware River. The Martins may have first lived in the Bucks / Northampton County, PA area known as the Forks of the Delaware that became "Hunter's Settlement".

There is still a nearby "Martin's Creek", midway between Mt. Bethel and Easton, PA, which is named for David Martin, who was born in 1698, the son of Joseph & Sarah [Trotter] Martin of Piscataway, NJ. I have researched David Martin, at one time thinking he may have been a relative of Hugh Martin; however, if he was – it would have been too distant to seriously contemplate. Briefly, I've found that David Martin owned the exclusive ferry rights and land on both sides of the Delaware River; i.e. Bucks / now-Northampton Co., PA and Hunterdon Co., NJ. David Martin leased his ferry rights to others as well as employing ferrymen. Although David was associated with the town of Easton / Forks of the Delaware River, he also served as the Sheriff of Hunterdon Co., NJ. He married Elizabeth [Doty] in Piscataway on March 9, 1714, and had three daughters: Sarah, b. 1714; Elizabeth, b. 1718; and Joan Martin, b. 1720. David was a close friend of Benjamin Franklin, who was instrumental in having David Martin named in 1750, as the

Rector of the Philadelphia Academy, later to become the University of Pennsylvania. David Martin died intestate in Philadelphia on December 13, 1751, and is buried in the Christ Church cemetery, Philadelphia.

The present-day City of Easton, PA, was originally the site named by the Indians as "The Forks of the Delaware". The "Forks" was a *"pebble-covered tongue of land that originally extended far out between the Delaware and Lehigh rivers at their intersection.* "The Forks of the Delaware" was sparsely populated by white settlers (in 1752, the residents only numbered about 40 families); originally it had been a meeting place for the Indians. The Lenni-Lenape came down the Lehigh River from the west; the Iroquois and the Delawares came from the North and would hold their joint peace conferences or meet to trade with each other.

Alexander Martin became ill and died soon after the family's arrival. Hugh must have felt a strong sense of responsibility for the care of his widowed mother and younger siblings. Hugh's youngest brother, Henry, born in 1720, was no more than a toddler when "orphaned". There should be some type of estate records in Bucks Co., PA for Alexander Martin – if nothing more than Orphan's Court orders for guardianship of Alexander's minor children, but to date, nothing has been discovered. Another of Hugh's worries must have been that it was not possible during those particular years to secure title to land in this region of Pennsylvania. Indeed, the Scots-Irish immigrants, who settled in the "Forks", were merely "squatters" on the land. These circumstances may have caused the Martins to turn their sights across the river to Hunterdon Co., New Jersey.

Although it's not known exactly when Hugh Martin moved from PA to NJ, it would seem Hugh had not yet relocated to NJ by 1722. The Hunterdon Co., NJ "1722 Tax List" and "Heads of Families in 1722" list no Martins as residents[18]. There are two very early references to Hugh Martin in Hunterdon Co., NJ:

---

[18] Hunterdon Co., NJ, Historical Society Newsletter – Spring 1977, p. 6-8 "Two Early Documents List Our First Settlers": Tax List of Hunterdon Co., NJ 1722 and Heads of Families 1722

A deed in the form of a Power of Attorney was found containing a reference to Hugh Martin as a Witness as follows:

"Hunterdon Co., NJ – Volume 1 of Special Deeds - Book One - Jan 31, 1716".

"Page 75: Power of Attorney - July 28, 1731. *Francis Moore of Amwell, Yeoman. To my trusty and well beloved wife, Sarah Moore.... especially regarding my 100 acre plantation in Amwell, bounded by William Lumase and Philip Peters. Witnesses: William Lumax, Catherine Lumax, HUGH MARTIN and HENRY MARTIN. Recorded: Oct 9 1731*".

At first glance, it would seem Hugh and brother Henry had witnessed the document; however, in 1731, Henry was only 11 years old. Under British Common Law, the minimum legal age for witnessing deeds in NJ was 14. If the witness was not "brother" Henry, who was he? Perhaps this adult Henry Martin was related to Hunterdon County Sheriff David Martin.

I don't know the identity of Francis Moore and wife Sarah, or whether Hugh was related in somehow to them. Could Sarah have been a Martin or Coughran? It's always wise to consider that a witness to a deed or will might be a relative, serving to protect the dower rights of the wife, etc. In fact, most adjoining neighbors in early America were related in some fashion, because the tendency was to "nest" together for protection, assistance in building homes, etc. The surety for the 1761 NJ administration of Hugh's brother Thomas was Moore Furman, who I've seen listed in unrelated NJ records as a judge and sheriff of Hunterdon Co. as well as the postmaster.

If not related to the Moores, Hugh was at the very least an adjoining neighbor. The Hunterdon Co., NJ Genealogical Society of NJ published a series of manuscript maps by D. Stanton Hammond, JD in 1967. Sheet "G" plats the property owners in the village of Ringoes and the Old York Road and delineates the property that would come to be purchased by Hugh Martin in 1730. To the east of Hugh's plantation was Francis Moore, William "Lummox", Philip Peters, Catherine "Lomax", Cornelius Ringo, Rudolph Harley and John Hous(h)ell. To the north was John Boss. To the southeast was Peter Fisher, Peter Rockefeller and Mt. Airy; the Old York Road led to Lambertville and Coryell's Ferry, which crossed the Delaware River to Bucks Co., PA.

Hugh had definitely purchased a plantation in Amwell township by the spring of 1730, as found in the book, "250 Years of Hunterdon County"[19]: I searched for years for the source of this property record cited:

*"Benjamin Field sold 300 acres to Henry Oxley, a long rectangle of land bounded on the north by Henry Boss, on the east by Boss, Rudolph Harley and Johannes Houshell, and on the west by John Heyden. The southerly boundary lay near the Old York Road where the Ringoes Drive-In Theater now stands, Henry Oxley sold the land in 1721 to James Burcham, who willed it to his son, Joseph. C. W. Larison, quoting from a deed he obtained from J. M. Hagaman, says that on May 11, 1730, Joseph **Burcham** sold the land to **Hugh Martin**, Hugh sold to **Thomas Martin**, who in turn willed it to his **son Daniel**. However, our research has not found this deed, which was apparently never recorded...."*. *"It lay on both sides of the Old York Road <Route 179> about a mile southwest of Ringoes..."*

I attempted to find a copy of the Burcham / Hugh Martin deed, as well as a deed from Hugh to his brother Thomas Martin, or some trace of Thomas Martin's estate, which might include this parcel of land. A researcher specializing in NJ Archives records conducted a search for me, but there was nothing to be found at the Archives; I personally searched the Hunterdon County deed book, and found none of these transactions. Yet, the Hunterdon Co. history book was accurate in portraying Daniel Martin as the son of Thomas Martin. That, in itself, was an astounding fact, because the only instance I had found which revealed that Thomas had a son named Daniel is in the Orphans' Court documents in Bucks Co., PA.

At long last, I recently discovered a very old book[20] published in 1890 regarding the family of Peter Fisher of Old

---

[19] The First 250 years of Hunterdon County, 1714-1964 - The dawn of Hunterdon / Norman C. Wittwer

[20] "Skech [sic] of the Fisher Family of Old Amwell Township in Hunterdon Co., NJ" by Cornelius Wilson Larison - 1890

Amwell Twp, Hunterdon Co., authored by Cornelius W. Larison, wherein he recounted being able to examine old documents in the possession of J. M. Hagaman, detailing the history of ownership for Mr. Hagaman's plantation. Mr. Larison's book reads in part:

"The land was commissioned to Andrew Hamilton on August 13, 1699. Hamilton sold 5,000 acres to one of the NJ Proprietors, Benjamin Field of Chesterfield, Burlington County, on May 19, 1701. Benjamin Field sold 300 acres to Henry Oxley on December 8, 1701. Oxley sold on February 2, 1721, to James Burcham, and upon Burcham's death, the land descended to his son Joseph Burcham. On May 11, 1730, Joseph Burcham sold his southerly half (150 acres) to Hugh Martin for £78 "silver money". Hugh Martin sold the same 150 acres to his brother Thomas Martin for £78 on December 3, 1736...."

[For additional detail pertaining to the progression of ownership of the plantation by Thomas Martin and his son Daniel, please refer to Chapter 5 – Thomas Martin.]

Mr. Larison's description of Hagaman's plantation in 1890 would be illustrative of Hugh's former home; i.e.,

"These several buildings <Hagaman's farm buildings> form an out-fit for a plantation that, in Hunterdon County, has rarely, if ever, been equaled; and for beauty and efficiency they seem to be, in the pursuit of agriculture, all that one could desire. The location of this villa is peculiar. Altho the eminence upon which it stands is not high, the pluvial waters never stand about the buildings. From the walls of the dwelling, the sward descends in every direction—forming a gentle but perfect drainage. The water from the roof on the south side of the barn finds its way to the Delaware thru a small tributary to the Alexsauken; that from the roof on the north, thru another tributary to the same rivulet; while the water from the roof upon the east side of the barn forms the head waters of one of the tributaries of the Neshanic and flows to the sea thru the Raritan".

Col. James in relating his parents' early married life, stated, "My father had bought a plantation in the township of Amwell in Hunterdon County, where my brother, Alexander, was born". Col. James was making a clear distinction between Hugh's original plantation at Ringoes, Amwell Twp, purchased from Burcham in 1730 – as opposed to Hugh's later residence in Annandale, Lebanon

Township, where Col. James always contended he had been born on May 21, 1742.

Hugh purchased the Amwell plantation in 1730, and his sale to brother Thomas Martin is recorded as being in 1736. It may be that Thomas shared the living quarters with Hugh as I don't believe Thomas married until the the early 1750's. Both Thomas & Hugh were recorded as official residents of Amwell Twp in the 1738 Voter List, as well as the April 15, 1742, Freeholders List.

Col. James Martin said his father Hugh had kept an English school for a year or two before he married Miss Jane Hunter. If, as Col. James remembers his father saying, Hugh was still a bachelor at near 40 years old, and that his mother was about 18 when the two first met; then the year of their meeting would have been about 1735. It's fascinating to speculate as to how their first meeting came about. Could it have been in conjunction with Hugh's teaching school? As you will later see, Jane was educated enough to help with tutoring duties in the 1760's. Or, did Hugh happen to meet Jane on the PA side of the ferry while on business? Or was their meeting church-related? "The Scotch-Irish of Northampton Co." book states, *"This brings us to a change in ecclesiastical jurisdiction caused by developments on the New Jersey side of the Delaware River, opposite to Hunter's Settlement."* In 1738, according to the Synod of Philadelphia, *"That the petition be granted, and that all to the northward and eastward of Maiden Head and Hopewell unto the Raritan River...* [i.e., Hunterdon Co., NJ]" Obviously, the New Jersey Presbyterians would have lobbied for support from their PA church brethrens, and possibly Hugh was selected to meet with members of the Hunter's Settlement.

The Hunter Family

Col. James continues his narration with an interesting biographical sketch of his maternal ancestry. *"My mother's family, the Hunters, had not come to this country"....."My father's and mother's families had never seen or heard of each other in Ireland."* I have read in several family histories that Hugh & Jane Hunter were "cousins"; however, Col. James' statements would definitely negate that hypothesis. The Hunters were undoubtedly Lowland Scots, among many induced to help colonize the north of Ireland, under the English "Confiscation Acts". The Hunters settled in County Antrim, as opposed to the Martins of Co. Tyrone; thus, there would be little chance of their meeting across such a distance.

Jane Martin was born in Co. Antrim in 1717. I would like to stress that her parents are not known. I have seen pedigree charts purporting Jane's father to be James Hunter, b. 4 July 1666, Scotland & her mother, Isabella Curry, born Feb. 1660. This couple is credited with having children:

    Alexander Hunter Oct 30 1698
    Karhol Hunter Sept 15 1700
    Janet Hunter June 14 1703
    George Hunter April 27 1704

Although, Jane [Hunter] Martin's brother Alexander Hunter was probably born about 1698, there is no accounting in the above for her elder brother John Hunter. I have seen some people convert the name "Janet" into Jane and erroneously declare Jane [Hunter] Martin to be born in 1703. Further research would have proved to them that Jane could not have been born in 1703. Jane's death at age 90 was reported in the 1807 newspapers. It seems someone found baptismal records in Scotland for this James Hunter, Isabella Curry, and their children, and misconstrued them as being our Hunter family. Of course, if the birth date of Isabella Curry / Currie is accurate, she must be ruled out as the mother of our Hunters. It is a fact that Jane was born in 1717, at which time Isabella [Curry] Hunter would have been 57 years old – hardly a candidate for motherhood. The other argument in dismissing the Isabella theory is that neither Jane, John nor Alexander Hunter named a daughter "Isabella". It is not reasonable during that era that none of these three children would honor their mother's memory.

Jane accompanied her two older brothers, John & Alexander Hunter, on the voyage to America. Looking at Col. James' statements concerning the Hunter history, one reads:

"They emigrated from Scotland to the north of Ireland and lived in the county of Antrim. My two uncles, John and Alexander Hunter, with

my mother, were all that came to this country." "They [the Hunters] came to Ireland two or three years after my father's family." "They, too, after landing at New Castle on the Delaware, came up to New Jersey, where my father first saw my mother. He, by this time (as I have heard him say) had got to be a pretty old bachelor about forty. My mother was then about eighteen. They soon made a match. She was very handsome." "My Uncle left a sister in Scotland, when he emigrated to Ireland. I have forgotten her name. She married a man named Lunman. I have not heard from her in a long time. This is all I can recollect from my mother's family."

Referring to the immigration of the Scots-Irish from Ireland to America, Robert W. Ramsey, wrote[21]:

"The fundamental causes of this movement were economic. Repressive trade laws, rack-renting landlordism, famine, and the decline of the linen industry were major factors in stimulating the overseas movement of these Ulster Scots. The manufacture of woolens, northern Ireland's staple industry, was restricted in 1699 by the passage of an act forbidding the exportation of Irish woolen goods to any part of the world except England. This act deprived the Ulsterites of their foreign markets. Between 1720 and 1728 thirteen Scotch-Irish churches were established in Pennsylvania and in New Castle County, Delaware". "According to Proud, such was the volume of immigration that an estimated six thousand Scotch-Irish landed in New Castle or Philadelphia in 1729 alone".

It is apparent there were at least four Hunter siblings; i.e., Mrs. Lunman, b. c1695; John Hunter, b. c1698; Alexander Hunter, b. c1700; and Jane Hunter, b. 1717. My theory is that the Hunter parents immigrated from Scotland to Co. Antrim about 1715; that the oldest daughter was already married to Mr. Lunman in Scotland, and thus stayed behind. Possibly by 1730, Jane's parents had both died, leaving her a young orphan. I believe that John Hunter was already married in Ireland to Elizabeth [Steele], had young children of his own, but took on the guardianship of his youngest sister. The economic times in Ireland were difficult, and the brothers opted to better their situation by immigrating to America. Jane was brought with them and helped care for her

---

[21] The Scotch-Irish Migration from Carolina Cradle, Settlement of the Northwest Carolina Frontier, 1747-1762 by Robert W. Ramsey - Chapter XII

young nieces & nephews. I doubt that the Hunters departed Ireland much before 1734, when Jane was about 17 years old; however, a Lehigh Valley, PA, historian, Matthew Henry, contended that Alexander Hunter settled in then-Bucks County in 1730. Unfortunately, the Hunters' arrival "window" from 1730 to 1735 exists, and cannot be narrowed. There were no deeds or land grants made in the area prior to the 1737 "Walking Purchase" made by William Penn from the Delaware Indians; even then, Penn was not able to gain any control over the region until 1742. For the purposes of research into the Martin family; however, it is not a critical factor to know whether Jane Hunter arrived at age 13 or 18.

According to Judge Walter M. Hunter, "*The early Scotch-Irish who followed the course of landing at New Castle and coming on up into Pennsylvania to settle, generally went on westward to the Susquehanna River area, but some stopped and established themselves near the border with NJ in what is now Northampton Co. The first settlement in the area above the Forks was that of a group led by Thomas and William Craig in 1728 and became known as the Craig or Irish Settlement. Its location was west of the present Easton and near the Lehigh River. Two years after, a rather extensive settlement was made along the Delaware River above Easton by other Scotch-Irish under the leadership of Alexander Hunter and bore the designation of Hunter's Settlement*".[22]

Col. James stated, "*My Uncle Alexander Hunter moved and settled in the forks of the Delaware, six miles above Easton. The Indians were then thickly planted with their wigwams over the country, and were very troublesome though not at open war. My Uncle Alexander, being a very strong, stout, athletic man, was the only one in that part, who could keep them in order. As to ability of body, he was said to have excelled all others anywhere to be found in the country, for the Indians went all over the nation and country to get someone who would be able to foil him in wrestling. Several trials of strength were made, but they all proved abortive. At length the Indians gave up, and always behaved in a very submissive manner when he was in their company, and would have no*

---

[22] The Hunters of Bedford Co., VA – Notes and documents on the family of James Hunter, Regulator leader of NC, including forebearers in PA, VA, NC, LA & TX" by Walter Marvin Hunter, Polyanthos, Cottonport, LA – 1973. Page 15

more to do with him. He afterwards, moved to Bedford or Buckingham County, Virginia, where he died. He was the father of Colonel James Hunter of Beaver Island, Rockingham County."

From "The Scotch-Irish of Northampton Co."[23] – p. 430-431 "Hunter Settlement", *"The expression 'Forks of the Delaware'…. was that [locality] lying between the Lehigh – the West Branch, and the Delaware proper – North Branch. The Craig Settlement was on the West Branch…. and included the neighborhood of Bath westward to the Lehigh River. The Hunter, or North Settlement, embraced the section of country on the Delaware, from the neighborhood of Martin's Creek northward through the Townships of Lower and Upper Mt. Bethel." "In the Minutes of the Synod of [the Presbytery] of Philadelphia for 1731, the name of Elder Thomas Craig appears"* with inference that he was from the Craig Settlement, *"but no reference seems to be made to the Hunter Settlement"*.

"Alexander Hunter And Presbyterian Followers -1730 - Permanent Settlement…Neighborhood Of Martin's Creek." "Early Settlers Were Miller, Moore, Lockard, Lyle, Moody, MARTIN, Nelson, Buchman, Hutchinson, Ross, McFarren McCracen, Silleman, Crawford, Galbraith, Boyd And Others." "Members Of The Familes of Copland, Gaston, Moore, Galraith, Wilson, Boyd, Hutton, Moody, Morris, Miller, McFarren, Mason, Nelson, Benward, Morr, Beard, Silleman, Scott, Henderson, Covert And Foresman emigrated westward to undeveloped sections of the country[24]."

The first mention made of Hunter's Settlement is found as entries in Rev. David Brainerd's Diary[25]. Rev. Brainerd was a famed Presbyterian missionary to the Indians, and his diary reads in part:

May 13, 1743: I arrived at a place called by the Indians "Sakauwatung" within the Forks of the Delaware.

Matthew Henry, Lehigh Valley historian wrote to Thomas Brainerd that Sakauwatung is the Indian name for "the mouth of a creek,

---

[23] "The Scotch-Irish of Northampton County, Pennsylvania", Northampton County Historical and Genealogical Society, John Cunningham Clyde, J. S. Correll, printer, 1926
[24] "History of Northampton County" - William J. Heller - 1920
[25] The Hunters of Bedford Co., VA – Notes and documents on the family of James Hunter, Regulator leader of NC, including forebearers in PA, VA, NC, LA & TX" by Walter Marvin Hunter, Polyanthos, Cottonport, LA – 1973.

where some one resides" and is now called "Allegheney Creek". It was here where Alexander Hunter lived; and he had a farm of 300 acres and a ferry across the Delaware River, in Upper Mt. Bethel township – about 3 miles east of the town of Richmond. Mr. Henry contended that Alexander Hunter arrived from Ireland in 1730, and further indicated that Rev. David Brainerd's cottage was within about ¼ mile of an Indian town "Clistowacki", meaning "fine land". Brainerd stated that the Indian village was three miles down river from Mr. Hunter's. A 1753 plat of the Forks area shows that Alexander Hunter owned a ferry across the Delaware – about 5 miles above Easton, PA.

Rev. David Brainerd actually made his home at Alexander Hunter's house until Brainerd had erected a small stone cottage for himself in 1744 at nearby Martin's Creek. Rev. David Brainerd was succeeded by his brother Rev. John Brainerd, whose diary shows:

October 7, 1749: Took leave of Mr. Lewis and his spouse, and came on my journey to the Forks; but, being hindered several hours at the ferry, did not arrive at Mr. Hunter's till after sundown.

October 8, 1749: "...Spent some time in conversation with Mr. Hunter and others, but felt poorly, and so retired to my lodging room, the same that my dear brother David used to lodge in when he preached to the Indians at the Forks." A footnote by Thomas Brainerd states, "This room was said to be an addition, probably of logs, to the home of the good Mr. Hunter of Easton, PA."

October 10, 1749: "Took leave of Mr. Hunter and his family and proceeded on my journey".

October 18, 1749: "Spent the forenoon with Mr. Lawrence, the weather being stormy; but in the afternoon, the storm being abated, took leave of him and other friends, and came to Mr. Hunter's, upon the north branch of the Delaware in the evening."

From the book, The History of Bucks County, "Alexander Hunter, a Presbyterian from the north of Ireland, arrived in the Forks of the Delaware with about 30 families in 1730. He took up 300 acres of land on the North Branch, near the mouth of Hunter's Creek* where he established a ferry. 'Hunter's settlement', as then called, was planted at three points, near Martin's Creek**." "These locations were all in Mount Bethel Township, later divided into Upper & Lower Mount Bethel."

Mount Bethel was generally hilly, with numerous mill-seats and slate & stone quarries.

*Note: Hunter's Creek was also called Allegheny Creek.

**Note: Martin's Creek was also known by its Indian name of Tunam.

Due to lack of land records, I cannot corroborate Mr. Henry's contention that the Hunters arrived in 1730. It is clear, however, that the Hunters settled in PA – not NJ as some have interpreted Col. James' family history.

~ ~ ~ ~ ~ ~ ~ ~ ~ ~ ~ ~ ~ ~ ~ ~ ~ ~

Hugh Martin & Jane Hunter were married about 1737, and their eldest son, Alexander, was born between 1738 and 1740.

The 1738 Voter List for Hunterdon County, NJ[26] lists men who were landowners and eligible to vote and elect General Assembly Representatives. The candidates were John Emley, Benjamin Smith, Daniel Coxe, Josh Peace, Abram Van Horne, Jno. Coate and Marten Reyarson. It is amusing to note that Hugh and brother Thomas Martin were in disagreement (no secret ballots) as to who would better represent their county at the colonial assembly:

"Pole <sic> of Freeholders of the County of Hunterdon for Representatives to serve in General Assembly of the Province of New Jersey for the County of Hunterdon, taken per Christopher Search, one of the Clerks, Oct 9, 1738, Before David Martin, Esq., High Sheriff."

Hugh Martin of Amwell, voted for Daniel Coxe & Josh. Peace

Thomas Martin of Amwell, voted for John Emley, Benjamin Smith

The Fundamental Constitutions of the Province of New Jersey in 1683 provided that "The Persons qualified to be Freemen...shall be every Planter and Inhabitant dwelling and residing within the Province, who has acquired rights to and is in possession of Fifty Acres of Ground, and hath cultivated ten Acres of it; or in Boroughs, who have a House and three Acres; or have a House and Land only hired, if he can prove he have Fifty Pounds in

---

[26] Hunterdon Co., NJ, Historical Society Newsletter – Winter, 1993 – p. 658-660

Stock of his own.." Juries were selected from "Freemen above five and Twenty Years of Age."

From the "County of Hunterdon Freeholders Book 1741"[27]:

The King agst. Wm. Tenent

Trenton April 14: 48 they agreed before me which I have numberd as they were named. ~ Ro: H: Morris.

Jury struck April 15: 1742:

<u>Amwell Township</u>: (selected entries only)

Adam Tates – [Juror #18]

Peter Midage

Francis Mason

John Burcham

Benjamin Severns

Jacob Moor

John Moore

Hugh Martin

Thomas Martin

I believe Hugh & Jane moved to their Annandale, Lebanon Twp, home between the April 15, 1742, jury selection and May 21, 1742, which was the birth date of their son James.

The description of Hugh's 419 acre Annandale plantation can only be derived from the May 6, 1774, deed[28] executed by Col. James Martin when he sold out of Hunterdon Co. to move to North Carolina: [For the full deed, please refer to Vol. II - Col. James Martin]

"For a certain Track of Land situate in Lebanon aforesd bounded as follows, viz: Beginning at a Post Corner near Adam Runkles Meadow running thence East 113 ch. along land belonging to the Estate of John Anderson, Esqr., dec'd & Andw. Bray, Esqr. to a post Corner, thence South 37 ch & 10 links along the Lands of Steven V. Rutherford to a Post Corner, thence 113 ch West along the land belonging to Corns. Low & Theodore Cramer to a Stone Corner standing in the Great Road leading to Rariton landing, thence North 37 ch & 10 links, along the lands belonging

---

[27] The Genealogical Magazine of NJ – May 1962 – Volume 37, No. 2, p 49-56

[28] Transcribed by Francie Lane from copy obtained from Hunterdon Co., NJ Clerk's file – Mortgage Deeds - Volume I, p. 195

to the sd. Adam Runkle to the Beging. containing 419 Acres Together with &c: ~"

Although the Genealogical Society of NJ's manuscript map, Sheet D (1978), by D. Stanton Hammond, JD, does not specifically name Hugh Martin as the property owner, but rather "Mathias Crammer / Kremer – 419 acres", it's clear from Col. James Martin's above deed that Hugh's plantation in Lebanon township was that self-same parcel, located a half mile south of Annandale, and adjoined Andrew Bray & John Anderson on the north; Adam & Jacob Runkle on the west; and Theodore Cramer on the south. It would seem from the map that Steven V. Rutherford's land was purchased in 1782 by John Bray. About two miles southwest of Hugh's plantation was that of his half-brother James Martin and a half mile below James' land was Samuel Rogers.

Hugh was a slaveholder as early as 1746, as indicated by the following notice printed in the "Pennsylvania Gazette":

July 3, 1746: Jack, Negro, age c. 22 - runaway from **Hugh Martin** *of Lebanon, Hunterdon Co.*[29]

The minutes of the Presbyterian Church's Synod of Philadelphia[30] reflects that on May 17, 1749, their Synod met at Maidenhead, Hunterdon Co., NJ, and Hugh Marten (sic), an Elder of the church was present. Present as Ministers were Aaron Burr, John Brainerd, Gilbert Tennent, James Campbell, Andrew Hunter, John Rogers and Samuel Finley. Hugh Martin was also recorded as present as a church Elder from The Minutes of Presbytery of Philadelphia's Synod of October 3, 1753, meeting in Philadelphia.

From Col. James narrative: *"Uncle Henry, after he came to my father's, signified he wished to have some education, that he might study divinity and fit himself for the University. Not having funds of his own, my father and his other brothers, Thomas and Robert, contributed each their share, and sent him to Newark College." "He* [Uncle Henry] *was*

---

[29] PA Colonial Records – Abstracts from Benjamin Franklin's "PA Gazette" - FTM CD#512
[30] "Records of the Presbyterian Church in the United States of America: Embracing the Minutes of the: Presbytery of Philadelphia from 1706 to 1716; Synod of Philadelphia from 1717 to 1758; Synod of New York from 1745 to 1758; Synod of Philadelphia and New York from 1758 to 1788" by the Presbyterian Board of Publication, James Russell, Publishing Agent, 1841

the cause of father's sending my brother, Alexander, to the same college, which was before it was moved to Princeton, where he learned very well, and in due time, graduated."

Perhaps a wee bit of Jane's "Irish" humor is portrayed in Col. James recollection of his brother Alexander Martin, later to become Governor of North Carolina, Speaker of the NC General Assembly. and U.S. Senator: *"I have heard my mother say he never spoke a word until he was four years old; but he learned to speak well enough afterwards."*

Hugh prepared his oldest son Alexander well for college, enrolling him in the Francis Alison Academy at New London, Chester Co., Pennsylvania, later known as the New London Academy. Alexander was also listed as an alumnus of the Nottingham Academy, also located in Chester Co., PA. Both academies were under the ecclesiastical control of the Presbyterian Church.

From "Irish Preachers & Educators in Early History of the Presbyterian Church in America"[31], *"Rev. Samuel Finley, D.D., a native of Co. Armagh, Ireland, came to Philadelphia in 1743 and within a year became Pastor of the Presbyterian Church at Nottingham in Chester County. Here he founded Nottingham Academy, and from 1744-1761 was engaged in preaching & teaching until elected to the Presidency of Princeton College in 1762. Among his alumni was Governor Alexander Martin of North Carolina".*

It has been said that Hugh was involved in the founding of Princeton College. He definitely had a strong belief in a college education as three of his sons attended Princeton. Alexander actually received his B.A. under the College of New Jersey in 1756, but was in the first class to attend newly established Princeton's Nassau Hall as he continued his education for a Master's degree, conferred in 1759. Hugh's sons James and Thomas were both attending Princeton at the time of Hugh's death in 1761.

---

[31] Irish Preachers & Educators in Early History of the Presbyterian Church in America, Journal of the American-Irish Historical Society, By American-Irish Historical Society, Volume 24, p. 162-174 - 1925

From a book on the alumni of Princeton University[32]: *Alexander Martin – Class of 1756 "The father, born in County Tyrone, migrated from Ireland in the 1720s. In New Jersey, Hugh became a moderately prosperous farmer (he left an estate inventoried at £362 and four slaves) and served as a justice of the peace for Hunterdon County.*

While it's true that Hugh's 1761 estate was valued at £362, his Inventory actually contained six slaves; namely, a man Jack (likely the 1746 "runaway"); 2 women – Rach & Kit / Kate; 2 boys – Bram & Prince; and a girl named Bett.

From New Jersey Colonial Records of 1751, it is clear that Hugh was a judiciary officer for Hunterdon County[33]:

Certificate of the Judges in the Province of New Jersey, in behalf of William Morris Esqr. Recd. with Mr. Richd. Partridge's Memorial.
To all persons whom it may Concern –
Greeting –
Whereas William Morris of Trenton, Esqr. hath Communicated to us the Subscribers, The Judges of His Majesty's Court for holding of Pleas, in & for the County of Hunterdon in the Province of New Jersey, and others his Majesty's Justices of the Peace for the said County of Hunterdon now sitting at Trenton at a General Quarter Sessions of the Peace for the said County, an Extract of a Paragraph of a Letter lately Arrived from London wrote by Mr. Benja. Morris and Expressed in the following words (Viz:) "Some days past I (Benja. Morris) went with Richard Partridge to one of the Board of Trade and Plantations, in Order to Defend the Reputation of our Uncle Wm. Morris which had been Scandalously slurr'd by Chief Justice Morris who is here. He had Carryed his Point so far That the Lords of Trade Designed to Reprimand Governor Belcher for Recommending to his Majesty a Bad Man for one of his Council a Man who was a Disturber of the Publick Peace and Concern'd in the late Riots here." We therefore in Common Justice to the Character of the said Wm. Morris Do hereby Certify That the said Wm. Morris neither to our Knowledge or belief, nor

---

[32] "Princetonians: A Biographical Dictionary" – James McLachlan, Princeton University Press, 1976.
[33] "Documents Relating to the Colonial History of the State of New Jersey", William A. Whitehead, Volume VII - Part of Administration of Gov. Jonathan Belcher - 1746-1751", Daily Advertiser Printing House, Newark, NJ – 1883 – p. 605-606

by any *Rumour* or *Report whatsoever was ever in his life time accounted a Disturber of the Publick Peace or Directly or indirectly Concerned in the late Riots in this Province but on the Contrary in all his actions and Conversation that we ever heard of, hath Condemned such proceedings and opposed as far as in him lay all such Unlawful Measures, And That the late Governor Morris Father of the above Chief Justice Morris upwards of seven years ago, Granted him a Commission under the Great seal of this Province to be first Judge of the Inferior Court of ye Common Pleas of this County of Hunterdon as a fitt and Proper person, and that by and under such Commission he now Acts as such.*

Theo: Philips
John Garrison

Philip Ringo	*Wm. Cleayton*
Charles Clark	*Benj. Biles*
Saml. Stout	*Cornelis. Ringo*
Hugh Martin	*Theo. Severns*
Saml. Johnson	

From "John Reading's Diary"[34] an entry in January, 1757, read that John Reading had received money from "Justs Martin" which had been recovered from Jo. Willson. Although author David R. Reading had indexed the entry as pertaining to a "Justin" Martin, I correspondence in 2011, with Mr. Reading, suggesting that his ancestor had abbreviated the title "Justice" to read "Justs". Mr. Reading agreed with my conclusion and his future editions, or published addenda will read "Justice Hugh Martin".

Hugh's mother, Martha [Coughran] Martin died on May 11, 1753, at the age of 74, and was buried at Hugh's plantation near Annandale.

All of Hugh & Jane [Hunter] Martin's children will have their own chapter, but I believe a brief sketch of each is warranted here:

---

[34] "John Reading's Diary – The Daily Business Record of the First American-Born Governor of New Jersey", edited by David R. Reading from original transcriptions by Dorothy A. Stratford,The Mount Amwell Project, Alexandria, VA 22314, 2010.

ALEXANDER MARTIN was born c1739. Upon receiving his Master's Degree from Princeton in 1759, he tutored for one year in VA, before settling permanently in North Carolina. He was appointed King's Attorney in NC; served as Colonel of the 2nd NC Line during the Revolution; served numerous terms as Speaker of the NC State Assembly; elected to several terms as Governor of North Carolina; and served as U.S. Senator from NC. He had one child, Alexander Strong Martin, b. 1787. Governor Martin died at his Danbury Plantation, Rockingham Co., NC, on November 2, 1807.

JAMES MARTIN was born May 21, 1742. Attended Princeton for a short time prior to his father's death, but chose to leave college to work his father's farm. He married in 1763 to neighbor Ruth Rogers, and remained in Hunterdon Co. until May, 1774, when he joined his mother and siblings in NC at the urging of his brother Alexander. James served as Colonel-Commandant of the Guilford Co., NC Militia throughout the Revolutionary War. After the War, Col. Martin acquired over 2,000 acres of land in Stokes Co., NC, and established the Union Iron Works (a lime kiln, ironworks and forge). James and Ruth [Rogers] Martin had eleven children. After Ruth died in 1795, James married for the second time to Martha Loftin, widow of Will Jones, and had five more children. Col. James Martin was active politically and served terms as Legislator in the NC State Assembly. Col. James died at his Snow Creek Plantation on 31 October 1834, at the age of 92.

THOMAS MARTIN was born about 1743. Thomas was educated at Princeton University, receiving his A. B. degree in 1762. On June 14, 1767, he was ordained a deacon in the Church of England in the Chapel Royal at St. James' Palace, London, and ordained to the priesthood on June 24, 1767. On July 8, 1767, he was assigned as Rector of the Old Brick Church, St. Thomas' Parish in Orange County, VA. Rev. Thomas also served as the tutor for the children of one of his parishioners, James Madison, Sr. Rev. Thomas Martin moved into the Montpelier Plantation and completed the college preparatory education of James Madison, Jr. – the future U.S. President. During a visit with his widowed mother in NJ, it was decided that Jane would move and live with Thomas in VA because she worried about his declining health. Rev. Thomas never married; he died young, about 27 years old in September, 1770, at Orange Co., VA.

MARTHA [MARTIN] ROGERS was born about 1745. Her future husband, neighbor Samuel Rogers witnessed her father Hugh's will in 1761. Martha and her brother James Martin married brother & sister, Samuel & Ruth Rogers. Martha & Samuel moved to Rockingham Co., NC, where he died. They were the parents of nine children, and Martha lived with her adult children after their move to TN. She died in 1825, Montgomery Co., TN

SAMUEL MARTIN was born about 1748. Served as a Lt. in the Revolutionary War. He served as County Clerk of Mecklenburg Co., NC. Delegate to the First Provincial Congress held August 1775. Samuel married and had at least two children. He was a merchant in partnership with Adlai Osborne in Charlotte, NC. Samuel died intestate on 11 March 1790, Charlotte, Mecklenburg Co., NC.

ROBERT MARTIN was the youngest son, born about 1750. Robert lived near his brother Alexander on the Dan River, Rockingham Co., NC, and inherited from brother Alexander's estate. Robert married Martha [?Denny] and was the father of four children: Sarah {Martin] Napier, Robert, Jr., John and Rachel [Martin] Broach. Robert maintained the closest relationship of any of the Martin family to nephew, Alexander Strong Martin, son of Governor Alexander Martin. Robert Martin died on June 1, 1822, in Rockingham Co., NC. It was Robert's granddaughter, Martha Denny Martin who married U.S. Senator Stephan A. Douglas.

JANE [MARTIN] HENDERSON was born 23 August 1759. She was not quite 2 years old when her father died. She was about 10 years old when her mother took her to live at Montpelier, Orange

Co., VA. Jane married Thomas Henderson in Guilford Co., NC, on November 10, 1778. Thomas Henderson was born March 19, 1752, the tenth of twelve children of Samuel and Elizabeth [Williams] - the prominent Henderson family of Granville Co., NC. Jane & Thomas Henderson had 7 children: Dr. Samuel Henderson, Alexander Martin Henderson, Mary [Henderson] Lacy, Col. Thomas Henderson, Jane [Henderson] Kendrick, Fanny [Henderson] Springs and Nathaniel Henderson. Jane [Martin] Henderson preceded her husband in death on or about March 31, 1815, Rockingham Co., NC.

Hugh's father Alexander was described by Col. James as being "a leading Elder in the Presbyterian Church near where he lived." We have records of Hugh as an Elder attending the regional Presbyterian Synod from 1749 to 1753; and Jane [Hunter] Martin had a strong Presbyterian family background. Additionally, Hugh's youngest brother Henry became a Presbyterian minister; brother Robert Martin bequeathed much of his estate to the propagation of the Presbyterian faith; and brother Thomas was buried in a Presbyterian graveyard. However, Hugh's son Thomas became an ordained Anglican Priest. Daughter Jane's husband Thomas Henderson's background was no doubt Anglican. Son Gov. Alexander Martin is often described as "Anglican" – even to the extent of his biographical sketch in the Presbyterian-run Princeton Alumni book stating, "[Alexander Martin] lived not far from the NC Moravian settlement and, although himself an Anglican, over the years became the Moravians' close friend, attending their prayer meetings and looking after their land interests and political affairs". Obviously, Hugh was raised as a Presbyterian; however, it is apparent that he was open-minded and allowed his children to choose their own faith. As the eldest brother of the orphaned Martin children, Hugh most likely gave his blessing for his sister Agnes' marriage to a Quaker, Thomas Dawson. Politically, Hugh received a "Royal" appointment as a Justice of Hunterdon Co. England's official position had relaxed a bit with the Act of Toleration, but I've wondered whether Presbyterians were merely "tolerated" or were they allowed to become His Majesty's Judges?

The first of Hugh's siblings to die was Thomas. His death must have been unexpected, because he died intestate on August 27, 1760. Hugh was present in Bucks Co., PA by the following day, August 28, 1760, to post the required bond to administer his brother's estate, along with Thomas' widow Mary and brother Rev. Henry Martin, as evidenced by the following excerpt from the bond:

"Know all men by these presents that we, Mary Martin of Middletown in the County of Bucks, Widow, and the Reverend Henry Martin of the said County, Clerk and Hugh Martin of Hunterdon County in the Province of West Jersey Yeoman And Anthony Tate and John Slack all of the said County are held and firmly bound unto William Plumsted, Esqr. Register General for the Probate of Wills and Granting Letters of Administration in and for the Province of Pennsylvania in the full and just sum of Five Hundred Pounds lawfull money of the said Province.........."

Six months later, on February 21, 1761, Hugh Martin appeared at the Hunterdon County, NJ, Court to serve as Administrator for his brother, Thomas Martin's New Jersey estate.

HUGH MARTIN[35]
ADMR.
THOS. MARTIN
~ BOND ~
Entered in Lib. No 10, Folio 460
Hunterdon County
1761
3540J
Letters Sealed

"Know all men by these presents, that we, Hugh Martin, Esq., of Lebanon, in the County of Hunterdon, and Province of New Jersey, &c

---

[35] Transcribed by Francie Lane - Hunterdon Co., NJ – Probate Records – FHC Film #461817.

and Theophilus Severns of Hunterdon ..., are held and firmly bound unto his Excellency Thomas Boone, Esq., Governor of New Jersey in the Sum of Five Hundred Pounds, Proclamation Money, to be paid to the said Governor or his successors or assigns: To which Payment well and truly to be made, we bind us, our Heirs, Executors and Administrators, jointly and severally, firmly by these Presents, Sealed with our Seals and Dated the Twenty first day of February, Anno Domini One Thousand Seven Hundred and Sixty One.

The Condition of the above Obligation is such, That if the Abovebound Hugh Martin, Esq. Administrator of all and singular the Goods, Chattels and Credits of Thomas Martin, late of the County of Bucks & Province of Pennsylvania, deceased, do make or cause to be made, a true and perfect Inventory of all and singular the Goods, Chattels and Credits of the said Deceased, which have or shall come to the Hands, Possession or Knowledge of the said Hugh Martin or into the Hands of any other Person or Persons for his use, and the same so made, exhibit or cause to be exhibited into the Registry of the Prerogative Court, in the Secretary's Office at Burlington, on or before the Twenty first Day of June next ensuing; and the same Goods, Chattels and Credits of the said Deceased, at the Time of his Death, or which at any Time after, shall come to the Hands or Possession of the said Hugh Martin or unto the Hands or Possession of any other Person or Persons, for his Use, do well and truly administer according to Law; and farther do make or cause to be made, a just and true Account of his Administration on or before the Twenty first Day of February now next ensuing the Date hereof; and all the Rest and Residue of the said Goods, Chattels and Credits, which shall be found remaining upon the Account of the said Administration the same being first examined and allowed of, by the Judge, for the time being, of the said Prerogative Court, shall deliver and pay unto such Person or Persons respectively, as the said Judge for the time being, of the said Court, by his Decree or Sentence, pursuant to the true Intent and Meaning of an Act of Parliament, made in the 22d and 23d Years of the Reign of King Charles II, entituled An Act for Settling Intestates Estates, shall limit and appoint. And if it shall hereafter appear, that any last Will and Testament was made by the said Deceased, and the Executor or Executors therein named, do exhibit the same into the said Prerogative Court, making Request to have it allowed and approved accordingly: If the said Hugh Martin, Esq. being thereunto required do render and deliver up the said Letters of Administration, Approbation of such Testament being first had and made in the said Court, then the above Obligation to be void, or else it shall stand in full Force and Virtue.

H: Martin

Sealed and Delivered in
  the Presence of

Rachel Hooton[36]   Theo Severns

New Jersey }
Hunt County }

    Be it Remembered that on the Twenty first day of February Anno Domini 1761 – Personally appeared before me Theo. Severns, duly authorized to qualifie admrs for their Truste &c Hugh Martin. Who being Sworn on the Holy Evangelists of Almighty God did acknlge that Thomas Martin dyed without a Will as far As he knows and as he verily believes and that he will well & Truly administer all and singular the Goods Chattels & Credits of the said Deceased which have or shall come to his hands or Possession or to the hands or possession of any other person or persons for his use and that he will make a True & perfect Inventory of the said Goods & Chattels Rights & Credits and exhibit the Same into Prerogative office at Burlington, and render a just & True Acct. of his Administration.

H: Martin

Sworn before me
the day & year above written
Theo. Severns, Juris.

---

[36] Note: Hunterdon Co., NJ records reveal "Hooton" was used interchangeably as "Houghton"

A short two weeks later, on March 5, 1761, Hugh wrote his own will, stating he was very sick and weak in body, but of perfect mind and memory. Four days later, on 9 March 1761, Hugh died.

It should be noted that there was an influenza epidemic that struck North America in c1761. Brother Thomas Martin died in August, 1760; sister-in-law Elizabeth [Slack] Martin died October, 1760; Hugh died March, 1761; and half-brother James Martin died in December, 1761.

HUGH MARTIN[37]
LAST WILL AND TESTAMENT
& INVENTORY
Recorded in Lib. No. 11, Folio 45
538J
Hunterdon County, New Jersey
1761

In the name of God, Amen. March the Fifth, One Thousand Seven Hundred Sixty One, I, Hugh Martin, in Lebanon, in the County of Hunterdon, in West New Jersey, Esquire, being very sick and weak in body, but of perfect mind and memory, thanks to God for it, but calling to mind my mortality, do make and ordain this my last will and testament; ie., first I give and recommend my soul to the hands of god who gave it, and my body to be decently buried at the discretion of my Executors nothing doubling, but at the general remuneration. I shall receive the same again by the mighty favor of God, and as regards my worldly estate where it hath pleased God to bless me in this life, I give and dispose of in the following manner and form:

First, I order all my lawful debts and burying charges to be paid.

Item: I order an inventory to be taken of my estate - real and personal.

Item: I order, give and bequeath my whole personal estate to my beloved wife and two daughters, Martha and Jane, to be equally divided

---

[37] Transcribed by Francie Lane - Hunterdon Co., NJ – Probate Records – FHC Film #461817.

among them, and to wit my children have their victuals, clothes, lodging and schooling free until the age of seventeen, and if any of my children die before they come of age, or marry, their part falls into the real estate.

Item: I order my two sons to wit are at college, to be brought through, out of the real estate, and after they are cleared at college, I order each of my sons, Alexander, James and Thomas to receive twenty pounds to be paid out of the real estate by the Executors.

But if my son, James, choose rather to come home and work the farm, then I order my real estate to be equally divided among my three sons, James, Samuel and Robert. And if any of these, my sons James, Samuel or Robert, die before they come of age, or marry, their part must fall to the survivors.

As it has been mentioned, to wit, if any of those to whom the personal estate was left, should die, the part of the deceased shall fall to the survivors, to wit the personal estate was left to and not to fall into the real estate.

Item: I order my sons, James and Samuel, Executors of this my last will and testament, and Brother, Robert Martin, Trustee, and I do hereby utterly disallow and disannul all former wills, legacies and Executors by me before named, ratifying this and no other to be my last will and testament in witness whereof, I have hereunto set my hand and seal the day and year above written.

Signed, sealed and pronounced and witnessed in the presence of the subscribers to be my last will and testament in witness of subscribers.

H: Martin   {Seal}

Witness:
John Hanna
James Martin, Jr.
Martha Martin

March the 6th, 1761 -- My will is that my Negro man, Jack, shall belong to the private Estates and the horses, and that my dearly beloved wife, Jean Martin, shall have my Negro wench, called Cate, and a horse and saddle and her maintenance during her widowhood.

Item: That my well beloved daughter, Martha Martin, shall have the little Negro wench, called Bett.

Item: That my dear son, Alexander Martin, shall have the young Negro boy, called Bram, and my dear son, James, to have the other boy, called Prince.

Item: And that my son, Alexander, shall be one of my Executors. ("crossed out" of my son Samuel, who is not of age); with my son James and Samuel, and Item that my daughter Martha shall have sixty pounds paid from the Real Estate and that my daughter, Jean, shall have sixty pounds and the bed and horse and saddle from the real estate. This is my last codicil --

H: Martin   {Seal}

Signed, Sealed and Delivered
in the presence of us:
/s/ James Martin, Jr.
/s/ Samuel Rogers
/s/ Martha Martin

James Martin, Jr. and Samuel Rogers, two of the witnesses to the within will and codicil, being sworn on the Holy Evangelists of Almighty God, did severally depose that they saw Hugh Martin, the Testator within named, sign and seal the same and heard him publish, pronounce and declare the within will and codicil to be his last will and testament and that at the doing thereof, the said Testator was of sound and disposing mind and memory, as far as these Deposers know, and as they verily believe, and that John Hanna and Martha Martin signed their names as witnesses to the said will and codicil in the presence of the said Testator, and in the presence of each other.

James Martin, Jr.
Samuel Rogers

Sworn the 12th day of May, 1761, before me.

Theo. Severns, Justice

Alexander, James and Samuel Martin, Executors named in the within will and codicil, being sworn on the Holy Evangelists of Almighty God, did severally depose that the within instruments contains the true last will and testament of Hugh Martin, the Testator within named, so far as they know and as they verily believe, and that they will well and truly

perform the same by paying first the debts of the said deceased and then the legacies in the said testament specified, and so far as the goods, chattels and credits of the said deceased can thereunto extend and that they will make a true and perfect inventory of the said goods, chattels and credits and exhibit the same into the Prerogative office at Burlington, and all and singular the said goods, chattels and credits will have or shall hereafter come to their knowledge or possession, or to the possession of any other person or persons for their use and render a just and true audit when lawfully required. /s/ James Martin
Sworn the 12th day of May, 1761, before me. /s/ Theo. Severns, Justice

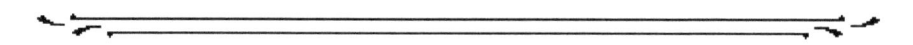

The Inventory of the moveable Estate of Hugh Martin, of Lebanon, in the County of Hunterdon and Province of New Jersey, deceased, taken and appraised to the best of our knowledge and judgment, the sixth day of May, Anno Domini, 1761.

		£	P	S
For	8 cowes @ 3 pounds each	24	0	0
	11 ewes & 11 lambs at 6 ea	6	12	0
	16 old sheep at 10 ea	8	0	0
	8 haffers at 1-10 ea	12	0	0
	3 yearling kine	3	0	0
	4 caufs at 10 ea	2	0	0
	15 hogs at 10 ea	7	10	0
	A black racing horse	10	0	0
	A gray trotting horse	45	0	0
	An old black horse	2	0	0
	An old brown mare	2	0	0
	An old brown mare with a starr in her forehead	6	0	0
	A 3 year old mare	5	0	0
	A bald horse with a wall eye	4	0	0
	A brown horse	4	0	0
	A yearling Colt	5	0	0
	A Negrow fellow Jack	40	0	0
	A Negrow winch called Rach	10	0	0
	A Negrow winch called Kit	45	0	0
	A Negrow boy called Bram	15	0	0

A Negrow boy called Prince	10	0	0
A Negro child called Bett	5	0	0
A Waggon and gers & tacklin	8	0	0
2 Plows and 2 harrows & tacklin	8	0	0
A windmill & ridler & Cuting & 2 slades	2	0	0
A peace of wheat suposed to be 40 acres	25	0	0
2 Scith	0	7	6
A bed & beding & furniter	10	0	0
2 beds In Ye rum	15	0	0
2 tables In Ye rum	1	0	0
A glass & warming pann	1	0	0
A 3 pair of hand irons & shovel & tongs	1	5	0
20 bushels of wheat	4	10	0
	303	4	6
Cash in hand at Hugh Martin's	40	0	0
Cash received for wheat	18	0	0
A chest	1	0	0
	362	4	6

Appraiser of the within Inventory being sworn on the Holy Evangelists of Almighty God did depose that the goods, chattel and credits in this Inventory set down and specified were by him appraised according to their just and true respective rates and values after the best of his judgment and understanding and that consented in all things in the doing thereof and that they appraised all things that were brought to their view for appraisal.

Sworn the 12th day of May, 1761, before me.

/s/ Theo. Severns, Justice

Alexander, James and Samuel Martin, Executors of this last will and testament of Hugh Martin, did being sworn on the Holy Evangelists of Almighty God, did depose that the within writing contains a true and perfect Inventory of all and singular the goods, chattel and credit of the said deceased which hath come to their knowledge, possession or to the possession of any other person or persons for their use.

Sworn the 12th day of May, 1761, before me.
/s/ Theo. Severns, Justice   /s/ James Martin

Hugh's LWT was witnessed by his nephew James Martin, Jr., and probable niece Martha Martin, children of half-brother James Martin, a near neighbor in Lebanon. Witness John Hanna was a medical doctor as well as ordained and assigned in 1761 to preach at the Presbyterian Church in Kingwood Twp. Witness Samuel Rogers, the son of Thomas Rogers, would soon become the husband of Hugh's daughter, Martha. Wife Jane [Hunter] Martin was referred to as "Jean" throughout Hugh's will – as was their daughter Jane. The body of the Will names sons James and Samuel as Executors, along with Hugh's brother Robert Martin to act as a Trustee. Later by way of a codicil, Hugh names son Alexander as one of the Executors, even though Alexander was living in Rowan Co., North Carolina. Hugh seems to delete Samuel as an Executor making a notation that he is not of age. This may tend to indicate that Samuel was born about 1748. It is clear from Hugh's deteriorating handwriting overnight from March 5th to the codicil dated March 6th, that he had taken a turn for the worse. Comparing Hugh's signature from his February 21st administration bond, which was strong and bold, one can see that his illness was very sudden.

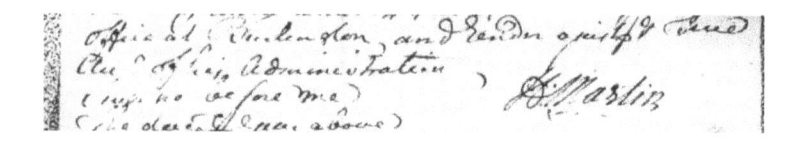

Above is Hugh's signature from February 21, 1761, and is consistent with his signature throughout the years.

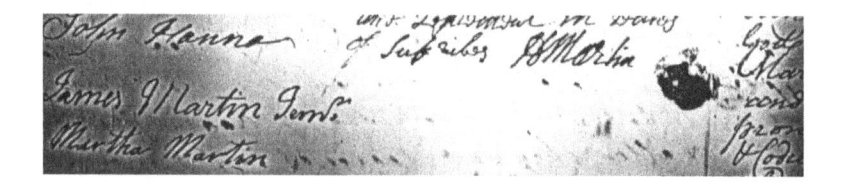

Above is Hugh's signature from LWT written on March 5, 1761

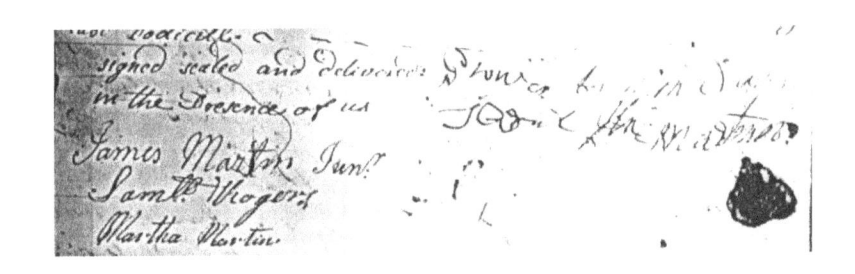

Above is Hugh's signature - LWT's Codicil, dated March 6, 1761.

Hugh's LWT is very interesting from the aspect of bequeathing his whole personal estate to Jane and his two daughters Martha & Jane, and in providing his children with their victuals, clothes, lodging and schooling free until the age of seventeen. As Hugh did not specify schooling be extended only to his sons, it must be assumed that the girls were also expected to attend school until age 17.

Hugh called one woman slave by the name of "Cate"; however, the inventory lists her as "Kit". She is called Kate when mentioned in Rev. Thomas Martin's 1770 letter to his brother Col. James as being the center of a dispute between Rev. Thomas and his Uncle Robert Martin, who had been designated the Trustee in the execution of Hugh's Will. It is interesting that Kate remained with the family for at least nine years after Hugh's death.[The full text of the letter is found in Chapter 10 – Rev. Thomas Martin]

The Inventory contains a considerable number of livestock, but fascinating is the listing of a black racing horse, a gray trotting horse, an old black horse, an old brown mare, an old brown mare with a star in her forehead, a 3 year old mare, a bald horse with a wall eye, a brown horse, and a yearling colt. This is an unusual number of horses for a "moderately prosperous" farmer. It's said that the Irish love horses and racing, and so it seems to have been with Hugh. The only indication of crops grown was the 40 acres of wheat and 20 bushels of wheat on hand.

From the "History of Hunterdon and Somerset Counties, New Jersey", compiled by James P. Snell (Philadelphia: Everts & Peck, 1881), p.538-539.

"There is an old burial-place on the John Fulkerson place, near Annandale, but, save in the cases of two graves that have been especially cared for, the resting-places of the dead in that spot are unmarked except by here and there a fragment of a headstone. The two graves alluded to are those of Hugh Martin and Martha, his brother's wife. About these graves David Fraser years ago built a stone wall, which fronts the highway." [38]

David Frazer, who built a stone wall surrounding the graves, married Rachel Anderson, daughter of John Anderson, Esq., next-door neighbor of Hugh Martin. David Fraser remained a friend to Col. James Martin, as evidenced by personal correspondence, dated 26 November 1795[39]. The pertinent paragraph of Frazer's letter, relating the news of old friends and neighbors, states: (See this letter fully transcribed in Volume II - Col. James Martin)

"...Adam Runkle & family is well. The old gentleman is happy in having your letter read, *he wishes you was his Neighbour* as I do. Old Peter Young was struck with the Palsey and Buried a few days ago ~ Coxes Familly, Dunhams, Herbert Rodenbough, Pickles, Apgars, John & Andw. Brays famillys all well, ..."

The Federal Census is missing for the years 1790 through 1820, so the first preserved census for Hunterdon Co., NJ was 1830, and fortunately, it was a neighborhood enumeration as opposed to an alphabetical listing.

By 1830, the Martin plantation was the property of John Fulkerson, and by viewing his 1830 neighborhood, one can still see the descendants of Col. James' neighbors living in their family homesteads. It would seem Rachel [Anderson] Frazer's brother may have been Fulkerson's next-door neighbor: Richard Anderson, age 90-100 years old:

<u>1830 US Census - Hunterdon Co., NJ - Lebanon Twp - p. 417-419</u>[40]:
p. 417:

---

[38] History of Hunterdon and Somerset Counties, New Jersey, compiled by James P. Snell (Philadelphia: Everts & Peck, 1881), 538-539.
[39] Letter from David Frazer, of Lebanon, Hunterdon Co., NJ, to Col. James Martin, of Snow Creek Plantation, Stokes Co., NC. The original letter is in the possession of Mr. Robert Upshur of Columbia, SC, a direct descendant of Col. James Martin, and transcribed on October 13, 2003, by Francie Lane.
[40] 1830 US Census – Hunterdon Co., NJ – Ancestry.com Census Images 1&3/40.

RODENBOCK, Herbert H <Rodenbough>
p. 418:
BRAY, John F.
BRAY, Andrew
Chrystie, James
Morgan, Asher
RUNKLE, Euphemia
APGAR, Peter (son of Peter)
Hoffman, John H.
FISHER, Anna
Ten Eyck, Peter, Capt..
FULKERSON, JOHN
ANDERSON, Richard (90-100 & blind)
Hoffman, Henry
YOUNG, PETER G.

Both Hugh and his mother's graves have subsequently been moved to Clinton, N.J., toward the rear of the Evergreen Cemetery, amongst contemporary burial sites. Charles Martin, a descendant of Col. James Martin advised me that the graves had been moved twice – once in 1946 due to widening of a Federal highway; then again in 1975 due to construction of the Interstate Highway. Charles Martin stated that Hugh Martin's gravestone was placed in 1804 by his sons Alexander & James.

From the inscription "His weeping sons in North Carolina", it is clear that the stone was not cut in 1761, but rather later, at a point in time when all of Hugh's sons, Alexander, James, Samuel and Robert, were residing in North Carolina. It would be reasonable to assume that Governor Martin contracted for the stone to be laid during his 1793-1799 term in the U.S Senate, then meeting in the nation's capitol of Philadelphia. I believe the epitaph was composed by Gov. Alexander Martin. As you will read later, Alexander was a published dramatist and poet.

Over Hugh Martin's grave is a white marble stone, inscribed as follows:

Here lies the remains of
Hugh Martin
who lived in this vicinity many years during which
possessing the confidence of his government
and his fellow-citizens
he discharged the duties of several offices
of profit and trust with integrity and honesty.
In the practice of the private and
public virtues, eminent;
as husband, father, relative, and friend, beloved;
as a magistrate, revered.
To religion a support, to science a patron,
and
to the poor, a friend.
He was born in Ireland, County Tyrone,
and
died March 7th, Anno Dom. 1761, aged 63 years.

Let sculptured marble vainly boast,
And birth and titles scan;
God's noblest work, of value most,
Here lies an honest man.
'His weeping sons in North Carolina
pay this tribute to his memory.

Go, traveler, and imitate his virtues.

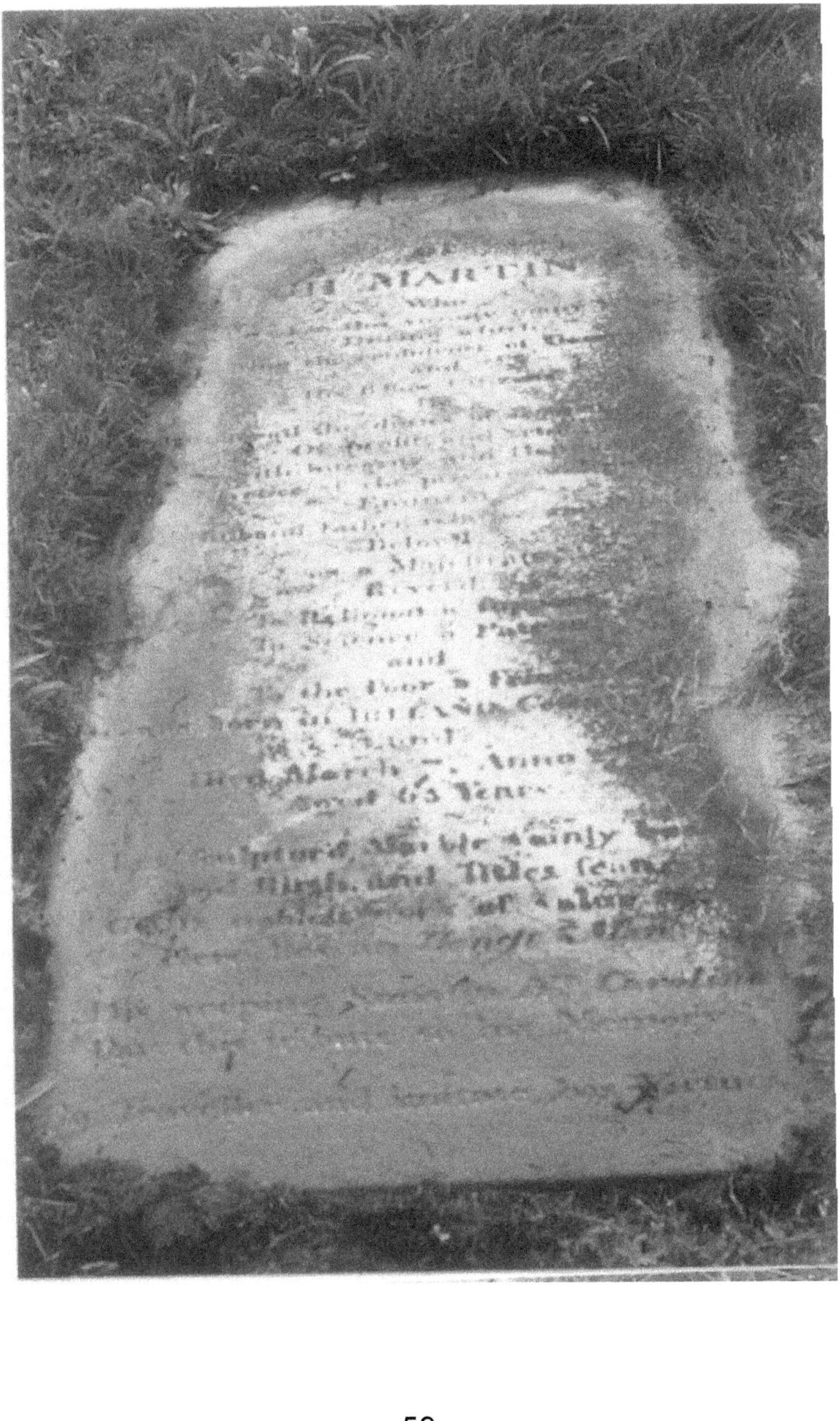
MARTIN

On December 10, 1761, the following article was printed in the *"Pennsylvania Gazette"*:

"Notice is hereby given to Alexander Martin, merchant, Salisbury, North Carolina, that his father, Hugh Martin of Hunterdon County, New Jersey, died 9th of March, last; and left him and his brother James executors of his will; wherefore said Alexander Martin, if not inconvenient to his business, is desired to return home to settle his late father's affairs, but if his coming should be attended with disadvantage to him, he is requested not to come, by his mother, Jane Martin."

In the June, 1802, Session of Stokes County, NC, Court, Robert Martin petitioned for a judgment against his brother Col. James Martin for failing to fully distribute the inheritance due from their father Hugh's estate. James defended the suit by stating he had acted as Executor of his father's will, and payment of 202 pounds, 9 shillings and 7 pence was made to Robert between May, 1776 and January, 1779, plus half-ownership of a stud horse. James further recited the various expenses incurred for their brother Thomas' education, and other legacies required by the terms of the will, concluding that Robert had received full satisfaction

State of North Carolina }
Stokes County   } June Session, 1802

The answer of James Martin to the petition of Robert Martin[41].

This respondent, now and at all times hereafter, saving and reserving to himself all manner and benefit of exceptions to the many uncertainties, insufficiencies, untruths and false allegations set forth in the complainant's petitions for answer thereto, or so much thereof, as this Defendant is advised is material for him to answer unto, answering saith that true it is Hugh Martin, father of the petitioner died some time in the

---

[41] Copy from Linda Vernon – Stokes Co., NC Records, NC Archives. Transcription by Francie Lane

year 1761, having made a last will and testament bearing date on or about the time set forth in the complainant's petition.

This defendant also states that there was a codicil annexed, bearing date the day following the date of said will. This defendant admits that there is a clause in the said will of the said Hugh of the tenor and effect set forth in the petition of the said Robert Martin, to wit that his two sons which are at College to be brought through out of the real estate, and after they are cleared at College, I order each of my sons, Alexander, James and Thomas to receive twenty pounds to be paid out of the real estate by the Executors, but if my son, James, choose to come home and work the farm, then I order my real estate to be equally divided among my three sons, James, Samuel and Robert, and if any of those, my sons, die before they come of age or marry, their part must fall to the survivors to whom the personal was left to and was not to fall into the real estate. This defendant admits and was always willing to admit that he, together with Samuel Martin and Alexander Martin, were appointed Executors of the last will and testament of their father, Hugh Martin, and that the defendant is the surviving Executors who qualified and that this defendant sold the real estate, the one third of which is claimed by the Petitioner under the devise contained in the said will of his father Hugh as his legacy at the price of one thousand six hundred pounds New Jersey currency dollars at seven shillings and sixpence as set forth in the petition. This defendant further states that the petitioner was well entitled to one third of the real estate sold by defendants above-mentioned, subject to the payment of the several legacies with which it is charged by the will with the codicil annexed of the said Hugh which this defendant prays may be received as part of this, his answer.

This defendant further states that it will appear from the will and codicil that the following special legacies ought to be deducted from the legacy of which the petitioner claims a share. Twenty pounds to Alexander Martin, twenty pounds to Thomas Martin, Sixty pounds to Martha Martin, sixty pounds and a bed and furniture, horse and saddle to Jane Martin, which legacies are to be considered in Jersey currency.

This defendant further states that he chose to come home from the College and his brother, Thomas Martin, remained. That they were the two sons who were to be brought through at College and this defendant *supported his said brother about two years at Princeton College, and expended at least thirty pounds upon said Thomas during said time, which legacy the said Robert claims an interest in was likewise chargeable with this expenditure on said Thomas. This defendant doth expressly deny that he appropriated the legacy the said Robert claims an interest in under the will wholly to his own use, but avers and so the truth is that he, the defendant, paid the said petitioner in part of the legacy aforesaid the sum of two hundred and two pounds, nine shillings and seven pence, Jersey money, exclusive of the different legacies and charges upon the legacy under which the aforesaid Robert claims, which payment of the aforesaid two hundred and two pounds, nine shillings and seven pence were made between May, 1776 and January, 1779. This defendant begs leave further to answer and set forth that after he sold the real estate of his father as set forth in the petition, before the purchase money was due, it was considerable depreciating and this defendant gave in bonds which he had taken to secure payment of the real estate so as aforesaid sold, to the amount six hundred and thirty three pounds, six shillings and eight pence Jersey money for a stud horse, which stud horse afterwards was received by Samuel Martin and Robert Martin, the legatees at the price above stated for and on account of said legacy from this defendant,*

    This defendant reasonably supposes after having a credit for the sum paid and deducting the charges upon the aforesaid legacy, the petitioner has received full satisfaction from this defendant for the legacy devised the aforesaid petitioner by the aforesaid will of his father, Hugh Martin, and this defendant prays that he may be hence dismissed. He prays that he may be allowed his reasonable costs for his acting as Executor.

                                                     Theophilus Lacy
                                              Attorney for Defendant

    James Martin maketh oath that the matters of fact set forth in this, his answer, that come to his own knowledge are true and those that do not come to his knowledge, he believes to be true.

                                                       Jas. Martin

Sworn to in open Court
Thomas Armstrong, DC

After Hugh's death, Col. James left Princeton to return home to work the plantation, and on August 10, 1763, married Ruth Rogers, daughter of Thomas Rogers. James paid the college expenses for his brother Thomas' continuing education at Princeton. Widow Jane remained at the plantation, raising the younger children (Martha, Samuel, Robert, and Jane).

The Rogers Family

For the sake of discussion, I will include speculation I've seen regarding the Rogers family. Hugh Martin's son, Col. James Martin, and daughter, Martha Martin, married respectively Ruth [Rogers] and brother Samuel Rogers, children of Thomas Rogers of Hunterdon Co., NJ. I have read claims that the Martin siblings and Rogers siblings were "cousins" and that Thomas Rogers' wife was Frances [Martin] Rogers. Certainly, James/Martha were not 1st cousins of Ruth/Samuel, and it's difficult to imagine why Col. James would have neglected to mention a Martin/Rogers kinship in his family history. If such a relationship truly existed, Mrs. Thomas Rogers might have been Hugh's 1st cousin, the daughter of an unknown brother to Alexander Martin. However, I would question whether Thomas Rogers' wife was named "Frances". Most traditional naming patterns reflect the oldest daughter to be named for her paternal grandmother; the second daughter named for her maternal grandmother. James & Ruth [Rogers] Martin named their 2nd eldest daughter, Mary Ann Martin; Samuel & Martha [Martin] Rogers named their 1st eldest daughter, Mary Rogers. Although Ruth [Rogers] Martin had a daughter Frances, she was the 6th daughter and the tenth of eleven children. Of the two daughters of Samuel Rogers, none were named "Frances".

I don't believe Mrs. Thomas Rogers could be placed into an earlier Martin generation, because of the birth dates of her Rogers children. In order to place her into a later generation, as a daughter of Alexander, one would have to wonder why Col. James would outline all of his aunts, uncles and half-uncles, but omit his own mother-in-law. The James/Ruth Martin marriage took place in 1763; the Samuel/Martha Rogers marriage probably was about 1765. Thomas Rogers, however, had earlier purchased a secondary plantation in Lebanon twp., which adjoined the Martin land. Another coincidence is that Hugh's half-brother, James Martin wrote his LWT in 1761, which was witnessed by William Rogers, son of Thomas Rogers. Further, Thomas Rogers' LWT was witnessed by "James Martin, Junior", presumed to be the son of Hugh's half-brother, James Martin, Sr. It is apparent that there were close ties between the Rogers and Martins, predating these two children's marriages. In all likelihood, Hugh's father had siblings; if so, they would have been apt to immigrate to America along with Alexander's immediate family.

Another more likely scenario, if the "cousin" relationship is to be believed, could involve Thomas Rogers being the younger brother or nephew of Alexander Martin's first wife, whose identity is unknown, but was the mother of Hugh's half-brothers James & William Martin. From the few Rogers facts known, it seems as though Thomas Rogers gravitated more toward Hugh's half-brother James Martin. [For more information on the Rogers family, please see Volume II – Col. James Martin / Martha [Martin] Rogers]

According to the Hunterdon Co., NJ Tax Lists of 1778-1780, James Martin was listed as owning the Lebanon Township plantation, which coincides with James' statement that the final sales payment was made in 1779.[42]

Rev. Thomas Martin graduated from Princeton, was ordained an Anglican Priest in England, 1767, and appointed Pastor of the Anglican "Old Brick Church", in St. Thomas Parish, Orange Co., VA. The Old Brick Church no longer stands, but it was originally built in c1755 upon a hill, where the Pamunkey Road crosses Church Run[43]. Rev. Thomas was simultaneously employed by James Madison, Sr. as a tutor for the Madison children at the nearby Montpelier plantation. It is apparent from correspondence

---

[42] "Revolutionary Census of NJ, Based on Ratables During the Period of the Revolution" by Kenn Stryker-Rodda.
[43] "A History of Orange Co., VA" by W. W. Scott. - Everrett Waddey Co., Richmond, VA, 1907

of [U.S. President] James Madison, (Jr.) that Rev. Thomas had been living at Montpelier with the Madison family until Jane made the decision to move herself, and children (Samuel and 10 year old Jane) to live with son Thomas. Because of the responsibility for, and number of dependents, now sharing quarters with Thomas, it was necessary for Rev. Thomas to move from Montpelier Plantation, and made plans for his mother and younger siblings to move into the glebe, where he established a school.

Unfortunately, Rev. Thomas died the following year, 1770. It was undoubtedly soon after that Samuel Martin left Virginia to join his eldest brother Alexander in Salisbury, Rowan Co., North Carolina. Young Jane remained with her mother, and moved with her into Montpelier, under the hospitality of James Madison, Sr.

From biography of President James Madison,[44]

"..Reverend Mr. Martin lived with the Madison family at Montpelier; Slaughter, in his parish history, that he [Rev. Thomas] lived with his mother and sister on the church glebe. The two statements are not really in conflict, for it was not until after Madison left for college that the rector brought his mother and several younger brothers (making no mention of a sister) to Virginia."

From a letter written by James Madison, Nassau Hall, August 10, 1769, to Rev. Thomas Martin, while in Hunterdon Co. visiting his Mother Jane: *"Sawney [Madison's slave] tells me that your mother and brothers are determined to accompany you to Virginia; my friendship and regard for you entitle them to my esteem, and assure them that with the greatest sincerity I wish, after a pleasant journey, they may find Virginia capable of giving them great happiness."*

"Tutoring the Madison children had been a problem since the illness and death of the Reverend Thomas Martin in 1770. At that time the elder Madison's thought had been to employ in his home a member of the class graduating at Princeton. He put the suggestion before James, Jr., who replied on July 23, 1770: 'I have spoken to several of the present senior class about living with you as tutor, but they will determine nothing

---

[44] "James Madison: The Founding Father", Robert A. Rutland – Macmillan, NY – 1987 ISBN: 0029276012 – UCD E342.R88 1987

unless they know what you would allow them...Let me know the most that you would be willing to give...'

"Nothing seems to have come of that, and the work may have been taken over temporarily by Mrs. Martin, the rector's mother. At any rate, though her sons went to North Carolina to join their eldest brother, Alexander, she remained at Orange, apparently entering the Madison household. More than a year later (October 7, 1771), Madison wrote from Princeton that one of the Martin boys, James, had been at Princeton during commencement, where he had news of "his brothers and friends in Carolina by a young man lately come from thence... You may tell Mrs. Martin he left his family at home all well." Since the Brick Church glebe had passed to a new rector, this appears to place Mrs. Martin in the Madison household."

"The Rev. Thomas Martin succeeded Mr. Marye in 1767...... Death removed him from the scene of his labours and his usefulness not long after he entered upon the duties of the parish. He was followed by the Rev. John Barnett. His name occurs officially in 1771."[45]

I was fortunate enough to visit Orange, Orange Co., VA, and tour the elegant Montpelier Plantation. I was overwhelmed at the realization that I was standing on the very steps, walking through the same rooms, and gazing at the same beautiful rolling countryside that were once "home" to my 5th Great Grandmother.

It was probably in 1774 that Jane accompanied her son James, his wife and children in their move to Guilford County, NC in what would become Rockingham County. Jane's son Alexander purchased a Granville Grant in 1761 on the Dan River at Jacobs Creek, shortly after his father's death, and was in conjunction with a similar purchase by his Uncle John Hunter. I feel Alexander contemplated building his Danbury Plantation for the purpose of providing his Mother with a home near to her Hunter family as well as her children and grandchildren. Indeed, Jane lived with her son Alexander at Danbury until her death on 6 November 1807, at the

---

[45] "Old Churches, Ministers and Families of Virginia" by Bishop William Meade, originally published: Philadelphia – 1857; reprinted by Genealogical Publishing Co., Inc., Baltimore, MD - 1966

age of 90. She outlived her son Governor Alexander Martin by four days.

Alexander Martin wrote his Last Will & Testament on February 20, 1807, making provision for the care of his Mother Jane:

"Item: I bequeath and devise my Danbury Plantation, where I now live, to the use of my Brother-in-law Thomas Henderson, and his wife, Jane Henderson, my sister, for and during their natural lives each, on this condition that they maintain and support my Mother, Jane Martin, in as decent and proper a manner with regard to clothing and provisions as she has been accustomed to have during her residence with me -- and to enjoy and have the use of her own chamber, bed and furniture for and during her natural life - and should the said Thomas and Jane, or either of them, die before my said Mother, she is to have the like support from their successors hereinafter named, ...",

"Item: I give and bequeath to the use of my Mother aforesaid for and during her natural life, my man Prince and Negro woman, There, with her husband Billy, to aid the said Thomas Henderson and Jane his wife, in the support and maintenance of my said Mother. After the death of my said Mother, my will and pleasure is that my said servant, Prince, be set free by order of the County Court or General Assembly for the many faithful and meritorious services the said Prince hath rendered me in my life time -- ..."

Abstracts of Vital Records from Raleigh, NC Newspapers – 1799-1819, Volume I, compiled by Lois Smathers Neal. The Reprint Co., Spartanburg, SC – 1979:

3166 MARTIN: D. At his seat in Rockingham county, on the 2d inst., the Hon. ALEXANDER MARTIN, LLD – And – On the 6th, his mother, at the advanced age of ninety years. RR Thurs 19 Nov 1807 3:4 / TM Thurs 19 Nov 1807 3:2

According to county and family lore, Jane was buried at Danbury Plantation in the family crypt, built near the Dan River on a beautiful wooded spot. About thirty years later, a freshet washed the vault into the river; however, Alexander's, and presumably Jane's, bodies were recovered and buried elsewhere. There is speculation that their graves may now be located in the Robert

Martin family cemetery in Rockingham Co., NC, which will be discussed in a later volume.

Charles D. Rodenbough, a historian who has spent many years researching the political career of Gov. Alexander Martin, told me he once had contact with a Martin descendant in Alamance Co., NC, who had shown him Jane [Hunter] Martin's prayer book. The woman has since died, and the whereabouts of Jane's prayer book is unknown. It was an Episcopalian Prayer Book, with "Jane Martin" embossed in gold lettering. Inside the cover was Gov. Alexander Martin's Society of the Cincinnati blue ribbon.

CHAPTER FIVE

THOMAS MARTIN
(1708 - 1760)

Thomas Martin was born in 1708, County Tyrone, in what is now Northern Ireland, the son of Alexander and 2nd wife Martha [Coughran] Martin.

It was in the early 1720's that Thomas arrived in America with his parents and siblings. It was probably about the spring of 1730, when Thomas would have accompanied his older brother Hugh in the move from the west bank of the Delaware River across to Hunterdon Co., NJ.

From a book[46] published in 1890 concerning the family of Peter Fisher of old Amwell, Hunterdon Co., author Cornelius Wilson Larison, stated he had been able to examine old documents in the possession of J. M. Hagaman, which detailed the history of Hagaman's plantation; i.e., the land was commissioned to Andrew Hamilton on August 13, 1699. Hamilton sold 5,000 acres to one of the NJ Proprietors, Benjamin Field of Chesterfield, Burlington County, on May 19, 1701. Benjamin Field sold 300 acres to Henry Oxley on December 8, 1701. Oxley sold on February 2, 1721, to James Burcham, and upon Burcham's death, the land descended to his son Joseph Burcham. On May 11, 1730, Joseph Burcham sold his southerly half (150 acres) to Hugh Martin for £78 "silver money". Hugh Martin sold the same 150 acres to his brother Thomas Martin for £78 on December 3, 1736. Upon Thomas' death, the land descended to Thomas Martin's only son Daniel. Daniel Martin first leased the land to Abraham Hagaman for the term of one year, commencing on March 31, 1787, for £35 Gold or Silver money plus payment of current taxes. On May 4, 1792, Abraham Hagaman purchased the "northerly part" from Daniel Martin, for £1,000 "a

---

[46] "Skech [sic] of the Fisher Family of Old Amwell Township in Hunterdon Co., NJ" by Cornelius Wilson Larison - 1890

plantation of 105 acres, lying on both sides of the York Road, about a mile southwest of Ringos". The southerly part, being 105 acres, was the "one-third part of one ninetieth undivided one hundredth part of a tract then known as the Proprietary Tract of Robert Dimsdale in West Jersey, and on the 23rd and 27th days of February 1682 one Nicolas Lucas conveyed it to P. Robert Dimsdale which descended to John Dimsdale, and he sold it to Richard Smith and Ebenezer Large on the 28th and 29th days of March 1746, who sold the same to Thomas Martin on the l0th of August 1750 for £150 which land then descended to Daniel Martin the only son and heir at law of Thomas Martin, deceased, and Daniel sold the same to Abraham Hagaman on the 21st day of May 1793". Abraham Hagaman lived on the land for about 44 years; died and left a part of the plantation to his son Peter Hagaman, who lived on the land for about 44 years, leaving the plantation to his son J. M. Hagaman, who owned it for about ten years up through 1890. Daniel's 1787 lease stated he was "of Middletown Township in the County of Bucks and State of Pennsylvania". C. W. Larison described Daniel Martin as "a brother <sic – should read "nephew"> to Hugh Martin, who, as a joint partner with Peter Boss, owned 300 acres adjoining said tract on the east, as shown by a Will in possession of J. M. Hagaman; also that Daniel Martin was a lawyer who wrote an excellent hand – "all his papers are drawn with neatness and plainness."

    C. W. Larison's description of the history of the land conveyances is somewhat confusing, because Joseph Burcham's "southerly half" as it progressed through the years from Hugh Martin's purchase in 1730, became known as Daniel Martin's "northerly half". Daniel's "southerly half" was purchased by his father Thomas from Richard Smith in 1750, and adjoined property purchased near the same time by Derrick Hogeland (Hoagland). For clarity, my interpretation of the history of Thomas' land was a total of 210 acres, comprised of the following:

#1: 105 acres (north half): The owners and purchase dates progressed as follows:
>   Andrew Hamilton (1699)
>   Benjamin Field (May, 1701)
>   Henry Oxley (December, 1701)
>   James Burcham (1721) then inherited by son
>   Joseph Burcham
>   Hugh Martin (1730)
>   Thomas Martin (1736) then inherited by son
>   Daniel Martin (1760) then leased in 1787 to:
>   Abraham Hagaman (1792)

#2: 105 acres (south half): The owners and purchase dates progressed as follows:
>   Nicholas Lucas
>   Robert Dimsdale (1682) then inherited by:
>   John Dimsdale
>   Richard Smith & Ebenezer Large (1746)
>   Thomas Martin (August 10, 1750) then inherited by:
>   Daniel Martin (1760)
>   Abraham Hagaman (May, 1793)

Larison stated, *"These several buildings <Hagaman's farm buildings> form an out-fit for a plantation that, in Hunterdon County, has rarely, if ever, been equaled; and for beauty and efficiency they seem to be, in the pursuit of agriculture, all that one could desire. The location of this villa is peculiar. Altho the eminence upon which it stands is not high, the pluvial waters never stand about the buildings. From the walls of the dwelling, the sward descends in every direction—forming a gentle but perfect drainage. The water from the roof on the south side of the barn finds its way to the Delaware thru a small tributary to the Alexsauken; that from the roof on the north, thru another tributary to the same rivulet; while the water from the roof upon the east side of the barn forms the head waters of one of the tributaries of the Neshanic and flows to the sea thru the Raritan".*

As an aside, I am curious as to the identity of Abraham Hagaman. Hugh & Thomas' brother, Rev. Henry Martin died intestate in 1764, Bucks Co., PA, and one of the sureties for the administration bond was shown as John Hagerman; signed as John Hegeman of Northampton, Bucks Co., PA. Obviously, John Hegeman was well acquainted with the Martins in Bucks Co. The history of Bucks Co., Pennsylvania, makes mention of a riot in 1766 at Gregg's Mill, near Newtown. The cause of the rioting is not detailed; however, the rioters were indicted and John Hagerman was the first so subpoenaed to stand trial.

In 1738, Thomas was 30 years old, and his brother Hugh was age 40. The 1738 Voter List for Hunterdon County, NJ lists men who were landowners and eligible to vote and elect General Assembly Representatives. The candidates were John Emley, Benjamin Smith, Daniel Coxe, Josh Peace, Abram VanHorne, Jno. Coate and Marten Reyarson. It is interesting to note that the election was not a secret ballot vote, and Hugh and Thomas disagreed over who the better colonial assembly candidates were.

"Pole of Freeholders of the County of Hunterdon for Representatives to serve in General Assembly of the Province of New Jersey for the County of Hunterdon, taken per Christopher Search, one of the Clerks, Oct 9, 1738, Before David Martin, Esq., High Sheriff."
Hugh Martin of Amwell, voted for Daniel Coxe & Josh. Peace
Thomas Martin of Amwell, voted for John Emley, Benjamin Smith

From the "County of Hunterdon Freeholders Book 1741" both Hugh & Thomas Martin were selected for jury duty at Trenton on April 15, 1742, drawn from Amwell Township.

When Thomas' youngest brother, Henry, indicated his desire to study divinity at Newark College, Thomas together with his brothers Hugh and Robert contributed to provide funds for Henry's education.

Thomas was the only son of Alexander & Martha [Coughran] Martin to engage in construction. Col. James wrote, *"My Uncle Robert kept a school for several years, and my Uncle Thomas had learned the stone-mason's trade, and they both by their industry made a considerable property."* Many of the Hunterdon Co., NJ and Bucks Co., PA buildings of that era were constructed of stone.

From "John Reading's Diary"[47], April 1747 begins the first of many entries concerning Thomas Martin, wherein "Tho: Martin Payed me in cash sent from Sam'l Furman".

In June, 1747, Reading indicated that Thomas Martin was building a house for his son, John Reading, Jr. Later, Thomas Martin contracted for work on a home for Reading's son George Reading.

August 6, 1747, John Reading "Payed Mr. Richard Smith 30p for Tho: Martin took his Receipt whereof was due to said Martin for building of Johns house".

The above was very important, because it indicates that Thomas Martin had already selected Richard Smith's parcel for purchase as early as 1747. According to Larison's book, Richard Smith sold the 105 acre on August 10, 1750 for £150, which became known as Thomas Martin's "Southerly part". Obviously Thomas was making payments to Richard Smith as early as 1747, and money due Thomas for construction of John Reading, Jr.'s home was applied toward the mortgage.

March 25, 1748, John Reading went to Derrick Hogeland's to divide a tract recently purchased by Derrick, son John Hogeland and Joseph Boss. The following day, Reading ran out some land of a tract <u>now</u> Richard Smith's on behalf of Thomas Martin and Derrick Hogeland.

October, 1749, Reading paid Thomas Martin for work done within the month.

August 13, 1750, Thomas Martin paid John Reading for a deed.

[Note: I feel this was not land purchased by Thomas from John Reading, but rather the payment of Mr. Reading's fees for

---

[47] "John Reading's Diary (1747-1767) – The Daily Business Record of the First American-Born Governor of New Jersey", edited by David R. Reading from original transcriptions by Dorothy A. Stratford,The Mount Amwell Project, Alexandria, VA 22314, 2010.

recording Thomas' deed from Richard Smith, which according to Larison's book occurred on August 10, 1750.]

November 8, 1750, Reading stated he "Received from Rich'd Smith jur for surveying of <u>Mart:</u> D Hog'd and P. Fishers Lands by him with Eb: Large sold to them."

This is another very important diary entry as it implies that it was Richard Smith, Jr. paying for the survey of the land purchased by Thomas Martin, Derrick Hogeland and Peter Fisher with confirmation that Ebenezer Large was the joint seller of the land. Peter Fisher is shown on the Hunterdon Co. historical map, Sheet G, as residing on 228 acres, adjoining the southeast boundary of Hugh & Thomas Martin's plantation at Ringoes.

March, 1751, Reading made note that Thomas Martin had finished George Reading's cellar. Two months later, John Reading recorded that Thomas Martin had finished his work at George Reading's house.

May 25, 1751, "Tho: Martin had 24 yds of Ozenbridge." One might wonder whether Thomas' need for 24 yards of Ozenburg linen was in preparation for furnishing a home for his bride. I've estimated that Thomas married between 1751 and 1752; his only child Daniel was born in 1753.

January 20, 1752, John Reading's entry read: "James Martin by Thomas Martin paid for a Deed."

October, 1752: "Tho: Martin Debtor to one days work."

In May, 1753, a partially illegible entry spoke of Thomas Martin's Plantation upon Muskonetcong River.

[Note: Thomas resided at Ringoes in Amwell Township, well to the south of the Muskonetcong River. Might Thomas have purchased property on the Muskonetcong containing a quarry as a source for his building stones?]

May 25, 1754, John Reading accounted money owed Thomas Martin for Mason's work at the House due to him for work done at Georges House 4:/4s, for Dls <Dilts> House per Agreement and further for 33 days work at 4s per day 6:12 in all £34:16:0.

In December, 1754, Reading stated Thomas Martin had worked about 2 days in Jobs charged 8s, and Reading paid him in 2 bushels of Wheat @ 5s per bushel. Thomas paid him 2s in cash.

January, 1755, "Some time this month Joseph Worford answered Tho: Martin by Di_t <Dilts> which paid sum is in full all Accounts between us vizt: Tho: Martin and myself".

May, 1755, Reading received payment from Jos: Boss and Thomas Martin for Writing and Surveying. June, 1757, Reading paid "towards the Parsonage House to Tho: Martin the further sum of 0:01:6.

I feel that Thomas remained single until approximately age 44. One would imagine that his wife was much younger, because she was of child-bearing age, giving birth to their son Daniel in 1753. What we do know is that Thomas married a woman, named Mary, by 1752. Mary's parents are not known. I had originally thought Mary was a Teate/Tate daughter or perhaps from the Slack family, because those two families participated in Thomas Martin's probate; however, I believe now that Anthony Tate & John Slack acted as sureties in the administration of Thomas' estate merely because they were prominent members of Rev. Henry Martin's church, and were readily available to comply with the rushed, but necessary, court requirements.

I've felt that Thomas' wife Mary had close family in Bucks Co., PA, and specifically, Middletown Twp, Bucks Co., PA, causing Thomas to establish his home there for Mary, as well as keeping his business interests in Hunterdon Co., NJ.

I have considered the possibility that Mary was a daughter of Benjamin Field, Sr., who named an unmarried daughter Mary in his Will[48] of 1749; or the unmarried daughter Mary named in the 1740, Will of Joseph Wildman, Sr., both of Middletown Twp, Bucks Co., PA.

Benjamin Field was the early landowner of Thomas Martin's property in Hunterdon Co., NJ. Benjamin at the time of his death in February, 1749 (O.S.), still owned land in "West New Jersey" as well as Middletown. Benjamin's heirs were: Wife Sarah; sons: Benjamin

---

[48] Bucks Co., PA – Will Book 2, p. 178 <277/382>

(Jr.), Thomas, Edward & Jennings; daughters: Sarah Stockdale, Susana, Ann, Elizabeth and <u>Mary</u>. Witnesses were familiar "Martin family" associates: William Blakey, Joseph Stackhouse and William Paxson.

Benjamin Field witnessed the Middletown Twp, Bucks Co., PA. Will of Joseph Wildman[49] in January 20, 1739/40; other witnesses were John Hunter and Euclydus Longshore.[50] Euclydus Longshore (Sr. and Jr.) were later neighbors of Thomas' son, Daniel Martin. John Hunter was Hugh Martin's brother-in-law. Joseph Wildman, Sr.'s LWT named heirs: Wife Sarah; son Jacob was the only child of age and was devised two Middletown tracts (1) bought of Robert Heaton and (2) bought of Thomas Yeats. Sons under age were John and Joseph, Jr.; daughters under the age of 21 and unmarried were: Rebecca, <u>Mary</u> and Rachel. Executors were: Wife Sarah Wildman , son Jacob, and trusty friend, Thomas Jenks. On May 7, 1740, Euclydus Longshore attested by giving solemn affirmation; John Hunter appeared to at court to give his corporal oath.

Joseph Wildman (Jr.) of Middletown Twp. wrote his LWT on January 22, 1807, stating he would be 77 years old on February 2, 1807. He stated he lived on the West Side of Newtown & Bristol Rd; and devised his land on the East Side of Newtown & Bristol Rd. to his son Solomon Wildman, stating the land was purchased of Daniel Martin. Joseph named his heirs: Sons Solomon, Martin, Joseph (III), William and Thomas. Daughters were: Abigail & Rachel Wildman. Granddaughter Elizabeth Wildman, daughter of Solomon. Witnesses were: John Warner, John Wildman & Isaac Hicks, who proved the Will on May 8, 1809.

As one can read in the probate records, there were a number of transactions concerning the Wildman families, often an indication of kinship, which could only have come about through Mary [ ] Martin Marple.

A further clue that Thomas Martin descendants may wish to further investigate, would be the family of Daniel Howell. You will

---

[49] Bucks Co., PA Will Book 2, p. 3 <186-382>

read later in Chapter 8 – Esther [Martin] Mason that her husband Francis Mason was a witness to the Last Will & Testament[51] of Daniel Howell of Amwell Township, Hunterdon County, NJ, written 9 September 1733."

Daniel Howell, Yeoman; Eldest son, Daniel Howell, Jr.; Son, John, "a mare bought from Thomas Lambert." Sons, Joseph and Benjamin, the copper furnace. Two daughters, Elizabeth and Mary, household goods, etc., "which was their mother's income from the mill and plantation," for bringing up of minor children. Sons, Daniel and John (under age), the corn or grist mill. Plantation where testator lived, fronting on the river. To daughters, Elizabeth and <u>Mary, the plantation "at Alias Hokk in the Township of Amwell."</u> Executors--brother-in-law, John Reading and William Rightinghouses. Witnesses--Samuel Fleming, <u>Francis Mason</u>, Walter Cane. Proved October 24, 1733.
Lib. 3, p. 382.

Daniel Howell, who died 1733, may have been the son of Daniel Howell, who wrote the following LWT in 1725, but was not deceased until 1732:

Name: Daniel Howell
Date: 30 Aug 1725
Location: Trenton, Hunterdon Co.

Blacksmith; will of. Wife, Mary. Son, David, land on east side on the middle road, Trenton; lot on the west side of Kings Street, Trenton, adjoining John Severam <sic Severin?> lot of meadow in Maidenhead great meadows, adjoining James Price's land, said lot bought of Samuel Hunt. Son, Daniel, when 21, house at Trenton which <u>John Severin</u> lives in; half of meadow lot in Maidenhead great meadows, bought of Ralph Hunt, Senior. Son, Joshua, 100 acres of plantation where testator lives, adjoining Ebenezer Prout and John Dean; also lot in Trenton, adjoining Josiah Howel's lot. Son, John, balance of plantation where testator lived, when of age; lot in Trenton. Daughters--Phebe, Elizabeth, Hannah, <u>Mary</u> and Prudence, when aged 18. Testator bequeaths "my son Daniel unto my son David that he may live with him," until he is aged 20 years; Daniel to be taught trade of glazier. Executors--son, David, and friend Nathaniel Moor. Witnesses--George Woolesey, John Carpenter, Moses Dickinson.

---

[51] New Jersey Calendar of Wills, p. 248

1732, April 21. Codicil. Son, Hezekiah, having been born since writing of will, to him a lot of land with a house, and a bond due from Hezekiah Bonham and Johanas Anderson, of Maidenhead. Witnesses--Ann Yearley, Henry Woodward and Enoch Armitage. Proved August 2, 1732. Lib. 3, p. 204.

1732, June 3. Inventory (£418) includes 24 swine, 50 sheep, negro man Jack about 50 years old (£20), negro woman and her child (£40), and bonds of Samuel Everit, Samuel Ruckman, Isaac Reeder, John Moor, Richard Morril, David Davis, Jonathan Davis, William Merril, Isaac Hutchinson, Henry Oxley, John Smith of Maidenhead, Matthew Rigby, Nicholas Roberts and Edward Hart. Made by Enoch Armitage and Jonathan Davis.

From "Stockton, New Jersey - 300 Years of History" by Iris H. Naylor: *"John Reading, a proprietor of West Jersey, one of the first surveyors of the wilderness area that is now know as Hunterdon County and one of the men chosen to meet with the Indians in 1703 in order to purchase this land. He chose for himself a large tract of land bordering the Delaware river. Part of this land contained the present day Stockton. Reading established a ferry across the Delaware and the area became known as Readings Ferry. When John Reading's daughter Mary married Daniel Howell part of her dowry was a square mile tract of land fronting the river. This property included the location of the ferry. The name was then changed to Howell's Ferry".*

From the "History of Sussex and Warren Co., NC"[52]: *"Martin's Creek is a name applied to a locality <u>partly in Pennsylvania and partly in New Jersey</u>, at the mouth of a stream of the same name. In Pennsylvania it is also known as the Three Churches, - from the Presbyterian, Lutheran and Reformed churches that have been there so long; or as Howells, from <u>David Howell,</u> for many years the main property holder there.*

As one can see while reading chapters in this book, the two Daniel Howells are connected to our Martin associations with Francis Mason, the Severns and John Anderson. However, the most important factor may well rest with the fact that the only known child of Thomas & Mary Martin was named "Daniel", which is not

---

[52] "History of Warren County, NJ" by George Wyckoff Cummins, Ph. D., M. D., Lewis Historical Publishing Company, 1911

a name found in the known Martin side of the family; therefore, was Daniel Martin a namesake of his maternal grandfather?

Thomas & wife Mary may have had more than one child, but only Daniel, born in 1753, survived to 1760. It is not known when Thomas moved from Hunterdon Co., NJ, to Middletown, Bucks Co., PA, which was his residence at the time of his death. It is apparent from Thomas Martin's probate documents that he continued to maintain his business interests in Hunterdon Co. as well as his plantation at Ringoes on the Old York Road. It is indeed unfortunate for our study of the Martin family that so little is known of Thomas' life.

Thomas' death must have been unexpected, because he died intestate on August 27, 1760. Thomas was buried in Newtown in the church graveyard of his brother Rev. Henry's Presbyterian church; however, his remains and gravestone were moved to the Sycamore Street Presbyterian Cemetery sometime prior to 1868. His original gravestone read[53]:

"Here lyeth the body of
Thomas Martin
Who departed this life
August 27, 1760
In the 52nd year of his age

Oh thou disappointing world
How has thou mankind in confusion hurled
In thee we toil the body and perplex the mind
Still on hope some happiness to find
But in vain till we get to yonder land
Where pleasure flows in God's right hand
Which this internal joys his eternal bliss
And given him by our lord his righteousness"

---

[53] Cemeteries with Connections to the Presbyterian Church of Newtown – Slack Cemetery – by Elinor Slack Campbell – p. 16 LoC – Catalogue Card #94-070943.

"Frank Fabian and Charles Swartz carefully removed the stones that were visible, as well as the few mortal remains of the brave pioneers who were buried there and, with quiet dignity, saw to it that they were laid to rest in the Presbyterian churchyard on Sycamore Street". A white monument was erected, listing all those graves which were moved. A photo of the monument can be found at:
http://www.findagrave.com/cgi-bin/fg.cgi?page=gr&GRid=9052070

Hugh Martin was present in Bucks Co., PA on August 28, 1760, the day following Thomas' death, to post bond to administer his brother's estate, along with Thomas' widow Mary Martin & his brother Rev. Henry Martin. Brother Robert Martin witnessed the following bond:

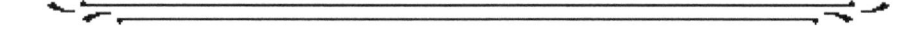

THOMAS MARTIN
Bond for Administration of Estate
Bucks Co., Pennsylvania
28 August 1760

Know all men by these presents that we, Mary Martin of Middletown in the County of Bucks, Widow, and the Reverend Henry Martin of the said County, Clerk and Hugh Martin of Hunterdon County in the Province of West Jersey Yeoman And Anthony Tate and John Slack all of the said County are held and firmly bound unto William Plumsted, Esqr. Register General for the Probate of Wills and Granting Letters of Administration in and for the Province of Pennsylvania in the full and just sum of Five Hundred Pounds lawfull money of the said Province To be paid to the said William Plumsted, Esq. or to his Certain Attorney his Executors Administrators Or Assigns to which Payment well and Truly to be made. We Bind Our Selves our Heirs Executors and Administrators jointly and Severally firmly by these Presents Sealed with Our Seals Dated the Twenty Eighth day of August ~ Anno Domini 1760

The Condition of this Obligation is such that if the above Bound Mary Martin, Henry Martin and Hugh Martin – Administrators of all and singular the Goods and Chattels Rights and Credits of Thomas Martin, Late of the County aforesaid, Yeoman, Deceased do make or cause to be made a True and perfect Inventory of all and singular the Goods Chattels and Credits of the said Deceased which have or shall come to the hands possession or knowledge of them the said Mary Martin, Henry Martin or Hugh Martin or into the hands and possession of any other person or persons for them and the same is made do Exhibit or Cause to be Exhibited into the Registers Office for the County of Bucks at or before the Twenty Eighth Day of September Next Ensuing and the same Goods Chattels and Credits of the said Deceased at the Time of his Death Or which at any time after shall come to the hands or possession of them the said Mary Martin, Henry Martin and Hugh Martin or into the hands possession of any other Person or Persons for them Do well and Truly Administer According to Law and further Do make or Cause to be made a True and Just Account of the Administration at or Before the Twenty Eighth of August In the Year 1761 and all the Rest and Residue of the said Goods and Chattels Rights and Credits which shall be Found Remaining upon the said Administrators Account the same being first Examined and allowed of by the Orphans Court of the said County of Bucks shall Deliver and Pay unto such Person or Persons Respectively as the said Orphans Court by their Decree or Sentence shall Limit and appoint and if it shall hereafter appear that any last Will and Testament was made by the said Deceased and the Executor or Executors therein Named Do Exhibit the same into the Registers Office Requesting to have it allowed and Approved Accordingly if the said Mary Martin, Henry Martin and Hugh Martin above Bound on being thereunto Required Do Render and Deliver up the said Letters of Administration (Approbation of Such Testament being First had and made in the said Registers Office) Then this Obligation to be Void or Else to stand and Remain in Full Force and Virtue in the Law ~

Sealed and Delivered }   *Mary (her "m" mark) Martin*
In the Presence of Us }   *Hen: Martin*

Robert Martin
Richd Gibbs

H: Martin
Anthony Teate
John Slack

The inventory of Thomas' estate was fascinating to me in regard to the personal property he owned – as well as the phonetic spelling used by his appraisers; i.e., barl & cagg <barrel & keg>, 56 Penns of glass <panes>, sasers & spuns & tea cattle <saucers, spoons & tea kettle>, a 3 Cornert harrow <three-cornered>. Thomas was evidently quite prosperous:

Thomas' inventory combines the money in his purse and his wearing apparel as valued at £40.10.0, but I doubt his clothing amounted to more than the 10 shillings. His brother Hugh also had £40 cash at the time of his death. Thomas had a servant girl and a "Negrow fellow", but their names were not given.

Thomas' real estate included an orchard, a pasture with meadow; a pasture of oats; a pasture of staked ground & stubble; and a piece of fallow ground.

As expected, Thomas owned masonry tools – as well as carpentry tools. Among some of the sundry farming tools were: 2 hoes, maul and wedges; 2 axes, a spade and a pick axe.

Of Thomas' livestock, the inventory separated "his" horse & saddle, valued at £7.5.0, from the 2 other horses, plus a mare and colt. There were 14 head of cattle (cows, bulls, steers and heifers, each descriptively differentiated); a total of 42 pigs (7 barrows, sows, etc.). 20 sheep and 11 geese. There were also 5 Beehives.

Thomas had a supply of Indian corn, wheat, rye, buckwheat, and hay; 5 cider barrels and 2 butter churns.

The home contained a Spinning wheel; a supply of flax and wool, and 18 yards of cloth. Oddly, the inventory listed Sail & Tackling, but Thomas was at least six miles distant from the Delaware River.

Thomas owned a clock with case; his bedroom contained a feather bed and bedroom furniture, including a pair of chests. The main house had a dining table with 6 chairs; a tea table; a mirror; 2

chests and 7 chairs; and room for a library and books. In the "little room" was a feather bed, probably for son Daniel. The kitchen furniture included a cupboard and a squire table <square table>; tin ware candlesticks, pewter dishes <putter Dichess>, stone pots and earthen ware pottery.

Thomas' probate file, unfortunately, did not contain the Estate Sale, which would have been helpful in seeing whether Mary's family might have been purchasers, or at least to have provided better clues as to the neighbors.

"The Inventory of the goods & Cattles <sic Chattels> & Rights & Credits of the moveable Estate of Thomas Martin of Midletown <sic>, In the County of bucks and Province of Pennsylvania Decs'd and taken in before us and prised to the best of our knowledg & we the undernamed subscribe our hands this first day of September 1760"

	£	S	P
First to his Purs & apperrel	40	10	0
To his hors and sadle	7	5	0
To a brown mare & colt	7	0	0
To a surrel hors	3	10	0
To a bay hors	3	15	0
To a beall cow	3	5	0
To a red cow with a white strick on ye buttock	3	10	0
To a red cow	3	5	0
To a payed cow	3	15	0
To a black hafer	3	0	0
To a brown haffer	3	5	0
To a brown haffer with a white tail	3	5	0
To a black bull with a white face	2	0	0
To brindle bull	1	5	0
To a brindle hafer	2	0	0
To a red haffer with a white face	1	12	0
To a red haffer	1	12	0
To a white steer	1	5	0
To a black haffer	2	10	0
To 7 Barrows & one speyed sow	8	0	0

To 10 open sows at 12/pece	6	0	0
To 24 Piggs at 21/6, Pece	3	10	0
To 2 Pieese of Indien corn	1	10	0
To a Pece of Buckwheat	1	0	0
To a waggon & sweling trees neck yoke & coillers	5	0	0
	122	19	0
To a great wheel & little & cards	0	10	0
To 10 baggs	1	5	0
To a meal chest & dow trough	0	4	0
To a Parsell of raye	1	1	0
To flax & ton & low yarn	1	10	0
To wheat	0	12	0
To 2 hatchets and a reel	0	12	6
To 2 ridles & 1/2 bushel	0	5	0
To a small sack & 6 pens of glass	0	3	6
To a stand & salt box	0	1	9
To Parsel of carpenders tools & mason tools	0	15	0
To old Iron & sundreys, Ets	0	7	0
To a bed steed	0	6	0
To 4 sickels	0	5	0
To a passel of wool	0	10	0
To an old trunk & side sadle	0	15	0
To 2 baskets and a lantren	0	0	6
To hows mall and wadges	0	6	0
To 2 axes spaid and Pick	0	6	0
To a colter & Plow & old Irons	0	5	0
To 3 Powdering tubs	0	6	0
To 5 cyder barls	0	12	0
To a lye tub	0	5	0
To 3 tubs	0	5	0
To sundreys of old casks in the saller	0	2	0
To 2 Churns & 2 Locllers	0	3	0
To an old barl and cagg	0	1	0
To a slay bank and old bed cloths	0	10	0
To a chain & Cleves & three forks	0	15	0
To 5 bees haves & several Empy gums	1	10	0
To a saill & takling	0	5	0

To 56 Penns of glass & some Puty	1	5	0
To a 3 Cornert harrow	0	10	0
To oats in ye great barrel	2	0	0
To a grinstone	0	3	0
To hay In ye great berrel	6	0	0
to hay In little barreck	2	0	0
Pasture & meadow	2	10	0
	29	2	9
To a Servant Girl	7	5	0
To a negrow fellow	45	0	0
To goods In the room	0	0	0
To a Clock & Case	10	0	0
To a fether bed & furniture with 2 pare chests	8	0	0
To a Table	2	5	0
To a tea table	1	5	0
To 1/2 dosen of chairs	1	7	0
To a looking glass	1	0	0
To tea cups sasers & spuns & tea cattle	2	10	0
To his libery and books	1	0	0
In the little room			
To a fether bed and cloths	5	0	0
To 2 Chests a small table & box	0	15	0
To 7 Chairs	0	15	0
In the kichen			
To Iron Pot & cattle	1	10	0
To a pot & poot hooks			
To a box Iron & flat Irons	0	10	0
To hand irons fire shovel & tongs	1	5	0
To frying pann grid Iron & bake Iron	0	7	6
To a poot tramel	0	15	0
To a Pair of stilerds	0	15	0
To a cuberd Dresser	0	12	0
To a squire table	0	7	6
To buckets pails trees & tranchers	0	7	6
To mortar strainer & butter Print	0	3	0
To knifes forks tine were Candlesticks	0	5	0
To stone poots or Earthen were	0	2	0

To putter Dichess & Plates	3	0	0
	95	0	6
the 4 lbs Corn			
To 20 sheep at 7/ a Peace	7	0	0
To 11 gees at 1/3 ye head	0	13	9
To a harrow culling ____ & box	2	8	0
To Pasture and meadow	2	5	0
To flax	1	0	0
To a pace of lincy cloth	0	5	0
To 18 yards of Cloth at 8/6 pr yard	3	3	0
To pasture of oats ground & orchard	0	10	0
To Pasture ground stak ground & stuble	0	12	0
To a flax break	0	0	6
To a table cloth	0	5	0
To a Pece of fallow ground	7	0	0
Less or more at 8/ per <?acre>	16	2	0
To sundreys Debts Due by			
John Willeman & James Fluck	3	10	
To several Debts unpaid & unsettled to ye ____	10	0	0
Due by bonds to ye Province of New Jarsey ?		2	
To a bond of Slack & Whithead	28	6	0
To 3 bonds Due at several times	250	0	0
from Jacob Starr <probably should be: Jacob Barns>			

Signed: Anthoney Teate
    John Slack
    Robert Martin

Six months later, Hugh Martin appeared at the Hunterdon County, New Jersey Court to serve as Administrator for his brother Thomas Martin's New Jersey estate on February 21, 1761.

HUGH MARTIN[54]
ADMR.
THOS. MARTIN
~ BOND ~
Entered in Lib. No 10, Folio 460
Hunterdon County
1761
540J
Letters Sealed

"Know all men by these presents, that we, Hugh Martin, Esq., of Lebanon, in the County of Hunterdon, and Province of New Jersey, &c and Theophilus Severns of Hunterdon, are held and firmly bound unto his Excellency Thomas Boone, Esq., Governor of New Jersey in the Sum of Five Hundred Pounds, Proclamation Money, to be paid to the said Governor or his successors or assigns: To which Payment well and truly to be made, we bind us, our Heirs, Executors and Administrators, jointly and severally, firmly by these Presents, Sealed with our Seals and Dated the Twenty first day of February, Anno Domini One Thousand Seven Hundred and Sixty One.

The Condition of the above Obligation is such, That if the Above-bound Hugh Martin, Esq. Administrator of all and singular the Goods, Chattels and Credits of Thomas Martin, late of the County of Bucks & Province of Pennsylvania, deceased, do make or cause to be made, a true and perfect Inventory of all and singular the Goods, Chattels and Credits of the said Deceased, which have or shall come to the Hands, Possession or Knowledge of the said Hugh Martin or into the Hands of any other Person or Persons for his use, and the same so made, exhibit or cause to be exhibited into the Registry of the Prerogative Court, in the Secretary's Office at Burlington, on or before the Twenty first Day of June next ensuing; and the same Goods, Chattels and Credits of the said Deceased, at the Time of his Death, or which at any Time after, shall come to the Hands or Possession of the said Hugh Martin or unto the Hands or Possession of

---

[54] Transcribed by Francie Lane - Hunterdon Co., NJ – Probate Records – FHC Film #461817.

any other Person or Persons, for his Use, do well and truly administer according to Law; and farther do make or cause to be made, a just and true Account of his Administration on or before the Twenty first Day of February now next ensuing the Date hereof; and all the Rest and Residue of the said Goods, Chattels and Credits, which shall be found remaining upon the Account of the said Administration the same being first examined and allowed of, by the Judge, for the time being, of the said Prerogative Court, shall deliver and pay unto such Person or Persons respectively, as the said Judge for the time being, of the said Court, by his Decree or Sentence, pursuant to the true Intent and Meaning of an Act of Parliament, made in the 22d and 23d Years of the Reign of King Charles II, entituled An Act for Settling Intestates Estates, shall limit and appoint. And if it shall hereafter appear, that any last Will and Testament was made by the said Deceased, and the Executor or Executors therein named, do exhibit the same into the said Prerogative Court, making Request to have it allowed and approved accordingly: If the said Hugh Martin, Esq. being thereunto required do render and deliver up the said Letters of Administration, Approbation of such Testament being first had and made in the said Court, then the above Obligation to be void, or else it shall stand in full Force and Virtue.

H: Martin

Sealed and Delivered in
  the Presence of

Rachel Hooton   Theo Severns

New Jersey }
Hunt County }

    Be it Remembered that on the Twenty first day of February Anno Domini 1761 – Personally appeared before me Theo. Severns, duly authorized to qualifie admrs for their Truste &c Hugh Martin. Who being Sworn on the Holy Evangelists of Almighty God did acknlge that Thomas Martin dyed without a Will as far As he knows and as he verily believes and that he will well & Truly administer all and singular the Goods Chattels & Credits of the said Deceased which have or shall come to his hands or Possession or to the hands or possession of any other person or persons for his use and that he will make a True & perfect Inventory of the said Goods & Chattels Rights & Credits and exhibit the Same into Prerogative office at Burlington, and render a just & True Acct. of his Administration.

/s/ H: Martin

Sworn before me
the day & year above written
Theo. Severns, Juris.

Hugh Martin died on March 7, 1761, less than three weeks after having posted the Administration Bond for Thomas' New Jersey estate. The administration of Thomas' estate and guardianship of young Daniel wrangled on for several years in Bucks County between Thomas' brother Rev. Henry Martin and widow Mary.

Bucks Co., PA – Orphans Court Records[55]: June 10, 1761 – p. 172
Mary Martin's Petition   File: 313
The Petition of Mary Martin was Read as Follows:
Humbly Sheweth That your Petitioners Late Husband Died Sometime in the month of August Last, and left the said Daniel his only Child now upwards of Seven Years of Age, and Left a Considerable Real and Personal Estate which Descends to the said Daniel, may it therefore Please your Worships to appoint a Guardian for the said Daniel to take Care of his Person and Estate, and Your Petr. Will Pray.
/s/ Mary Martin
Which being Considered by the Court, it is Ordered That the Petitioner, and Henry Wynkoop be Guardians to the said Minor.
And Now Henry Martin an Uncle to the Minor, and one of the Administrators of his Father's Estate appears and **Prays the Court to Reconsider this Course, alleging that the said Mary is not a proper**

---

[55] Transcribed by Francie Lane - Pennsylvania Probate Records, 1683-1994 – Bucks Co. Orphans Court Records 1752-1765, Vol. 1 <172/271>

Person for Guardian. *Therefore it is Ordered that Henry Krewson, be added, and be One of the Guardians of the said Minor.*

Within a year of Thomas' death, his widow, Mary remarried on 29 July 1761[56], to David Marple of Bucks Co., PA.

Bucks Co., PA – Orphans Court Records[57]: September 16, 1761 – p. 177

The Petition of Henry Martin one of the Admrs. Of Thos. Martin Decesased 313
The Petition of Henry Martin One of the Administrators of Thomas Martin late of Middletown Deceased was Read in these records Vizt: Humbly Sheweth That your Petitioner became One of the Administrators of the Goods, Chattels and Credits of his Brother Thomas Martin, Deceased and your Petitioner Humbly Prays that you'll please to Inspect his accounts or appoint Auditors as you in your Wisdom may see most need and your Petitioner as in Duty Bound will Ever Pray   /s/ H: Martin
Which being Considered it is Ordered by the Court that Gabriel Vanhorne, Robert Heaton, and Henry Jamison, Do view, Examine and Adjust, the Petitioners Account, of what he has Received and Paid, of the said Intestate Estate, and Report thereon to the next Court.

Petition of Mary Marple late Martin Adminx. Of Thomas Martin   313
The Petition of Mary Marple, late Mary Martin Widow and One of the Administrators of Thomas Martin, Late of Middletown Deceased was Read as Follows Vizt: Humbly Sheweth that your Petitioner became one of the Administrators of the Goods and Chattels, Rights and Credits of Her Former Husband Thomas Martin Late of Middletown Deceased, and your Petitioner humbly Prays that you'll please to Inspect her Accounts Relating to her Administrating what part of the Deceased Estate as hath

---

[56] Pennsylvania Marriages Previous to 1790: PA Archives, Series II, Vol. II
[57] Transcribed by Francie Lane - Pennsylvania Probate Records, 1683-1994 – Bucks Co. Orphans Court Records 1752-1765, Vol. 1 <177/271>

been in her Power to Transact, and your Petr. Will Pray. /s/ Mary Marple

Which being Considered by the Court it is Ordered that Gabriel Vanhorn, Henry Jamison and Robert Heaton, Do Examine and Settle the Petitioners Account, of her Administration of the said Estate, and Report thereupon to the next Court, and it is also Ordered that the Petitioner do Produce to the said Referees the Vendue Bills or an Account of Sales, together with an Office Copy of the Inventory of the said Intestate's Estate
~

The Petition of Henry Wynkoop and Henry Krewson, Guardians to the Minor Son of Thos. Martin, Deceased   313

The Petition of Henry Wynkoop and Henry Krewson Guardians appointed at last court to a Minor Son of Thomas Martin late of Middletown Deceased was Read as follows Vizt: Humbly Sheweth that Whereas by an Order of this Court we your Petitioners are appointed Guardians to the Child of Thomas Martin Deceased in Conjunction with Mary Martin, Widow to the said Martin, and as **the said Widow hath behaved her Self in a manner unsuitable to the Trust this Court hath Reposed in her by marrying to a Person of a Low Character and Leading a Disorderly Life with her Neighbours, we your Petitioners humbly Pray that Either the said Widow be Discharged from being a Guardian to said Child, or your Petitioners be Exempted from Engaging in a Case, which we Conceive may not Only be Troublesome to Our Selves, But likewise Frustrate the Good Design of this Court,** and Your Petitioners as in Duty Bound shall Ever Pray &c   /s/   Henry Wynkoop, Henry Krewson

Which being Considered by the Court the Judgment thereon is deferred till Mary Marple the other Guardian and Mother of the said Minor appear, and Ordered that She have Notice to attend on Friday next, at which Day to wit on the day the 18th Day of September the said Mary Marple, as well as the Petitioners being fully heard, It is Considered by the Court, That **in the Present Circumstances of the said Mary Marple it is not Proper to Continue her in the Guardianship of the said Son, and Ordered That She be Discharged**, from that Trust, and that the said Mary Marple, do Account with Henry Wynkoop and Henry Krewson for all the Minor's Money or Estate in Her hands, and Pay the whole to the said Wynkoop and Krewson, who are wholly Trusted with his Person and Estate ~

Mary and new husband David Marple jointly filed for administration of Thomas Martin's estate located in Hunterdon Co., NJ, as evidenced by the following:

DAVID & MARY MARPLE[58]
ADMRS.
THOS. MARTIN ESTATE
~ BOND ~
Entered in Lib. No 11, Folio 132
Hunterdon County
1761
540J
Letters Sealed

"Know all men by these presents, that we, David Marple and Mary Marple late widow and relict of Thomas Martin Dec'd of the province of Pensylva. and Moore Furman of Trenton in the County of Hunt. New Jersey are held and firmly bound unto Josiah Hardy, Governor of the province of New Jersey in the Sum of Five Hundred Pounds, Proclamation Money, to be paid to the said Governor or his successors or assigns: To which Payment well and truly to be made, we bind us, our Heirs, Executors and Administrators, jointly and severally, firmly by these Presents, Sealed with our Seals and Dated the Thirteenth Day of Novr - Anno Domini One Thousand Seven Hundred and Sixty One.

The Condition of the above Obligation is such, That if the Above-bound David Marple and Mary Marple late widow & relict of Thomas Martin Dec'd - - - Administor & administratrix of all and singular the Goods, Chattels and Credits of Thomas Martin, late of Pennsylvania, deceased, do make or cause to be made, a true and perfect Inventory of all and singular the Goods, Chattels and Credits of the said Deceased, which have or shall come to the Hands, Possession or Knowledge

---

[58] Transcribed by Francie Lane - Hunterdon Co., NJ – Probate Records – FHC Film #461817.

of the said David Marple and Mary Marple or into the Hands of any other Person or Persons for their use, and the same so made, exhibit or cause to be exhibited into the Registry of the Prerogative Court, in the Secretary's Office at Burlington, on or before the Thirteenth Day of Feby next ensuing; and the same Goods, Chattels and Credits of the said Deceased, at the Time of his Death, or which at any Time after, shall come to the Hands or Possession of the said David & Mary or unto the Hands or Possession of any other Person or Persons, for their Use, do well and truly administer according to Law; and farther do make or cause to be made, a just and true Account of their Administration on or before the Thirteenth Day of Novembr. now next ensuing the Date hereof; and all the Rest and Residue of the said Goods, Chattels and Credits, which shall be found remaining upon the Account of the said Administration the same being first examined and allowed of, by the Judge, for the time being, of the said Prerogative Court, shall deliver and pay unto such Person or Persons respectively, as the said Judge for the time being, of the said Court, by his Decree or Sentence, pursuant to the true Intent and Meaning of an Act of Parliament, made in the 22d and 23d Years of the Reign of King Charles II, entituled An Act for Settling Intestates Estates, shall limit and appoint. And if it shall hereafter appear, that any last Will and Testament was made by the said Deceased, and the Executor or Executors therein named, do exhibit the same into the said Prerogative Court, making Request to have it allowed and approved accordingly: If the said David & Mary being thereunto required do render and deliver up the said Letters of Administration, Approbation of such Testament being first had and made in the said Court, then the above Obligation to be void, or else it shall stand in full Force and Virtue. David Marple
Sealed and Delivered in Mary Marple
 the Presence of Moore Furman

George Douglass
Theo Severns

New Jersey }
Hunt. County }

Be it Remembered that on the Thirteenth day of Novr. Anno Domini 1761 – Personally appeared before me Theophilus Severns, duly authorized to qualifie admrs for their Trust &c David Marple and Mary Marple, late Widdow and relict of Thomas Martin Dec'd. Who being Sworn on the Holy Evangelists of Almighty God did depose that they will well and Truly administer all and singular the Goods Chattels & Credits of the said Deceased wch. have or shall come to their hands knowledge or possession or to the hands knowledge or possession of Any other person or persons for their and that they will make a True and perfect Inventory of the said Goods Chattels and Credits & Exhibit the same into the prerogative office in Burlington and render a just & True Account of their Administration.

            David Marple
Sworn before me   Mary Marple
 Theo. Severns, Juris.

Inventory of the Goods & Chattels of Thomas Martin Late of Amwell deceased Taken and appraised this Fourteenth day of November 1761 by Benja. Johnson & Moore Furman

Purse	£100 –
One Bond from Jacob Barn dated Feby. 24, 1757 Payable April 1762	100 -
One other Bond from Jacob Barn dated at the Same time payable April 1763	50 -
One note from Joseph Reading dated Sept. 10, 1760 Payable 20 June Ensuing	7 –
	£257 -

Appraised by us the day above ment'd.
 Benjamin Johnson
 Moore Furman

David Marple and Mary Marple late Widdow and relict of Thomas Martin Dec'd being sworn on the Holy Evangelists of Almighty God did Severally depose that the within Writing Contains a True and perfect Inventory of all and singular the Goods Chattels & Credits of Thomas Martin Dec'd wch. have Come to their hands knowledge or possession or to the possession of Any other person or persons for their use.

David Marple
Mary Marple

Sworn the 13th day of Novr. 1761
Theo. Severns   Juris

Bucks Co., PA – Orphans Court Records: December 16, 1761 – p. 297[59]
Mary Marple, Adminr of Thos. Martin   313
Mary Marple late Mary Martin One of the Administrators of Thomas Martin, Deceased, files here the Report of the Referees who at last court were Ordered to Adjust her Account, and the Report and Account is Read and Ordered to be further Considered till next court.

Henry Martin, Admr of Thos. Martin   313
Henry Martin another of the Administrators of the said Thomas Martin also produces here the Report of the Referees Ordered at last court to Adjust his account, and the Report and Account is Read and Ordered to be further Considered until next court, and it is also Ordered that the said Henry Martin Do then Exhibit to the Court the Receipts for the several Sums by him Charged ~

Bucks Co., PA – Orphans Court Records[60]: June 16, 1762 – p. 320
The Acct of Henry Martin Admr of Thos. Martin Dec'd   313
Henry Martin, One of the Admrs. Of Thomas Martin late of Middletown Deceased, Now produces the Receipts as Ordered at Last

---

[59] Transcribed by Francie Lane - Pennsylvania Probate Records, 1683-1994 – Bucks Co. Orphans Court Records 1752-1765, Vol. 1 <180/271>
[60] Transcribed by Francie Lane - Pennsylvania Probate Records, 1683-1994 – Bucks Co. Orphans Court Records 1752-1765, Vol. 1 <193/271>

Court, and the Court having Examined the Particulars, Charges and Vouchers the same is allowed as here stated:

Henry Martin Admr. Of the Estate of Thomas Martin
Dr.

To Sum of Goods Sold at Vendue	£126.2.5
To Sum ye taken per Appraisement	14.7.2
To Cash Recd of Mary Martin	33.12.-
To D°. Of John Connoly for Rent	1.-.-
To William Cartars Bond	13.13.-
To Cash Rec'd of his Brother Hugh Martin to pay Henry Slack }	15.-.-
To a Debt for Work done to the Parsonage	4.-.-
	£207.14.7

Cr.

By Sundry Sums pd. as per Rct.	£ 127.0.0
By Sundry Expenses in Exhibit Serv'd	8.11.8
By Comssn on Receiving £155.2.7 @ 5pc	7.15.1
By Comssn on Paying £131.1.6 @ 5 pc	6.11.1
By Expenses of Auditors	4.1.6
	£153.19.4
Bal. in Mr. Martins Hands	£53.15.2
	£207.14.7

It also appears that the said Henry Martin has in his Hands a Gun Belonging to the Intestate which he is still to Account for ~

Bucks Co., PA – Orphans Court Records[61]: March 16, 1763 – p. 347
Citation Summond agt. Thos. Martin's Extr.

Citation having been Issued to Henry Martin and David Marple and Mary his Wife, late Mary Martin, Admrs. Of Thomas Martin late of Middletown In the said County, Yeoman, Deceased, to Render to this Court a Just and full Account of their Administration of the said Intestate

---

[61] Transcribed by Francie Lane - Pennsylvania Probate Records, 1683-1994 – Bucks Co. Orphans Court Records 1752-1765, Vol. 1 <208/271>

Estate, and also to perform and abide the Order of this Court upon the Complaint of Henry Krewson and Henry Wynkoop, Guardians to Daniel Martin, a Minor Son of the aforesaid Thomas Martin Deceased. The said Adminrs. Appear and the Guardians also appearing the Citation is Read, and Henry Martin One of the Admr. Exhibits to the Court here his Petition which is Read in these words Vizt: The Petition of Hen: Martin To his Majesties Justices holding Orphans Court at Newtown in Bucks County the 16th Day of March 1763. Humbly Sheweth That Whereas there Remains some of the Accounts of the Estate of Thomas Martin Deceased to be Given into the aforesd. Court which should have been Settled before now, but as some of the Debts Lie in the hands of Backward People who have Shifted and put me Off with promises of Settlement and my Backwardness to force them by Law is the only Reason why I have not Complied with Orders ~ Therefore if your Worships will please to allow me One Interval or Space between this and next Court, I'll Endeavour to Give in the whole Accnt. And your Petr. As in Duty Bound will Ever Pray &c.

Which being Considered by the Court it is thereupon Ordered That the said Petitioner Henry Martin have time till next Court to Settle his Account, and that he do then Exhibit a Just, True and full Accnt. Of his Administration of the said Intestate's Estate. And it is also Ordered that Mary Marple late Mary Martin, the Adminx. Who now appears in Court, have the same Time to prepare her Accounts.

Bucks Co., PA – Orphans Court Records[62]: June 14, 1763 – p. 350

Mary Marple late Martin   Accnt of her Admin. Of Thos. Martin's Estate
313
Pursuant to an Order of Last Court Mary Marple late Mary Martin One of the Adms. Of Thomas Martin late of Middletown Deceased Now Exhibit here Additional Account which is Read as follows Vizt: 1762

---

[62] Transcribed by Francie Lane - Pennsylvania Probate Records, 1683-1994 – Bucks Co. Orphans Court Records 1752-1765, Vol. 1 <210/271>

*The Acct. of Mary Marple agt. The Estate of
   Thomas Martin Deceased Continued }*
Dr.
1762

April 16	To Cash Recvd of Joseph Redding	7.0.0
	To d⁰. Recd of John Whitehead In the Jerseys	22.10.0
June, 1763	To d⁰. Recd of John Davids For Rent }	21.0.0
April 6	To D⁰. Recd of Benjamin Stackhouse	6.0.0
11	To D⁰. Received of **Francis Mason** For 2 Years Rent For the Mill and place in The Jerseys	60.0.0
		£106.10.0

1762 Contra

	By Cash pd. Patrick Gregg the Provincial and County Tax	0.10.6
April 16	By d⁰. Pd. Peter Runyon in the Jerseys for weaving as per Rect.	1.2.3
May 12	By d⁰. Pd. Jos. Stackhouse As per Rect.	50.0.0
June 1763	By d⁰. Pd. Tim⁰. Smith as per Rect.	0.2.0
May 17	By d⁰. Pd. Jos. Stackhouse as per d⁰.	50.0.
June 6	By d⁰. Pd. Nathl. Ellicott	0.10.6
	By d⁰. The provincial and county Tax for the place John Davids lives on as per Rect.	0.12.3
	By d⁰. Pd. For the Oven and Wall bucket, for the [?end] of the	

Place John Davids Lives on	1.0.0
	£103.17.6
By d°. For Administering in	
The Jerseys	0.2.0
Mary Marple	£105.17.6

And the Court having Considered thereof it is Ordered that Her Account be allowed.

Bucks Co., PA – Orphans Court Records[63]: September 13, 1763 – p. 357

Henry Martin's Petition One of the Admrs. Of Thos. Martin Decd.   313

    The Petition of Henry Martin One of the Administrators of Thomas Martin Deceased was presented to the Court and Read in these words Vizt: Humbly Saeth That whereas some Accounts of the Estate of Thomas Martin Dec'd Remains unsettled and to be Exhibited to said Court, your humble Petitioner prays that you in Your Clemency would please to Receive those Accounts sd. Martin as Administrator has to give in, and as there are some attended with Difficulty your Petitioner has Consulted a Councilor, who will it is hoped Satisfy the Court, and your Petitioner will as in Duty Bound for Ever Pray ~   /s/Hen. Martin

    Find Now the said Henry Martin appearing it is Ordered that Gabriel Vanhorn, John Woolston, and William Paxson Do Settle and Adjust the said Petitioners further Account and Report to next Court.

Bucks Co., PA – Orphans Court Records[64]: December 12th, 1763 – p. 361

Additional Acct of Henry Martin Admin. Of Thos. Martin, Decd.   313

    Henry Martin One of the Admrs. Of Thomas Martin Late of Middletown Deceased, Now appears and Exhibits the Report of William Paxson, John Woolston, and Gabriel Vanhorn, who were Ordered to Settle

---

[63] Transcribed by Francie Lane - Pennsylvania Probate Records, 1683-1994 – Bucks Co. Orphans Court Records 1752-1765, Vol. 1 <214/271>

[64] Transcribed by Francie Lane - Pennsylvania Probate Records, 1683-1994 – Bucks Co. Orphans Court Records 1752-1765, Vol. 1 <216-217/271>

the remaining Acct. of the sd. Henry's Administration, on the sd. Thomas Martin's Estate, and the Acct. and Report are Read as follows:

The Estate of the Remaining Accnts. Of Tho: Martin's Estate in the Hands of Henry Martin Adminr. Unsettled to be Exhibited to Court:

Collected from Peter Scales in the Jerseys	16.0.0
Coll'd. from Wm. Cartar by J. Hecklin	
The Remaining part of the Bond }	15.0.0
Due on the Last Balancing Accts.	53.0.0
	£84.0.0
	00.15.00
	3.4.4
Paid to Wm. Blackfan a Bonds Interest	44.19.0
Paid to Jos: Stackhouse by Rect	10.11.0
To Nathl. Ellicot by Do	0.9.1
To John Blair by Do	0.3.9
Paid for 2 Petitions	0.10.0
Paid to Mr. Growdon's Office	2.10.7
Cash to Jno. Wildman, [?from] trying to settle the	
Mill Rent with James Dyer	0.7.6
For a Tomb Stone at Philada	15.0.0
Cash to an Attorney for Council	2.10.0
To Cambles Bill Insolvent	1.3.0
For a Petition	0.9.0
Cash for the Order to the Auditors	1.0.0
Cash paid to Nath'l Ellicot for Exht. Of Auditors	0.9.3
The Auditors Charge 2/6 Each 7/6	0.7.6
	£80.15.8

Bucks Co., PA – Orphans Court Records - September 13, 1763 – p. 362

    In Obedience to an Order of an Orphans Court held at Newtown this Twelfth Day of September last past we have Examined the above

Accts. Of Henry Martin Administrator on his Brother Thos. Martin's Estate and find a Balance Remaining in his hands of Three Pounds, four Shillings & Eight pence, Exclusive of his Commissions on Eighty Pounds fifteen Shillings and eight pence, which at 10pc is Eight Pounds, one Shillings & six pence, which makes a Balance due to the Administrator of Four Pounds, Sixteen Shillings & ten pence, which is nevertheless Submitted to the Court ~ Gabriel Vanhorn, John Woolston, Wm. Paxson.

But as the Guardians to the Minor Son of the said Intestate do not appear Nor is it proved that they had any Notice to appear here this Day, Therefore the further Consideration thereof is Continued, and Ordered that the sd. Guardians have Notice when the sd. Henry will again apply to the Court for Judgment that they the sd. Guardians may show their Exceptions to the said Acct. if any they have to show.

After which to wit on the 14th Day of December the sd. Henry Martin and the Guardians appear, and the Acct. being again Read, is not Gainsaid by the Guardians only as to 7/6 charged paid John Wildman for trying to settle the Rent with Jas. Dyer, which is Deducted, and the Rest Confirmed. ~

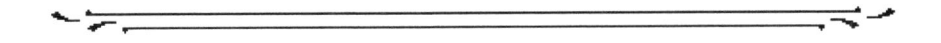

The published Bucks Co, PA Tax Records of 1693-1778[65]:
Middletown – 6th of ye 2nd mo. 1762:
MARTENS MILL & LAND   40£, 10 sh

In 1762, only Anthony Teate (45£,11sh,9d), identified as "one of the overseers of Middeltown"; John Gregg & Mill (70£,16sh, 6d); and William Paxson (50£, 12 sh, 6d) exceeded the property value of Thomas Martin's mill and land. There are no "Marple" families listed, but I did find other familiar names: Henery Slieght <Slack>, James Fluck, William Murrey, James Moon, Goarg Loman Slacks, William Carter, and James Hayhurst.

Two years later, the following newspaper advertisement appeared: From the Pennsylvania Gazette (1728-1789)

---

[65] Bucks County Tax Records – 1693-1778, compiled by Terry McNealy & Frances Waite. Bucks Co. Genealogical Society, PO Box 1092, Doylestown, PA 18901

MARTIN, Thomas - 16 Aug 1764 - <u>Mill, etc. in Middletown</u> - advertised by his <u>estate</u> (15:12).

Although Thomas' mill was advertised for sale in 1764, it's apparent from his son Daniel's estate in 1801, that Daniel had ownership of a "plantation and grist mill", which he had rented to Thomas Lloyd. The plantation and grist mill were sold by Daniel's executors in 1801 for $8,000.

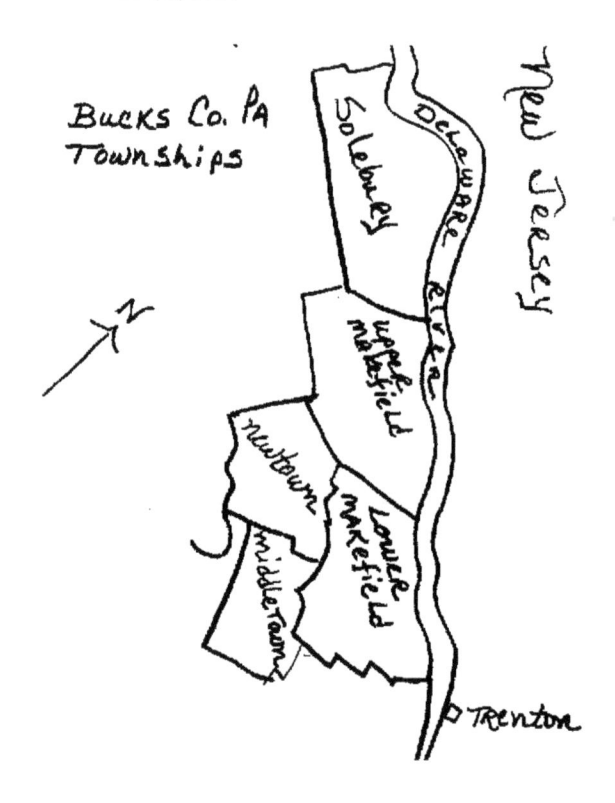

[Map: Bucks Co. PA Townships — Solebury, Upper Makefield, Newtown, Lower Makefield, Middletown; Delaware River, New Jersey, Trenton]

The following tax delinquency may not pertain to our Thomas, because the reference is to property owned in Buckingham; however, Solebury adjoins Buckingham, and 1761 was the year after Thomas' death, so a tax delinquency would be logical: Bucks Co., PA - Tax Lists:

Poor Tax - Township of Buckingham - 6 Apr 1761:
    MARTIN, Thomas   6£   1s

Thomas & Mary Martin had only one child living at the time of Thomas' death; i.e., Daniel Martin, born c1753. The Orphans Court removed his mother Mary as a guardian, and I've felt Daniel was likely placed in the home of guardian Henry Wynkoop. The court was responsible in approving guardians until the orphan turned 14 years old, at which time the orphan was permitted to choose his own guardian – with the approval of the court, which apparently was not forthcoming.

Bucks Co., PA - Orphan's Court Records[66] - December 12, 1768
p. 108
Daniel Martin's Petition   File #473
The Petition of Daniel Martin was Read as follows: Humbly Sheweth That your Petitioner is an Orphan above the Age of 14 Years and therefore prays your Worships to appoint David Marple for his Guardian to take care of his Estate during his Minority for which favours your Petitioner will Pray ~   /s/ Daniel Martin
And Ordered that the said Petition be Continued under Advisement to next Orphans Court ~

I have searched the subsequent Orphans Court sessions and found no further mention of Daniel's petition for the court to approve his step-father David Marple as guardian. It may be that in the three month span between court sessions, Daniel's mother passed away; or Daniel was convinced that the court wouldn't approve his choice due to the past reputation of Marple, so rather than debate the issue, Daniel decided to withdraw his petition.

At age 19, Daniel Martin entered Princeton as evidenced by the following newspaper article[67]:

1772: *"Prince Town, New Jersey, October 6*
On Monday the 28th ult. the Grammar School in Nassau Hall was examined, and the Scholars acquitted themselves greatly to the Satisfaction of the Gentlemen who were pleased to attend. The Senior Class, ten in

---

[66] Transcribed by Francie Lane - Bucks Co., PA - Orphan's Court Records 1766-1801, Vol. 1-2 <89/418>
[67] From Jeanie Smith Zadach – Extracts from American Newspapers Relating to Colonial New Jersey – Heritage Books Archives CD.

Number, were admitted into the Freshman Class in the College. In the Evening the Class performed a dramatic Piece in Latin, before a numerous and learned Audience.

On Tuesday the 29th, voluntary Competitions for Premiums, among the Students of the College in several Branches of Learning, were attended in the publick Library by a very respectable Number of Gentlemen of Letters, and Graduates from different Colleges. Seven judges were elected to decide in each Competition.... In "translating from English into Latin", the first to Samuel Waugh, the second to Isaac Keith, the third to Daniel Martin; the two latter from Pennsylvania, and of the Freshman Class."

"Princeton, Sept. 30, 1773:

On Monday last the 27th Instant, the Grammar School here was examined in Presence of the President and Officers of College, and several other Gentlemen of Letters; when after a full Trial of all the Classes, seven of the Senior Class were approved and admitted into the Freshman Class in College. Judgment was passed upon all the other Classes, and Prizes distributed to the Victors in each......Two Prizes for Writing the best Latin Versions, were assigned to Isaac Keith, and Daniel Martin, both of the Sophomore Class, and from Pennsylvania".

At age 23, on August 1, 1776, Daniel Martin witnessed the LWT of his Uncle Thomas Dawson of Solebury, Bucks Co., PA. Daniel's witnessing of the Will was probably to protect the rights of his Aunt Agnes [Martin] Dawson, although he may have been serving in the dual capacity as an attorney. Daniel Martin appears on many subsequent Bucks Co. documents as a witness or guardian in Orphans' Court cases, which was likely due to his serving as the lawyer for one of the parties.

I had long suspected that Daniel's wife Ann "Agnes" was a Murray daughter. Agnes' own Will had a bequest to her "Cousin Riselma Murray" and Agnes & Daniel's son was named William Murray Martin. But I was not successful in discovering her identity until January, 2012, when I stumbled onto the abstract of the Will of

Gen. Francis Murray of Newtown, Bucks Co., PA. A year later, I found a copy of his entire Will.

Briefly, Gen. Francis Murray was Scots-Irish, born about 1732, settled in Newtown, Bucks Co., PA, becoming a large landowner there. Francis had been commissioned as a Major by John Hancock and served under Col. Walter Stewart in the 13th PA Regiment, along with his brother Maj. John Murray. Francis was captured by the British in 1778, and held a prisoner of conscience at Long Island during the Revolutionary War. After the War, Francis served as the General of the local militia.

The LWT of Francis Murray, Esq. was written on April 20, 1811, with Codicil added on November 17, 1816[68]. The Will was submitted to the Bucks Co. Court of Probate on December 2, 1816, and contested by his Grandson John Dormer Murray, with the court issuing a verdict the following June 16, 1817. The Executors of Francis' estate were his sons-in-law Dr. Phineas Jenks and Jonathan Wynkoop. Witnesses were J. Morris, James Hicks & Asa Casey.

Due to its length & complexity, I've abstracted below portions of the Will of Gen. Francis Murray, Esq., and much information can be derived from his many bequests. Francis had been a widower, left with young children, and he must have acted as the Guardian for his orphaned niece, Agnes "Ann" [Murray] Martin, whom Francis nicknamed "Nancy".

Francis & his wife Martha had children:

Daughter Patience [Murray] Heaton had one son Joseph. Francis adopted Grandson Joseph Heaton as his own son, through the Will and actually renamed him "Francis Heaton Murray", which I found extraordinary, considering Patience was still living. Gen. Francis devised 120 acres and a home, in addition to one-third of his estate to Francis/Joseph, and named a Guardian for him. "… for my said adopted son and at his discretion to advance small sums of money at different times to Patience Heaton not exceeding ten dollars per annum and also small quantities of grain at his discretion such as Indian corn, buckwheat, rye & wheat, not

---

[68] Abstracted by Francie Lane - Bucks Co., PA Will Book 9, page 178 - Familysearch.org <111-116/256>

exceeding together ten bushels per annum during the minority of my said adopted son Francis H. Murray as a compensation to her for her attention & care over him during his age of nurture". "And it is my will and I hereby enjoin it as a duty on my said adopted son not to suffer his mother to come to want & that he assist her with the comforts of life as fully as I have permitted his Guardian to do during his minority. Joseph Heaton aka Francis Heaton Murray married Sarah [Mitchel], the granddaughter of Daniel & Agnes [Murray] Martin, through their daughter Ann "Agnes" Mitchel.

Son John Dormer Murray died in 1803, but had a son named John Dormer Murray (Jr.) whom Francis provided for in his Will, but wasn't quite convinced John, Jr. was truly his grandson, continually referring to him in the Will as "John Dormer Murray, the reputed son of my son John". John, Jr. contested the Will in 1816, and a Jury found in his favor; merely awarded him 6¢; but his suit held up probate for six months. John's daughter Emily was also referred by Francis as "the reputed daughter of my son John Murray" and bequested $1,000 to her in installments.

Son George W. Murray was deceased at the time of Francis' Will, but the Codicil made a bequest to George (Jr.) "the putative son of my son George W. Murray, deceased". Francis made several references to his "Lineal Descendants", which seemed to show his intention to differentiate between his "reputed" grandchildren of sons John & George W. Murray.

Daughter Frances "Fanny" [Murray] married Jonathan Wynkoop, son of Henry Wynkoop, Esquire, whom Francis Murray termed "my venerable friend". They had two sons, Francis & John Wynkoop, both under 21 at the writing of the Will in 1811, but by the time of Francis' Codicil of 1816, Francis Wynkoop at died.

Daughter Eliza E. [Murray] was born 1782, and married Dr. Phineas Jenks on March 20, 1806. Dr. Jenks graduated from University of PA and studied under Dr. Benjamin Rush. Eliza died a year after her marriage on March 16, 1807. Their one child, Eliza E. M. Jenks died at age 5 months, 9 days. Eliza and her daughter are buried in the Newtown Presbyterian Cemetery.

Son William Murray had no children at the time his Father wrote his Will, but by the time the Codicil was added, Francis provided for William's daughter, Rosalina Murray. I'm quite sure "Rosalina" was the same "Riselma" Murray who received a gold mourning ring through Agnes [Murray] Martin's LWT of 1822. The clerk's writing is quite clear in both Wills, so I don't know which name is correct, but it's probably "Rosalina". Rosalina was bequeathed $550 every year for her natural life.

Gen. Francis Murray died between November 17th and December 1st, 1816, a resident of Newtown, Bucks Co., PA. He willed "that a "tomb or head & foot stones be procured for myself, my wife buried at Newtown and all my deceased children such as my executors hereafter named at their discretion shall decree suitable…." His & wife Martha's large, flat gravestone is located in the Historic Newtown Presbyterian Church cemetery[69]. He owned 60 acres, adjoining the Newtown Common and the Meeting House lot, along with several other tracts. His "mansion house" on 4 acres, adjoined the Yardley Ferry Rd., Congress St. and the street passing in front of the Court House, which were devised to executors Dr. Phineas Jenks & Jonathan Wynkoop, then in trust to son William Murray and his children. Francis stipulated that the Executors shall not be liable for any of William's debts.

Gen. Francis provided for his sister Mrs. Mary Tracey, directing his executors to maintain decently & comfortably Mary Tracey during her natural life and to bury her. They were also to hold in trust $100 for the use of one or more of her friends or acquaintances as she by her Will shall direct.

The most important portion of Francis Murray's Will proves his relationship with Agnes "Ann" [Murray] Martin, although he uses the nickname of "Nancy":

"Item: I give and bequeath to **my niece Nancy Martin, widow of my friend Daniel Martin** *all my plates of every description, except the tea spoons included in a bequest hereinafter made for the use of my son Williams & his family in trust nevertheless for the uses and purposes herein after mentioned and for no other uses and upon no other trusts*

---

[69] www.findagrave.com

whatsoever that is to say, In trust that she my said niece will receive my silver teapot for her own use **as a token of respect due from me to her for the motherly care exercised over all my children & especially my daughter after the death of their mother** *and upon this further trust that she my said niece or some person by her appointed for that purpose will give and dispose of all the rest and residue of said plates to the daughters born or to be born to my son William in such order and proportions as she my said niece may be pleased to appoint, order and direct, and it is further my will and I do hereby order and direct that my executors hereinafter named put out one hundred pounds <sic> at interest & that they receive the interest thereof and pay the same to my said niece annually during the continuance of her natural life and it is further my will and I do hereby give and bequeath to my said niece one Hundred dollars, to be paid to her out of any part of my estate or her executors , administrators or assigns by said executors wherever they may conceive the circumstances of my estate will admit leaving them the sole judges and from and immediately after the decease of my said niece the hundred pounds <sic> to be considered as a part of the general residue of my estate for the purposes hereinafter mentioned".*

I learned that staff of the Bucks Co. Historical Society believed that Gen. Francis Murray's niece "Nancy Martin", was the wife of Daniel Martin and probably the daughter of a Philadelphia merchant, William Murray, who died in Philadelphia in September, 1762.

The Will of William Murray, Merchant, of the City of Philadelphia[70] was written on September 23, 1762; and proved on September 28, 1762. The abstract of his Will indicates his heirs to be his children: <u>Agnes Murray</u>, George Murray and an unknown child. His Co-Executors named were his wife Jane Murray, his <u>brother John Murray</u>, and merchants Abraham Usher and <u>Randle Mitchell</u>. Witnesses were: <u>John Mease</u> & James Sloan.

---

[70] Philadelphia, PA Will Book M, p. 359

Although I have not been able to acquire much detail of William Murray's life, it would appear that he was in partnership with his brother John in a dry goods mercantile business. John became partners with Andrew Bunner and Thomas Leaming, Jr. under the name style "Bunner, Murray & Co." although it's not known how early this firm was in existence. There are records of its operation during the Revolutionary War, because the company pledged £6,000 to supply the Continental Army wintering at Valley Forge. John Murray was born c1730 in Belfast, Co. Antrim and, as an Irish-born Philadelphian, was proposed as a member of Philadelphia's Society of Friendly Sons of St. Patrick[71]. His sponsor was John Mitchell, brother and partner of Randle Mitchell, both highly respected, wealthy merchants. Another member of the Friendly Sons was John Mease, born in Strabane, Co. Tyrone, who amassed a fortune as a merchant of Philadelphia. The Society of the Friendly Sons of St. Patrick also included members Colonels Walter Stewart and Charles Stewart.

Agnes was born at least by 1762, and as the oldest of 3 children, she was likely born c1756. It's not known when her Mother Jane died, but as a fatherless orphan, Agnes would have been placed under guardianship as a child. Usually the guardian approved by the court was not the same individual serving as the father's executor due to possible conflicts of interest. So rather than her Uncle John of Philadelphia, it's likely Agnes was under the care of her paternal uncle Gen. Francis Murray. Gen. Francis Murray attended the Newtown Presbyterian Church, which was served by Rev. Henry Martin until his death in 1764. Rev. Henry Martin's nearest neighbor was Henry Wynkoop, who was the Co-Guardian of Daniel Martin. It's very likely that Daniel's guardianship entailed removing him from his Mother's home, when the court agreed that Mary was not providing a wholesome environment for Daniel. I would suspect Daniel was placed in the Wynkoop home for proper supervision. Gen. Francis Murray's daughter Fanny married Jonathan Wynkoop, the son of Henry Wynkoop.

---

[71] Ancestry.com "A brief account of the Society of the Friendly Sons of St. Patrick"

Undoubtedly, both Daniel and Agnes attended church at Newtown Presbyterian.

From Bucks Co. Tax Records – 1693-1778[72]:
Middletown Township – 1778: Danl. Marton (sic)   6£, 3£

Daniel is not listed among the separate accounting of "Single Men", so we must assume he was married by the above 1778 tax record. Familiar neighbors include: the Paxsons (Thomas, William, Mahlon); and the Richardsons (Joshua, Samuel, William).

From the 1876 "History of Bucks Co., PA", Daniel Martin served in the Bucks Co. cavalry as a private in Capt. Jacob Bennett's Light Dragoons for the year 1781.

The Hunterdon Co., NJ Tax Lists for 1778-1780 - show Daniel Martin as owning property in Amwell Township.[73]

Bucks Co., PA Property & Tax Records – Middletown Township – 1779[74] & 1781:
Daniel Martin – 110 acres; 3 horses; 11 cattle, 0 servants

Daniel is also listed as property tax payer in Newtown Township – 1779, and again in 1781[75], he is listed as a married man, but having no acreage; 1 horse; no cattle; no servants.

In 1783 – Middletown[76], Daniel Martin is listed as having paid £3. 3. 4

1784 – Middletown: Daniel Martin: 1 Dwelling house; 4 White Inhabitants and 2 Black Inhabitants.[77]

1785 – Middletown: Daniel Martin was taxed for 120 acres; 4 Horses; 3 Cattle; and 1 Servant.

---

[72] Bucks County Tax Records – 1693-1778, compiled by Terry McNealy & Frances Waite. Bucks Co. Genealogical Society, PO Box 1092, Doylestown, PA 18901
[73] "Revolutionary Census of NJ, Based on Ratables During the Period of the Revolution" by Kenn Stryker-Rodda.
[74] Middletown Tax Records – 1779 – transcribed by Patricia Woodruff
http://pagenweb.org/~bucks/TaxRecords/middletwontwptax.html
[75] Newtown Tax Records of 1781- transcribed by Judy Jackson.
http://pagenweb.org/~bucks/TaxRecords/newtowntax.html
[76] Bucks Co., PA - Middletown Township Tax Records 1783 - Transcribed by Laurie VanSant
 http://pagenweb.org/~bucks/TaxRecords/middletowntax1783.html
[77] Bucks Co., PA - Middletown Township Tax Records 1784 - Transcribed by Laurie VanSant
http://pagenweb.org/~bucks/TaxRecords/middletowntax1784.html

A Middletown neighbor to Daniel Martin was presumably his stepfather, David Marpole (sic), whose tax assessment was minimal for 1786:

Daniel Martin: £1.3.4

David Marpole: £-.-.7[78]

I've not been able to find any additional records for Thomas' widow, Mary Martin Marple. Mary's parents are unknown and her death date has not been ascertained. The above tax listing is the last record I've found for Mary or David Marple.

Daniel Martin was a Bucks County Tax Collector for at least the year 1783, from the following PA Colonial Records:

The Supreme Executive Council met - Philadelphia, Tuesday, December 16, 1783:

"The accounts of John Thompson and Daniel Martin, Collectors of Excise for the county of Bucks, as the same were reported by the Comptroller General, were read and approved."

Daniel Martin served as a witness to the LWT of John Gregg, Yeoman, of Middletown Twp. On March 9, 1787[79]

In 1788, the State of PA required all slaveholders to register the children of slaves. Bucks Co. Prothonotary Records show on March 10, 1789, Daniel Martin, described as a Yeoman of Middletown, registered "John" age 3, born December 23, 1785, termed to be a slave until the age of 28.

1790 U. S. Census - Bucks Co., PA - p. 184:
Daniel Martin - 1 3 5 1 1

Daniel's household (in addition to himself) included three males under the age of 16, and four daughters by 1790. His closest neighbors were the Longshore, Gillam, Allen and Blakey families. Joshua Richardson and Michael Gregg were nearby.

The 1790 LWT[80] of Patrick Doyle of Middletown Twp referenced "debts against Daniel Martin, John Jenks and Mark Hapenny".

---

[78] Bucks Co., PA - Middletown Township Tax Records 1784 - Transcribed by Laurie VanSant http://pagenweb.org/~bucks/TaxRecords/middletowntax1784.html
[79] Bucks Co., PA – Will Book 5, p. 82
[80] Bucks Co., PA – Will Book 5, p. 161

The LWT of Richard Gibbs[81], Yeoman of Bensalem Twp, dated November 4, 1790, devised to his Rodman grandchildren "land in Newtown, Bucks Co., PA, bought of Daniel Martin".

Bucks Co., PA – Orphans' Court[82] records show several instances where Daniel Martin was appointed as a Guardian:

File #1078 – January 5, 1796: Aaron Hageman, Northampton Twp. Widow Mary (now Kroesen). Left five children under 14: Henry, Mary, Anna, John and Deborah. Daniel Martin appointed guardian.

File #1091 – May 2, 1796: William Carter, Northampton Twp. Children James and Rebecca Carter, over 14, petition for guardians. Daniel Martin appointed for orphan James; Dr. Joseph Fenton appointed for Rebecca Carter.

File #1107 – February 6, 1797: William Hayhurst, Northampton Twp. Grandchildren Rebecca and James Carter, over 14, children of William Carter, late of Northampton Twp, petition for guardians. Daniel Martin appointed for James Carter; Dr. Joseph Fenton appointed for Rebecca.

1800 U. S. Census - Bucks Co., PA - p. 307:
Daniel Martin - 31010-01210-00

In 1800, Daniel's household included 3 males under the age of 10; 1 male aged 10 not yet 16; 1 daughter aged 10 not yet 16; and 2 daughters 16 not yet 26. Daniel and wife Agnes were enumerated as being "26 not yet 45".

Daniel Martin died about the first of April, 1801:

---

[81] Bucks Co., PA – Will Book 5, p. 454
[82] Bucks Co., PA Orphans' Court Records 1685-1852, Thomas G. Myers. Willow Bend Books, Westminster, MD – 1999.

THE LAST WILL & TESTAMENT OF DANL. MARTIN[83]

WILL DATE: MARCH 26, 1801
WILL PROVED: APRIL 10TH 1801
BUCKS CO., PA
WILL BOOK NO. 6, PAGE 324 - 325
#3040

 Be it Remembered that I Daniel Martin of Middletown Township in the County of Bucks and State of Pennsylvania, Do this twenty sixth day of March the year of our Lord one thousand eight hundred and one make & put in writing this Instrument as and for My last will and Testament in Manner and form following:

 In the first place I will and order all my estate both Personal and Real be sold as soon as convenient after my Decease.

 Secondly I will that my Beloved wife Agnes have one hundred Pounds of the Money arising from those sales.

 Thirdly I will that my beloved wife leave one eighth of the remainder which legacies I consider in lieu of her Dower.

 Fourthly the Remaining seventh parts I order and direct to be put out to Interest upon good and sufficient security and to be equally Divided among my seven children; namely, Mary, Frances, Agness, Thomas, William Murray, Daniel and Charles Alexander share & share alike each Child's share to be paid when they arrive to the age of twenty one years, but if any of my said Children should Die before they arrive to the age of twenty one years, then their share or shares to be equally divided among the survivors.

 Lastly I Do Nominate constitute and appoint Peter Sharpe Esquire of Greenwich Township in the County of Sussex & State of New Jersey sole Executor of this My Last Will & Testament. In Witness whereof I have hereunto set My hand and seal the Day and year aforesaid.

 Dan: Martin {Seal}

---

[83] Transcribed by Francie Lane – December 29, 2013 - Bucks Co., PA Will Book 6, p. 324 – www.familysearch..org

*Sealed Signed Published Pronounced and
Declared By the said Testator as and for his Last Will and
Testament in the Presence of us:
Mahlon Gregg   Wm. Blakey, Junr.*

April 10 Anno Domini 1801 – Personally appeared Mahlon Gregg William Blakey the two subscribing witnesses to the within Instrument of writing and on their solemn affirmation did say that they were present at the execution thereof and saw and heard Daniel Martin the Testator therein named sign seal publish and declare the same as and for his Last Will and Testament and at the Time of his so doing he was of sound mind and memory & of a Disposing understanding to the Best of their Knowledge & belief.

/s/ James Hanna

Register's Office, Bucks County, March the 16th 1804

THE Heirs, Creditors, and other Persons interested, are desired to Take NOTICE, that Peter Sharpe, Executor of Daniel Martin ~ late of the township of Middletown Deceased, has filed in this Office the Accounts of his Administration to the estate of the said deceased, and that the same will be presented for approbation and allowance, to an Orphan's Court, to be held at Newtown, in and for the said County of Bucks, on the Seventh day of May next at 10 o'clock A.M.

Wm. Hart, D.R. Register

An Inventory of the goods & Chattles of Daniel Martin Deceas'd of Middletown in the County of Bucks & State of Pennsylvania ~ Appraised this 10th day of April 1801 by us ~   Wm. Blakey Junr.

Mahlon Gregg

	Dollars
Purse & Wearing Apparel	10.50
Desk $8 ~Desk & Book Case $12 ~ Bed Bedsteads & Beding $20	40.00
Coverlids & Blankets $20, dining Table $5 Dressing Table $3.50	28.50
Breakfast Table $4, Candlestand $2	6.00
Seven Windsor Chairs $5 Chanea & Glass ware in Cupboard $6	11.00
Looking Glass 60 Cents Books $12	12.60

Bible, Catechism, <?Sand> Book, 2 small dº	3.00
Clock $40 Looking Glass $4	44.00
Open Stove $10, And Irons Shovel & Tongs $2.50	12.50
Breakfast Table & Sundries $4 1/2 doz. Windsor Chairs $4	8.00
Table & Sunds. In Kitchen $2 And Iron Shovel & Tongs $3	5.00
Trammels & Sunds. $2.50, Pewter & Sunds. In Cupboard $4	6.50
2 Pewter dishes 1 doz plates 1/2 doz Knives & forks spoons &c	2.00
One Copper Kettle 1 Brass Dº, Tea Kettle	8.00
Rye Meal $8.50 SteelYards Chest &c $2	10.50
Two under beds $2, Cask & Grain $2	4.00
Chest, Scales & Weights, Warming pan	4.00
Two pair Bedsteads, Beds, & Beding $30, Box & Candles 50 cents	30.50
Bottles Trunk & Sunds. $2 ~ Sunds in Garret $4	6.00
Waggon $20 Cart body &c $10 ~ $30, Gun & Sunds. In out house $7	37.00
Sleigh $5 Hay $8 Boards $4 Potatoes & Sunds. $2	19.00
Bay Mare $20 Bay horse $20 Two Colts $50	90.00
Black Cow $20 one dº $16 one Heifer $12	48.00
Number of Rails & posts $8 A quantity of flax $2	10.00
Plow & Tackling $2 Harrow $3 Axes spades & Sunds. $8	13.00
Five Swine $12 Tubs $1, Tub & Soap $2.50	15.50
Saddle & bridle $4 Sund Casks in Cellar &c $4	8.00
Notes	14.00
	$507.10

Bucks P.   April 10th 1801 James <?Hagina>

  Personally appeared before me William Blakey, Junr. and Mahlon Gregg appraisers of the above Inventory and on their Solemn Affirmations did say that they appraised the same to the best of their knowledge.

  A portion of Daniel Martin's Probate File contained an accounting by the accountant, which stated in part:

  A 20 acre lot near Hughes' Forge was sold for $75 to Joseph Carling who agreed to pay $20 over two years.

  Daniel's plantation and grist mill was sold to Jacob Young for £3,000, with payments of £500 April 1, 1802; £300 on May 1, 1803 and the "Residue in eleven yearly payments of £200 ea, which amounted to $8,000.00

  On January 24, 1803, Rent of $361.34 was received from Thomas Loyd for the "above Plantation, Grist Mill, etc."

  In 1803, the estate received the following income:

William Welch - £11.1.3 for Arrears of Rent

    Sundry items such as 1,110 shingles, a crosscut saw, old iron, and boards.

    Payments for Settlements were received from Aaron Phillips, James Lenton and Samuel Blakey

    The estate sold various grain to the following:

Thomas Loyd & Jacob Sharpe – Grain

James Doughterty – 6 bushels of Oats

George Bidleman – Wheat & Rye

Peter Rope – 5 bushels & 1 peck of Rye

    In 1803, the estate received from Joseph Richardson $137.13, and various amounts from William Johnson, Jacob Vanhart & John Kirkbride.

    There were many familiar names listed in the probate account records such as: John Dyer, William Blakey, Jr., Joshua Paxson, Francis & John Murray, John, James & Solomon Wildman, Euclydus Longshore, Mahlon Gregg, Richard Tomlinson, Daniel Larue, and William & Joseph Jenks.

Last Will and Testament of Daniel Martin, late of Middleton Deceased, as well of and for such and so much of the Goods, Chattels as for his payments and Disbursements out of the same

1801		Voucher	Ye Contra, he Prays Allowance	
May, 5		1	For Cash paid Levi Bond for a Coffin $8.00	3.0.0
	20	2	For Cash paid Ann Jones $1.00	0.7.6
		3	For Cash paid Nathaniel Price	8.6.0
		4	Ditto paid John Simmons	2.15.5
		5	Ditto paid John Pitman	0.3.9
		6	Ditto paid Nathaniel Burrows	14.6.2
		7	Ditto paid John Dyer	0.14.5
		8	Ditto paid John Johnson	1.2.10
		9	Ditto paid Jesse Lovett	2.4.6
		10	Ditto paid William Huddleston	3.7.4
		11	Ditto paid William Blakey Junr	0.18.9
		12	Ditto paid James Worstall	1.13.10

13 Ditto paid Joshua Paxson	1.5.8
14 Ditto paid Francis Murray	13.16.10
15 Ditto paid James Wildman	2.7.9
16 Ditto paid Euclydus Longshore	8.10.8
17 Ditto paid John Brooks	1.19.6
18 Ditto paid Jacob Kisler	20.19.7
19 Ditto paid Isaac Reader	0.11.3
20 Ditto paid Jonathan Walton	0.19.2.5
21 Ditto paid Thomas Ray	3.11.5
22 Ditto paid William Allen	0.15.0
24 Ditto paid Robert Pidgeon	0.7.6
25 Ditto paid John Hellings	1.10.0
26 Ditto paid Susanna Torbert	0.17.4
28 Ditto paid Wm. Duane	0.7.6
29 Ditto paid Samuel Langcope	0.18.9
30 Ditto paid Mahlon Gregg	25.12.9
31 Ditto paid Christopher Melick	6.12.11
32 Ditto paid Nathl. Burrows for Wm. Torbert	1.17.9
	132.1.10 1/2
33 For Cash paid John Linton	0.12.4
34 For Ditto paid Cooper States	0.9.4
35 Ditto paid Jeremiah Brown Senr	1.17.7
36 Ditto paid Joshua H. Brown	8.2.8
37 Ditto paid Jeremiah Brown Junr	1.17.7
38 Ditto paid Joseph Luber	0.18.2
39 Ditto paid David Landis	3.15.8
40 Ditto paid Joseph Taylor	3.11.3
41 Ditto paid Isaac Tucker	2.17.7
42 Ditto paid William Aspy	14.15.6
43 Ditto paid Enos Yardley	1.5.4
44 Ditto paid John Wildman	17.10.9
45 Ditto paid Charles Goheen	0.3.0
46 Ditto paid Lambert Longshore	0.16.10.5
47 Ditto paid Richard Tomlinson	15.17.11
48 Ditto paid Thomas Wildley	2.4.2
49 Ditto paid James Flowers	5.4.10.5
50 Ditto paid Robert Croandale	1.8.1
51 Ditto paid John Birkey	5.10.1

	52 Ditto paid Samuel Y. Thornton	1.14.3
	53 Ditto paid Crandale & Gregg	11.15.10
	54 Ditto paid Francis Gregg Execr.	17.1.8
	55 Ditto paid Solomon Wildman	0.6.6
	56 Ditto paid Patrick Hunter	10.5.4
	57 Ditto paid Samuel Winner	2.16.1
	58 Ditto paid Thomas Ross $5.60	2.2.0
	59 Ditto paid John Murray $10.00	3.15.0
	60 Ditto paid Thomas Buckman	67.13.8
	61 Ditto paid Andrew McMinn	3.13.6
	62 Ditto paid Abram Chapman	0.16.8
	63 Ditto paid James Raquet	6.19.5
	64 Ditto paid William Tomlinson	5.3.10
	65 Ditto paid Ezra Thackray	13.8.8
	66 Ditto paid Henry Dudder	1.4.8
	67 Ditto paid James Gilkyson	8.10.0
	68 Ditto paid Danl. Larue Junr	6.9.7
		384.2.1 1/2
	69 For Cash paid Isaac Hicks	6.5.3
	70 for Cash paid Thomas Ross	1.10.0
	71 For Cash paid Nathaniel Huston	4.14.0
	72 Ditto paid Jonathan Woolston	14.14.0
	73 Ditto paid Samuel Thornton	1.0.3
	74 Ditto paid Samuel Johnson	1.3.2
	75 Ditto paid Phineas Paxson	10.4.4
	76 Ditto paid John Hulme & Son	13.7.2
	77 Ditto paid Phineas Paxson	3.5.5
	78 Ditto paid Mahlon Miller	0.15.4
	79 Ditto paid Willm. Buckman	3.12.5
	80 Ditto paid Josiah Addis	2.3.9
	81 Ditto paid William Jenks	2.17.7.5
	82 Ditto paid Cesar Wilkes	9.14.0
	83 Ditto paid Gerardus Wynkoop	0.11.3
	84 Ditto paid Abner Buckman	32.11.9
	85 Ditto paid Richard Tomlinson	2.18.4
	86 Ditto paid John Hibbs, Collr $2.32	0.17.5
1802	87 Ditto paid Nathaniel Shewell $80.00	30.0.0
Novr 26	91 Ditto paid James Hyndshaw	5.5.0

May 7, 1803	92 Ditto paid James Carter	12.12.2
	93 Ditto paid Abm. Chapman $12.26	4.12.0
Aug, 2	94 Ditto paid Benjn. Buckman	0.19.8
	95 Ditto paid Ditto	2.1.5.5
	96 Ditto paid Joseph Jenks	1.7.10
	97 Ditto paid Thomas Wiley Junr	2.10.4
	100 Ditto paid James Hannah Prothan $1.53	0.11.6
	101 Ditto paid Ditto $2.00	0.15.0
	103 Ditto paid Benjn. Buckman Esq. $1.00	0.7.6
	104 Ditto paid Jacob Thompson for Recording Mortgage	0.3.9
	by Book debt due from John absentia	1.3.0
	105 By Cash pd. Agness Martin <expences?> in	
	accomodating Arbitrators &c on settlement of Estate	15.0.0
	per Rect.	
	By fees pd Register Clk Orphan's Court &c	3.0.1
	By dº Clerk Orphans Court for copy for the Exr	0.12.0
	By Commissions Allowed for Compleating the whole	
	Trust	200.0.0
		777.8.10 1/2
	By Cash pd. For Cloathing for Widow & Children before	
	funeral ~ as pr. Rects.	11.8.7
	" Saml. Fitgraves Atty. dº	3.15.0
	" A. Chapman dº ~ dº	1.10.0
	Balance in the hands of the Executor to be disposed	
	of agreeably to the direction of the will	3540.19.1 1/2
		£4,335.1.7
	By Cash paid the Heirs & Guardians at Sundry Times	
	1801 (Viz)	
May, 20	23 By Cash paid William Richardson Junr as Guardian	17.19.6
dº	27 By Ditto paid Agness Martin (Heir)	75.8.3
	88 By Ditto paid Agness Martin (Heir)	308.3.10
	1802	
Novr 26	89 By Ditto paid Agness Martin (Heir)	41.16.5
	90 By Ditto paid Mary Martin (Heir)	37.10.0
	1803	
Aug, 2	98 By Ditto paid William Richardson (Guardian)	125.0.0

99 By Ditto paid Ditto   500.0.0
102 By Ditto paid Agness Martin (Heir)   28.2.6
   Last Will and Testament of Daniel Martin, late of
   Middleton Deceased, as well of and for such and so

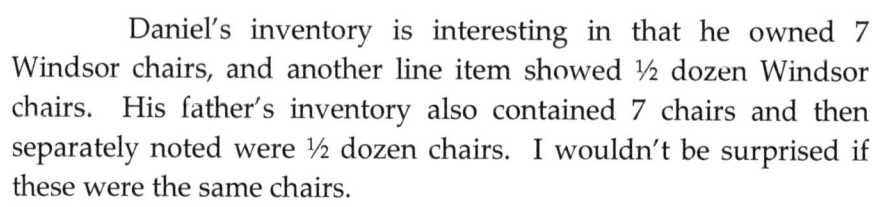

Daniel's inventory is interesting in that he owned 7 Windsor chairs, and another line item showed ½ dozen Windsor chairs. His father's inventory also contained 7 chairs and then separately noted were ½ dozen chairs. I wouldn't be surprised if these were the same chairs.

Daniel owned 20 acres near Hughes' Forge, which was sold April 25, 1801 for $75.

Daniel owned a plantation and grist mill, which was sold December 7, 1801, for $8,000.00 to Jacob Young in installments over eleven years. The plantation and grist mill had previously been rented to Thomas Lloyd and the estate received $361.34 in (past due) rent from Lloyd in January 24, 1803. I'm of the opinion that Daniel's plantation and grist mill had been inherited from his father, and that Daniel's primary residence was in the town of Attleborough, where he pursued his law practice, preferring to rent out his farmland and mills.

Daniel Martin's File in Orphan's Court is #1341:

May 4,1801, Middletown. Widow Agnes, 7 children, 3 under 14: William, Daniel, Charles. 3 children over 14: Mary, Francis, & Thomas. Agnes & William Richardson Jr. appt'd guardians.

July 27, 1801-Daughter Agnes, over 14, petitions for guardian. Agnes Martin & Wm. Richardson appt'd.

Until I could locate the complete Will of Daniel, I had relied on an abstract which was incorrect; i.e., Daniel's sons were listed in a Will Book abstract as "Thomas, William, Murray, Daniel and Charles". However, there was not a son Murray Martin. The abstractor incorrectly placed a comma between "William" and "Murray", when actually the son was William Murray Martin.

I tried to determine why Daniel chose Peter Sharp of Sussex Co., NJ, as his sole executor. Initially, I imagined that Peter Sharp was a probate attorney and possibly a friend and classmate during Daniel's years at Princeton, but I could not confirm that theory as there was nothing to be found concerning Peter's professional life. What I did discover was either extraordinarily coincidental or a clue to a closer relationship – unexplainable at this point. Peter Sharp[84] was the son of John & Joanna [Hager] Sharp of Greenwich, Sussex Co., NJ, whose Will was written June 31, 1770, naming Peter as the oldest son. The witnesses to the Will were Robert Martin and Alexander White. Could this Robert Martin have been Daniel's paternal uncle? The other mystifying, convoluted issue was that Peter's nephew Morris Sharp, Jr., owned a farm in Lebanon, Hunterdon Co., NJ and married Maria Cramer, daughter of Matthias & Anna Maria "Mary" Cramer. After Matthias' death in 1783, his widow Mary married John Sharp, son of Morris Sharp, Sr., who was Peter Sharp's brother. It had been Matthias Cramer who purchased Hugh Martin's plantation in Annandale, Lebanon Twp. in 1774 from Col. James Martin. The bio on the Sharps (aka Sharpenstine family) continues, stating that Morris, Jr's farm passed to his grandson Asa Sharp, who is shown on the Hunterdon historical maps (Sheet D) in 1860 as owning 120 acres of what had been Hugh Martin's 420 acre plantation.

1810 US Census[85] – Bucks Co., PA – Middletown <4/8>
MARTIN, Ann: 002-01121

1820 US Census – Bucks Co., PA – Middletown <3/8>
MARTIN, Agnes: 00001-01011

Agnes' home was located in the village of Attleborough, about six miles west of the Delaware River, in Middletown Township. Attleborough, which is officially only ½ square mile, was originally known as Four Lanes End, and since 1876, has been

---

[84] "The Early Germans of NJ" byTheodore F. Chambers – ebooksread.com – p. 47
[85] Ancestry.com

renamed Langhorne. Four Lanes End was descriptive of the location as it was the crossroads of the road between Trenton, NJ and Philadelphia, and the road from Bristol to Durham. These two roads were originally Lenni-Lenape Indian paths. Joseph Richardson, who married Mary [Paxson], settled Four Lanes End in the 1720's, operating a general store and inn at the intersection of the roads.

Daniel's widow Agnes Martin wrote her Will on October 25, 1821; and probate commenced on February 2, 1822. Agnes named all her then-living children:

AGNES MARTIN[86]
LAST WILL & TESTAMENT
WILL DATE: OCTOBER 25, 1821
WILL PROVED: FEBRUARY 2, 1822
BUCKS CO., PA WILL BOOK 10, PAGE 64
#4927

I, *Agness* alias *Ann Martin of the township of Middletown and County of Bucks, being weak in body but of sound and disposing mind and memory do make this my last will & testament.*

First I direct that my just debts and funeral expenses be paid by my executor hereinafter named and in order to enable him so to do ~

I direct my house & lot of ground in Attleborough (where I now dwell) to be sold by my Executor as soon after my decease as soon as he may judge proper together with my personal property not hereinafter devised.

Item I give and devise to my daughter Frances her choice of my beds – bedsteads in the front room, bed spread and curtains bed quilt lined with pink, the dark one that is not quilted, the red chairs that were her sister Mary's, the cherry breakfast table, Large looking glass in the parlour, my silver teaspoons & tea tongs.

---

[86] Transcribed by Francie Lane – December 29, 2013 – Bucks Co., PA Will Book 10, p. 64 www.familysearch.org <45/511>

Item I give & devise to my daughter Ann, wife of Augustine Mitchel, my silver tea pot, brass andirons, a bed quilt with blue lining, two table cloths.

Item the remainder of my linens I give & devise to my daughter Frances and any other part of my household goods that she may make choice of.

Item my clothing I leave to my two daughters by them to be equally divided without being appraised.

Item I give & devise to my cousin Riselma Murray a gold mourning piece which belonged to my Daughter Mary at the age of twenty one to remain in the care of my Executor until then if she does not live to heir it I give it between my two daughters.

Item the remainder of my estate I give & devise equally between my children; namely Frances, Ann, Thomas, William, Daniel & Charles.

Lastly I constitute & appoint my friend William Richardson my Executor to this my last will. In witness whereof I hereunto set my hand & seal this twenty fifth of October in the year of our Lord one thousand eight hundred and twenty one.

/s/ Agness A. Martin {Seal}

Signed sealed and declared by the said testatrix to be her
Last will & testament in the presence of us:
William Blakey, Jr. Mahlon Gregg

Bucks Co, Pa – Personally appeared before me on the 2nd day of February 1822, William Blakey, Jr. & Mahlon Gregg the subscribing witnesses to the foregoing last will & testament of Agness A. Martin deceased and on their solemn affirmations did say they saw & heard Agness A. Martin the testator therein named sign seal publish & declare the same as & for her last will & testament and that at the time of so doing she was of sound mind & memory & of disposing understanding to the best of their knowledge & belief.

Benjamin Field, Register

The known children of Daniel & Agnes [Murray] Martin were:

Mary Martin was born about 1780, and apparently named for her paternal grandmother, Mary [ ] Martin Marple. Miss Mary Martin wrote her Will September 7, 1819, and died by March, 1820. Oddly, Mary omitted any reference to her brother William Murray Martin. It may be that Mary had become a Quaker due to her Will phrasing, "Be it remembered ...." as opposed to the traditional preface of "In the name of God, Amen...." Mary's executor and "friend" Thomas L. Allen was heading his own household in the 1820 US Census, near Agnes Martin.

MARY MARTIN[87]
LAST WILL & TESTAMENT
WILL DATE: 7 SEPTEMBER 1819
WILL PROVED: 20 MARCH 1820
BUCKS CO., PA WILL BOOK 9, PAGE 391
#4709

Be it remembered that I, MARY MARTIN, of Middletown Township, Bucks County considering it prudent whilst in the full enjoyment of my natural abilities to provide for the distribution of my estate which it hath pleased divine providence to bless me with therefore I make and cause to be put into writing this my last will and Testament – as follows ~ I give and devise to my dear Mother Agness Martin the income or Interest of all my monies now in Bonds Notes and Bank Stock during her natural life ~ After her death that they (that is the Bonds Notes & Bank Stock) be divided into Six equal shares two of which I give unto my sister Frances ~ One to my sister Ann ~ One to my Brother Thomas ~ One to my Brother Daniel and one to my Brother Charles Martin, and their heirs and assigns individually and separately forever. I give and devise to my dear Mother Agness Martin all my household goods of every description for her own use and benefit forever ~ I give to my Brother Daniel Martin all my Library of Books (except Cox's Medical Dispensatory) for his own benefit

---

[87] Transcribed by Francie Lane – December 30, 2013 –Bucks Co. Will Book 9, p. 391 - www.familysearch.org <226/256>

& use forever ~ I give and devise to my friend Thomas L. Allen my copy of Coxs Medical Dispensatory for his own benefit forever ~ I appoint my friend Thomas L Allen to be the Executor of this my last will & testament hoping my affairs may be settled in a quiet and peaceable manner as possible ~ In witness whereof I have hereunto set my hand & seal this Seventh day of September 1819.

Mary Martin {Seal}

Witness present
Joseph Richardson, Jonathan Walton

Bucks County P. On the 20th of March 1820, Joseph Richardson & Jonathan Walton the subscribing witnesses to the foregoing writing purporting to be a last will & Testament of Mary Martin Appeared before me & on their solemn affirmations did declare and say that they were present & saw & heard Mary Martin the Executrix sign seal publish and declare the foregoing as and for her last will & Testament & that at the time of her so doing She was of sound mind & memory & of disposing understanding to the best of their Judgment & belief.
 H. M. Gearhart, D.R.

Bucks County P. Be it remembered that on the 20th of March 1820 the foregoing last will & testament of Mary Martin was duly proved when Letters Testamentary were granted unto Thomas L. Allen the Executor therein named he having first been duly Affirmed will & truly to Administer the estate according to law. Witness my hand & Seal of office
H. M. Gearhart, D. R.
Registered March 20, 1820.

Frances Martin was born October 15, 1783. She did not marry, and may be shown as "Francie Martin", (female) age 65, living with the John Warner (age 73) family in the 1850 US Census of Bucks Co., PA – Middletown. In the 1860 US Census of Bucks Co., Middletown Twp - Newtown, Frances age 75, is living with four similarly-aged, single women; Rachael Price, a confectioner, headed the household. Frances died on June 2, 1866 and is buried[88] in the "Historic Presbyterian Church Cemetery" in Newtown, Bucks Co., PA.

FRANCES MARTIN[89]
LAST WILL & TESTAMENT
WILL DATE: 8 SEPTEMBER 1851
WILL PROVED: JUNE 9, 1866
BUCKS CO., PA WILL BOOK 16, PAGE 401
#11869

I, Frances Martin of the township of Middletown in the County of Bucks and State of Pennsylvania, Single woman, Do make this my last Will and Testament in Writing in manner as follows Viz:

Imprimises – I order and direct all my just debts, funeral expenses and Will charges, fully paid and discharged by my Executor, out of my Estate.

Item: It is then my Will, after all legal charges and expenses in Settling my Estate are paid, that my remaining property and estate be divided into Six Equal Shares. I give and devise to Sarah Heaton, Widow of Joseph M. Heaton, and to Deborah Walker, wife of Phineas Walker, daughter of my Sister Agness Mitchell Each One of which shares and to their heirs, And to the Daughters of my Brother Thomas Martin, viz, Anna Childs, wife of Thomas Childs, Susannah Scott wife of Joshua Scott, Mary Martin and Eliza Warren, wife of Joseph Warren, Each One Share of my said Estate and to their heirs.

And Lastly I appoint my friend Michael H. Jenks, Executor to this my last Will and Testament giving him full power to sell and dispose of any part of my Estate for the purpose of carrying out this my Will.

In Testimony whereof I have hereunto set my hand and seal this 8th day of September, in the Year of our Lord One thousand Eight hundred and fifty one (1851)

Frances Martin {Seal}

---

[88]Findagrave.com – Memorial #25652171
[89] Transcribed by Francie Lane – December 30, 2013 - Bucks Co. Will Book 16, p. 401 – www.familysearch.org<524/566>

Signed Sealed and declared by the Testatrix to be Her Last Will and Testament in the presence of us who were in the presence of each other:
Edward Stapler, Kinsey B. Tomlinson

Bucks County S.S.

On the 9th day of June A.D. 1866, personally appeared before me H. K. Sager, Register of Wills in and for the County of Bucks, Edward Stapler & Kinsey B. Tomlinson the subscribing witnesses to the annexed Instrument of Writing purporting to be the Last Will & Testament of Frances Martin, deceased and being first duly affirmed according to Law, did depose and say that they were present and saw and heard Frances Martin the Testatrix sign and seal publish pronounce and declare the annexed paper writing as and for her last Will and Testament and that at the time of her so doing she was of sound mind and memory and of disposing understanding to the best of their Knowledge & belief. H. K. Sager, Register

Be it Remembered that on the 9th day of June A.D. 1866 the annexed last Will and Testament of Frances Martin deceased was duly proved when letters testamentary thereon were granted unto Michael H. Jenks the Executor therein named he having been duly affirmed will and truly to administer the goods, and chattels, rights and credits of said deceased according to law, And also diligently and faithfully to regard and will and truly comply with the provisions of the law relating to Collateral Inheritances and that the estate will not exceed the sum of $2,000.00

Register's Docket – Book 5, p.271   342/402

On the 9th day of June A.D. 1866 the last Will and Testament of Frances Martin, late of Middletown township, dec'd. was duly proved when letters testamentary thereon were granted unto M. H. Jenks Esq., Executor therein named.

Inventory Filed June 13th, 1866, Amt: $1,641.30
Settlement Rendered: Oct. 19th 1866
   Debits: $1,042.18
   Credits: 650.32
   Balance: $ 391.86

Thomas Martin was born about 1785, Middletown, Bucks Co., PA and married Mary Gillam, daughter of Simon & Anne [Paxon] Gillam, on October 17, 1811, Middletown Monthly Meeting, Bucks Co., PA.

1820 US Census – Bucks Co., PA – Middletown <3/8>
Martin, Thomas: 00112-3011

Thomas was a witness on August 3, 1823, for the LWT of Charles Jenks[90].

Thomas remained in Middletown, and had four daughters: Anna [Martin] Childs, wife of Thomas Childs; Susannah [Martin] Scott, wife of Joshua Scott; Mary Martin who remained single; and Eliza [Martin] Warren, wife of Joseph Warren. Thomas Martin died intestate in 1825, and his estate administration is in File #5483.

Agnes "Ann" [Martin] Mitchel, b. in c1787; m. Augustine Mitchel. Augustine Mitchell, wife and family are enumerated in the 1830 US Census – Bucks Co., PA, living in Northampton Township.

Augustine & Ann's daughter Sarah married the adopted son of Gen. Francis Murray; i.e., who had been given the name Francis Heaton Murray by Gen. Murray, but as an adult was known as Joseph Heaton, son of David & Patience Heaton.

Augustine Mitchel wrote his Will[91] on September 29, 1843, as a resident of Northampton Township, Bucks Co., PA, bequeathing to his beloved wife Ann the sum of $2,500, which was to be secured by his real estate, with interest annually paid to Ann. Augustine named his three daughters: Mary Ann LaRue, Sarah Heaton and Deborah Walker. His Executor was Michael H. Jenks. The Will was witnessed by Ezekiel Tyson and Robert Walker, and proved on October 20, 1843.

---

[90] Bucks Co., PA – Will Book 10, p. 210
[91] Abstracted by Francie Lane – December 30, 2013 – familysearch.org – Bucks Co., PA Will Book 12, p. 340 <201/358>

ANN MITCHEL[92]
LAST WILL & TESTAMENT
WILL DATE: 16 JUNE 1855
WILL PROVED: 29 AUGUST 1864
BUCKS CO., PA WILL BOOK 16, PAGE 167
#11412

In the name of God, Amen, I, Ann Mitchel of the town of Newtown, Bucks County and State of Pennsylvania being of sound mind and memory and considering the uncertainty of this frail and transitory life, do therefore make, ordain, Publish and declare this to be my Last Will and testament that is to say:

First that after all my lawful Debts and Expenses is paid, I bequeath to my Daughters Sarah M. Heaton and Debora Walker all my wearing apparel in equal Shares. I also further give to my daughters Sarah M. Heaton, Debora Walker and Mary Ann Larue Ten dollars each the residue of my estate to be divided between my grandchildren share and share alike. If at my death there should be any Minor Grandchildren, there shall be a guardian appointed and the money left by me to them shall be put to interest and remain until they are of age.

I also Constitute and appoint my Son-in-law Phineas Walker my Executor to this my last Will and testament hereof revoking all former wills by me made.

In witness whereof I have hereunto subscribed my name and affixed my seal the 16th day of June one thousand eight hundred and fifty five /s/ *Ann Mitchel {Seal}*

Witness: R. C. Nagel   William K. Carver

Bucks County S.S.   *On the 29th day of August A.D. 1864, personally appeared before me H. K. Sager, Register of Wills in and for the County of Bucks, R. C. Nagel and William K. Carver*

Letters Administration Cum Testamento Annexo were granted unto William B. Warner, he having been duly affirmed well and truly to administer the goods .... And truly comply with the provisions of the law

---

[92] Transcribed by Francie Lane – December 30, 2013 – www.familysearch.org Bucks Co. Will Book 16, p. 167 <395/566>

relating to Collateral inheritances and that the Estate will not exceed the sum of $5,000.00.

William Murray Martin was born about 1790. No further information has been found after his mother's Will in 1822.

Daniel Martin, Jr. was born about 1792, resided in Middletown, Bucks Co., PA, and wrote his will on August 1, 1822. The Will was submitted for probate on October 18, 1822, naming William Richardson as Executor. Daniel directed that his lot in Washington Village be sold. Daniel was single at the time of his death as his heirs were his brother Thomas and two sisters, Frances Martin and Ann, wife of Augustine Mitchell. "Washington Village" was also known as "Four Lanes End", then Attleborough, and finally Langhorne, Bucks Co., PA.

DANIEL MARTIN (JR.)[93]
LAST WILL & TESTAMENT
WILL DATE: 1 AUGUST 1822
WILL PROVED: 15 OCTOBER 1822
BUCKS CO., PA WILL BOOK 10, PAGE 116
#4967

I, Daniel Martin of Middletown Township, County of Bucks being weak in body but of sound and disposing mind and memory do make and publish this for my last will and Testament.

First I direct my Executor hereinafter named to pay all my just debts and funeral expenses out of such monies as may come into his hands of my estate.

Second I direct my executor to sell my real Estate consisting of two Lots of Land with their improvements in Washington Village

---

[93] Transcribed by Francie Lane – December 30, 2013 – www.familysearch.org – Bucks Co., PA Will Book 10, p. 116 <73/511>

Attleborough at such time as he may judge will be the Interest of my Estate. I also direct all my personal property to be sold by my Executor (except such as is hereinafter devised) as soon after my decease as may be convenient.

Third. I give and devise to my sister Frances Martin my Desk and Book case with all my Books including the Family Bible, together with my wearing apparel.

Fourth. The residue of the moneys arising from the sale of my estate after paying my just debts and necessary expenses, I direct to be devised into four equal shares two of which shares I give and devise to my sister Frances Martin, one share to my brother Thomas Martin and one share to my sister Ann Mitchell, wife of Augustine Mitchell for their own use.

Lastly I constitute and appoint my friend Wm. Richardson my Executor to this my last will and Testament in testimony whereof I hereunto set my hand and seal this first day of August in the year of our Lord one thousand eight hundred and twenty two.

Dan. Martin {Seal}

Witness:
Mahlon Gregg   Jonathan Walton

Mahlon Gregg & Jonathan Walton affirmed on 15 October 1822, by William Field, Dep. Register

Charles Alexander Martin was born about 1795. He was named in his Mother's Will of 1822, but he died intestate in 1824, Bucks Co., PA. The administration of his estate is found in File #5339. No further information is known.

CHAPTER SIX

ROBERT MARTIN
(c1710 – 1776)

Robert Martin was born about 1710, in County Tyrone, in what is now Northern Ireland, the son of Alexander and Martha [Coughran] Martin.

As a youngster in the early 1720's, Robert sailed from Ireland and settled with his parents and siblings in then-Bucks Co. Robert's father, Alexander became ill and died shortly thereafter.

Elder brother Hugh Martin had moved across the river to Hunterdon Co., New Jersey, by the spring of 1730, and apparently Robert accompanied him, from the following information, given to us by Robert's nephew, Col. James Martin:

"After the death of my grandfather, my grandmother moved where my father and his three brothers, Thomas, Robert and Henry then lived." *"My Uncle Robert kept a school for several years, and my Uncle Thomas had learned the stone-mason's trade, and they both by their industry made a considerable property."*

Brother Hugh had also kept an English school for a year or two before his marriage in c1738, so it's possible that Robert took over the school from Hugh. From a history of "The First 250 Years of Hunterdon Co. 1714-1964", published by the Hunterdon Co. Board of Chosen Freeholders: "Tradition also tells of a school built by the Anglicans at Ringoes as early as 1720." A deed from 1756 reflects the terms of a lease creating a "district" school near Pittstown in a joint effort of local Presbyterians, Anglicans and Quakers.

It's curious that Robert is not shown as a resident of Hunterdon Co., NJ, from either the 1738 Voter List for Hunterdon County, NJ listing all male landowners, nor in the 1741 list of

Hunterdon Co. Freeholders. A possible explanation is that Robert did not own property during those years, but rather lived with either Hugh or Thomas.

Robert contributed his share toward the college expenses of his youngest brother Henry Martin in obtaining his divinity degree.

It is clear from Robert's Will that he was a staunch Presbyterian, leading me to wonder whether he might have obtained a position as a teacher at either of the two Presbyterian academies in nearby Chester Co., PA; i.e., the New London Academy or the Nottingham Academy. Hugh enrolled his eldest son Alexander in both schools in preparation of his college education, and may have been drawn to these Chester County schools due to Robert's employment there.

In 1764, Robert posted a bond for the administration of his brother Rev. Henry Martin's estate in Bucks Co., PA, stating he was residing in Northampton Township of Bucks Co., PA, and was deemed a Yeoman.

Undoubtedly, Robert was beloved by his brother Hugh and sister Esther. Hugh named a son "Robert" in honor of his brother, and Hugh, in his LWT of March, 1761, chose Robert as a Trustee, even though half-brother James was a near neighbor, and brother Rev. Henry was still living at the time.

In 1764, Robert served as the Administrator of his brother Rev. Henry Martin's estate:

REV. HENRY MARTIN[94]
BUCKS COUNTY, PENNSYLVANIA
FILE #1143

Know all Men by these Presents that we Robert Martin of Northampton Township in the County of Bucks, Yeoman, Brother of the Reverend Henry Martin of the same place, Clerk, Deceased, John Hagerman of the same Township in the County of sd. Yeoman and John Slack of Lower Makefield Township in the same County, Yeoman and held

---

[94] Transcribed by Francie Lane – Bucks Co., PA Probate – File #1143

and firmly Bound unto William Plumsted, Esq. Register General for the Probate of Wills and Granting Letters of Administration In and for the Province of Pennsylvania in the full and Just Sum of Eight Hundred Pounds Lawfull money of the said Province To be Paid to the said William Plumsted Esq. Or his Successors Register Generals of the Province aforesaid, To which Payment well and Truly to be made we Bind Our Selves Jointly and Severally Each and Every of us by himself for the whole and the Heirs Executors and Administrators of us and Every of us firmly by the sd Presents Sealed with Our Seals Dated the Eighteenth Day of April Anno Domini 1764.

    The Condition of this Obligation is such that if the above Bounden Robert Martin, Administrator of all and Singular the Goods Chattels and Credits of Henry Martin ~ Late of the said County of Bucks, Clerk, Deceased do make or cause to be made a True and perfect Inventory of all and singular the Goods Chattels and Credits of the said Deceased which have or shall come to the hands Possession or knowledge of him the said Robert Martin, or unto the hands and Possession of any other Person or Persons for him and the same so made do Exhibit or Cause to be Exhibited into the Registers in the said County of Bucks at or before the Eighteenth Day of May next Ensuing and the same Goods Chattels and Credits of the said Deceased at the Time of his Death or which at any Time after shall Come to the hands or Possessions of him the said Robert Martin ~ or into the hands and Possession of any other Person or Persons for him do well and Truly Administer according to Law and further do make or Cause to be made a True and Just Account of his Administration at or before the Eighteenth Day of April In the Year 1765, and all the Rest and Residue of the said Goods and Chattels Rights and Credits which shall be found Remaining upon the said Administrators Account the same being First Examined and allowed of by the Orphans Court of the said County of Bucks shall deliver and pay unto such person or Persons Respectively as the said Orphans Court by their Decree or Sentence shall Limit and appoint and if it shall hereafter appear that any Last Will and Testament was made by the said Deceased and the Executor or Executors therein named do Exhibit the same into the Register Office Requesting to have it allowed and Approv'd Accordingly if the said Robert Martin above Bounden being thereunto Required to Render and deliver up the said

Letters of Administration (Approbation of such Testament being first had and made in the said Registers Office) Then the above Obligation to be Void or Else to be and Remain in full Force and Virtue.

Robert Martin
John Hegeman
John Slack

Sealed and Delivered
In the presence of Us
  Richd. Gibbs
  John Gregg

Bucks Co., PA Orphan's Court Records – September 9, 1765, p. 420
Petition of Robert Martin, Administrator of Henry Martin – File #385. Robert's petition was read in court, stating he had become the administrator of all Goods, Chattels, Rights & Claims of his brother Henry Martin, Deceased, and that the Justices "in your goodness please to appoint suitable persons to audit and settle ye accounts of the administration…" The Court so ordered and referred Robert's administration account records to be examined by John Woolston, Anthony Tate & David Twining, and make a report at the next Court.

Robert Martin had been appointed to act as Trustee over his brother Hugh's estate, and seems to have taken his job very seriously. The 1770 correspondence between Robert's two nephews Rev. Thomas and Col. James Martin, sons of Hugh, would indicate Rev. Thomas (then living in VA) was quite unhappy over business dealings with his Uncle Robert:

"Uncle Robert writes to me for the Money paid to V. Martin, in answer to him I have desired him to transmit Kate to me in Virginia, and I will pay Expenses and his Demand upon sight – if that cannot be done, to endorse the Bill of Sale to you, or some other Person. You or they to veil her at publick Sale, thence to satisfy himself, for he complains heavily & bitterly about it ~ most certainly she might be sold for thirty Pounds by any other Man than our Uncle ~ he has it in his Power to make himself

whole, and I have no Reason to lie out of the Use of that Money but no services were done ~ ..." [95]

My interpretation of the above paragraph is that Robert was demanding that money he had paid to a mysterious "V. Martin" on behalf of Rev. Thomas be repaid. Rev. Thomas felt the debt was unjustified, but he would readily reimburse his uncle if Robert would either sell Kate, who was the slave in Hugh's 1761 estate, to retain that portion of the sale that would have been Rev. Thomas' share of the proceeds, or to send Kate to Rev. Thomas so that he could sell her in VA. It would seem that Robert had either balked at having to personally be involved in the sale, or that the sale would not result in sufficient money to resolve Rev. Thomas' debt.

It would seem that Robert lived for awhile in his nephew William Mason's household. A provision in Robert's Will, forgave the debt owed by William Mason, because of Williams' favors to him "when I lived at his house." William Mason was born in c1741 and married in 1763, so possibly Robert lived with William & Mary [Van Dyke] Mason in the early 1770's.

Sister Esther [Martin] Mason took Robert into her home to live until his death in 1776. It is not known whether Robert ever married, but if so, he outlived a wife and had no children that survived him. Robert left legacies to his favorite nieces and nephews.

Robert's LWT makes for interesting reading in his choice of bequests. For instance, Robert gave £20 to nephew Alexander Martin, the eldest son of Hugh; however, Hugh's youngest son Robert was to receive £50. It's indeed interesting that no bequest was made to Hugh's son James, who had remained behind in NJ and was the executor of Hugh's estate – under Robert's trusteeship. This might indicate that James also had difficult business dealings with his Uncle Robert. It should be noted that Robert named his nieces and nephews as "cousins", which was then common terminology practice. Robert makes no mention of real estate holdings – only personality, but does have an inordinate amount of

---

[95] Francie Lane's transcription of the original letter from Rev. Thomas Martin to his brother James Martin, dated June 20, 1770, in the possession of Dr. Thomas Upshur.

cash on hand: £310 plus enough money to set up a trust account designated for the Presbyterian ministry in North Carolina. If Robert had ever owned land or a house, he perhaps sold it prior to moving into the Masons' homes.

ROBERT MARTIN
LAST WILL & TESTAMENT
JUNE 25, 1776
NORTHAMPTON COUNTY, PENNSYLVANIA
Recorded: JULY 16, 1776
WILL #693[96]

In the Name of God Amen ~

I, Robert Martin resident in Mount Bethel Township, Northampton County, in the province of Pensylvania, Yeoman, finding myself in a low state of health, but in a regular and composed state of mind and memory, blessed by the Lord for the present mercy, and knowing the certainty of death and the uncertainty of my time in this world, do think it proper to settle my temporal concerns, by constituting this to be my last will and testament, making void all others heretofore written ~

In the first place, I will and bequeath my soul to Almighty God, who gave it; and my body to the dust from whence it came to be decently buried at the discretion of my Executors, in hopes of a glorious resurrection and a crown of eternal life ~

And with respect to my temporal state which the Lord has been pleased to bestow upon me, I dispose of it after the following manner ~

I order all my funeral expenses, and just and lawful debts to be paid.

I will and bequeath to my Brother-in-law, Francis Mason the sum of ten pounds current money of Pensylvania, also my two sutes of apparel to him and his heirs Exrs, and assigns forever.

---

[96] Copy of original LWT from Josiah L. Mason, Ashland, OH (Aug. 9, 1999). Transcribed by Francie Lane.

Item – I give to my sister Esther Mason the sum forty pounds current money aforesaid, to her and her heirs exrs. and assigns forever, also my bed & furniture.

I also will and bequeath to my cousins, the children of Francis Mason the following legacies, current money of Pensylvania, to them and their heirs exrs and assigns forever ~

First, I give to my cousin Willm. Mason all that money which I lent to him, principle and interest for his favours to me when I lived at his house.

Item – I give to my cousin Henry Mason the sum of fifty pounds, also my saddle, bridle, new leather briches and my (?wearing) hat ~

Item – I give to my cousin Thomas Mason the sum of fifty pounds, also my riding horse and second beber hat ~

Item – I give to my Cousin Mary Mason the sum of thirty pounds

Item – I give to my Cousin Lidia Mason the sum of thirty pounds~

I also will and bequeath to my Cousin Alexander Martin, son of Hugh Martin, deceased, the sum of twenty pounds of the like money as above mentioned to him, his heirs exrs, and assigns forever ~

Item I give to my Cousin Robert Martin, also son of Hugh Martin deceased the sum of fifty pounds of the same currency aforesaid, to him and his heirs and assigns forever ~

Item – I give to the Revd. John Debow* the sum of thirty pounds money aforesaid to him, his heirs exrs assigns forever

Item – I will and bequeath all the remainder of my estate principle and interest for the education of the poor and pious youth who may design with the blessings of heaven, to enter into the ministerial character of the Presbyterian denomination, in North Carolina, and I do appoint the Revd. John Debow to be my Manager in this important affair, to dispose of said money for the pious purposes of propagating the people in those desolate parts, by giving at least five pounds to each poor young man designing for the ministry or ten pounds if the said Mr. Debow shall judge it realy necessary; And as this is a gratuity bequeathed to the Church, I order my Executors to collect the same and give it to the said Mr. Debow gratis without reducting as the law might insist to do for collecting and paying the same, and that the said Mr. Debow shall dispose of it gratis.

  I appoint my Executors to procure for my grave a marble toomstone, from John Cole, stonecutter in Philadelphia, in case I should be buried any where in these parts ~

  And for the management of these my temporal affairs, I appoint the following persons to be my Executors, Namely, Esther Mason, my beloved sister also my two legatees, Henry Mason & Thomas Mason, nothing doubting their fidelity in discharging the trust I do repose in them, And I do allow them two years to pay the above legacies in, but no longer and to reduct for their reward what the law allows them, that is ten pounds out of every hundred except the gratuity, and no more.

  And for the confirmation which I have hereunto set my hand & seal this twenty-fifth day of June in the year of our Lord one Thousand seven hundred & seventy six.

Signed sealed & Delivered }   Robert Martin {Seal}
in the presence of us }
John Debow
Thos. Ruckman
A. Mason
Mary Mason

Rec'd 16th July 1776 John Debow } Evid: Sworn
       Agnes Mason
       Henry Mason

---

  * Rev. John DeBow graduated Princeton with an A.B. degree in 1772; he was ordained and licensed as a Presbyterian Minister in 1775. Rev. DeBow was installed at the Upper Mount Bethel Church, Northampton Co., PA. In 1775 he served the Oxford, Warren Co., NJ Church; and later the same year settled the Hawfields Church, (now Alamance Co.), NC and served from 1775-1783. Rev. DeBow also served the Eno church in Orange Co., NC as well as the Little River Presbyterian Church in what's now Durham Co., NC. Rev. DeBow died at Hawfields, NC in September, 1783.[97]

---

[97] "The Colonial Clergy of VA, NC and SC" by Rev. Frederick Lewis Weis, Genealogical Publishing Co. – Baltimore - 1976

From the Presbyterian Church Synod Minutes, the New Brunswick Presbytery reported May 18, 1774, that John DeBow had been licensed, and the Synod directed that "Mr. John Debow, a probationer, under the care of New Brunswick Presbytery (was) appointed to go southward as soon as (he) conveniently can and supply under the direction of the Presbytery of Orange ... one whole year at least". By the minutes of the following year, May 17, 1775, it was reported that Debow had not fulfilled the mission to the southern colonies, but his reasons for omission were sustained.

May 22, 1776, minutes reflect that "Mr. Debow fulfilled his mission as appointed at our last", and he presented an application for supplies on behalf of North Carolina. The minutes of May 15, 1782, state John Debeau was absent. May 19, 1784, the Presbytery of Orange reported "Rev. Messrs. John Debow and James Campbell have been removed by death"[98].

NC State Land Grant #2337 to John DeBo(w) - – 13 Mar 1780 – 240 ac on the head Branch of the West fork of Eno River, adjoining Lindsey and Debo(w)'s own land.[99]

---

[98] "Records of the Presbyterian Church in the United States of America: Embracing the Minutes of the: Presbytery of Philadelphia from 1706 to 1716; Synod of Philadelphia from 1717 to 1758; Synod of New York from 1745 to 1758; Synod of Philadelphia and New York from 1758 to 1788" by the Presbyterian Board of Publication, James Russell, Publishing Agent, 1841, page 450, 451, 460, 463, 473, 497, 503

[99] Abstracts of State Grants – Vol. I – Margaret Hofmann - 1998

CHAPTER SEVEN

AGNES [MARTIN] DAWSON
(c1712 –1787)

Agnes Martin was born about 1712, in County Tyrone in what is now Northern Ireland, the daughter of Alexander and Martha [Coughran] Martin.

Near the age of 10, Agnes sailed with her parents to America, and settled in then-Bucks Co., PA. Agnes' father, Alexander became ill and died shortly thereafter.

Elder brother Hugh Martin moved across the river to Hunterdon Co., New Jersey, by the spring of 1730, and perhaps Agnes, about eighteen, accompanied her brothers to New Jersey. If so, her stay in New Jersey was short-lived, because she was married about the year 1734. It would seem more likely that Agnes remained in Pennsylvania, giving her more opportunity to meet and marry a prominent Bucks County Quaker.

Col. James Martin's narrative spoke of Agnes [Martin] Dawson: *"My Aunt Agnes married a Quaker by the name of Dawson, a respectable farmer who lived near Carroll's Ferry on the Delaware in Pennsylvania, and their descendants may be living there still. They had no sons."*

Agnes, in fact, married Thomas Dawson, and although I've not found a record of their marriage, it would seem that Agnes was "convinced", meaning she joined the Society of Friends. The Quaker marriage traditions were very strict, so had Thomas Dawson married outside the faith, he would have been excluded. As clearly shown in his father, John Dawson's Will, John's grandchildren were to be disinherited if they married "out of unity", so Agnes certainly converted for her marriage to Thomas.

Thomas & Agnes resided in Solebury Township, Bucks County, PA. I've not been able to locate a "Carroll's Ferry" in early

Pennsylvania maps. There was a "Coryell's Ferry" in Solebury, and I believe Col. James either confused the two similar sounding names, or perhaps the hand-written history by Col. James showed, "Coryell's", but was mistakenly transcribed as "Carroll's". John Coryell had operated his ferry from the New Jersey side of the Delaware River at Lambertville for many years, but in 1764, Coryell purchased the land and ferry rights on the western shore in Bucks Co., PA

The following is a brief description of the Dawson heritage and history of their community:

Thomas Dawson, born 13 September 1710, was the son of John & Catherine [Fox] Dawson of Solebury, Bucks Co., PA. John Dawson was born about 1669, of Chebsey, Staffordshire, England; and married Catharine Fox, b. c1675, of Eccleshall, Staffordshire, on 4 June, 1696, Staffordshire, England. John arrived in America in 1710, and resided on 500 acres in Solebury. John Dawson wrote his LWT[100] on May 31, 1753, and was proved May 26, 1759. Heirs were: Son Thomas Dawson, Executor; Daughter Anne Brown of Plumstead, Bucks Co., PA; Granddaughters: Elizabeth Brown and Martha Harvey of Makefield; Esther Dawson, Rachel Dawson and Sarah Dawson, daughters of Thomas Dawson. Witnesses: Samuel Eastburn, Rees Davis, and Henry Paxson, Jr.

John & Catherine [Fox] Dawson's other children were all born in Chebsey, Staffordshire, England, as follows:

John Dawson, b. 15 January 1696.

Margaret Dawson, b. 16 Dec 1698.

Elizabeth Dawson, b. 27 May 1701; married 29 March 1721, Buckingham, Bucks, PA to Thomas Brown, Jr., b. 1 Sep 1696, Barking, Essex, England, the son of Thomas & Mary [Ayer] Brown, Sr.; Elizabeth died 10 May 1733

Jonathan Dawson, b. 28 March 1703.

Ann Dawson, b. 3 April 1705; married 29 March 1729, Buckingham, Bucks, PA to Joseph Brown, b. 10 Dec 1707, the son of Thomas & Mary [Ayer] Brown Sr.; d. 26 Feb 1748, Plumstead, Bucks Co., PA. Ann died 7 January 1791, Plumstead, Bucks, PA

---

[100] From Jeanie Smith Zadach – FTM CD209 – PA Wills – 1682-1834 – p. 364

Thomas Brown, Sr. was born 27 May 1666, Barking, Essex, England; married on 17 July 1694, Plaistown, Essex, England, to Mary Ayer, born 17 May 1664, Lincolnshire, England, the daughter of Alexander Ayer, b. c1639, Burrow, Lincolnshire, England. Thomas Brown, Sr. died 27 December 1747, Plumstead, Bucks, PA; Mary [Ayer] Brown died 15 April 1748, Plumstead, Bucks, PA. Thomas Brown, Sr. was the son of George Brown, b. c1643; d. 1726.

From the book: "Place Names in Bucks County": "SOLEBURY *Village in central northwestern. Solebury Township at the intersection of Old York Road (Route 657) and the road from Peters Corner to Phillips Mill on Delaware River Road (Route 326). The greater part of the village stands upon land known in early times as the Dawson Tract. On 9th mo. 6th, 1681, William Penn gave a deed to Nathaniel Harding, basketmaker, of London, for 500 acres of land, which was taken up in Solebury Township and was bounded east by the Pike and Ely tracts, south by the Logan tract, west by the Scarborough tract and north by what later became the Upper or Old York Road. In 1719 Francis Harding, merchant, and Ralph Jackson, whitesmith, both of Philadelphia, son, son-in-law and heirs of Nathaniel Harding, sold the 500 acres to John Dawson, "yeoman, of Saulsbury," who appears to have been the first actual settler on the tract. Eventually the Dawson land was cut up into smaller tracts, the greater part going to the Blackfan family and the remainder to the Fell, Eastburn and other families".* "SOLEBURY TOWNSHIP *In central northeastern Bucks County, bounded northwest by Plumstead Township, northeast by Delaware River, southeast by Upper Makefield Township, southwest by Buckingham Township".* Buckingham and Solebury had *been one township prior to 1700; the division caused a need for a resurvey, and in 1703, the survey showed 23 landowners who held 28 tracts, and extended across the township in four irregular tiers, from the Manor of Highlands on the southeast to Paunaucussing Creek on the northwest. The first tier along the river, commencing at the manor line, is marked: Robert Heath 1,000 acres (two tracts of 500 acres), Joseph Pike 624 acres, Randal Speakman 500 acres, Richard Burgess 300 acres, Henry Paxson 100 acres. Second tier, commencing at the upper line of Robert Heath's land: Gilbert Dymock 220 acres, Randal Speakman 500 acres, William Croasdale now: Henry Paxson 250 acres, Jeremiah Lunghome 250 acres, Francis White now George Brown 250 acres; a large vacant uncharted triangular tract, extends along the river from the Brown and Lungborne tracts to the Paunaucussing. Third tier, commencing at the manor line: Great Spring tract of James Logan 500 acres (on the southeast this tract abutted the Heath tract), James Logan since William Scarborough (acreage not noted, but apparently same size as Great Spring tract which it adjoined), vacant tract 320 acres, Stephen Beakes 624 acres, Samuel Beakes 350 acres, Ezra Croasdale 200 acres, George Brown 200 acres, Joseph Pike 376 acres. Fourth tier (adjoining Buckingham Township line), commencing at the manor line: Thomas Bye now John Bye 438 acres, John Scarborough 504 acres, Isaac Pellar 100 acres, Proprietary's Land 500 acres, Roger Hartley 100 acres and allowance, Edward Hartley acreage not stated, Jedidiah Allen 230 acres, Thomas Canby 450 acres, Randal Blackshaw 500 acres. "Among other early families were the Dawsons, Blackfans, Elys and Eastburns".*

"The derivation of the name Solebury has been the cause of much interesting controversy over a long period of years". "Solebury may be a modification of Salisbury, the name of the country seat of Wiltshire, (England), from which large numbers of Friends came to Pennsylvania. A very common way of spelling the name in the early part of the eighteenth century was Saulsbury". "It seems probable that the name comes from 'SOLE'--a pond or wet place--plus 'bury,' a manor. The many springs, and the Great Spring in particular, would support this. We find this use of 'SOLE' in the English surname Nethersole. It is also possible that the SOLE here is one of the recognized forms of .SULL--a Plow (English 'Plough'). If this etymology were accepted it would make Solebury the equivalent of Plough Manor, or Ploughland —not a bad name for a rich agricultural neighborhood."

"A valuable collection of old documents relating to the Dawson tract and the Dawson and Blackfan families in Solebury shows the early changes undergone by the township name. In the oldest document in which the name occurs, a bond (Thomas Dawson to Ralph Jackson, Philadelphia), dated December 5, 1714, the name is Soulsbury. In two releases, 1719, it becomes Saulsbury. The present form, Solebury, first appears in 1720 in a lease 'between William Blakey, Jr., of Pennsbury, and John Dawson, of Solebury. In this lease it is spelled both Solebury and Soleburry. In all later documents in this collection, the latest dated early in the nineteenth century, the name is always Solebury, except in a release of 1731 and in the marriage certificate of William Blackfan and Esther Dawson, 1758, where it is Soleberry, and in the marriage certificate of Isaac Chapman and Martha Blackfan, 1809, which has it Solesbury"[101].

Solebury was a small township. The tax list for 1761 shows 138 taxables. In 1784, there were 980 whites, no blacks, 166 dwellings and 150 outhouses.[102]

From the Bucks County, PA Tax Records:

Solebury – 1751[103]:
Thomas Dawson	15£, 2sh, 6d
John Dawson	35£, 5sh, 10d
William Blackfan	35£,5sh, 10d

Solebury – 1761:
Thos. Dawson	40£, 10sh, 0d

Solebury Township – 1778:
Thomas Dawson	17£
John Coryell	10£, 10sh
Chrispin Blackfan	18£
Wm. Blackfan	7£, 10sh

Solesbury Township – 1781:
Thomas Dawson: 453 acres - 3 Horses - 4 Cattle - 0 Servants

Thomas Dawson wrote his Will on August 1, 1776, less than a month after the Declaration of Independence was signed in nearby Philadelphia. Possible worry regarding the oncoming

---

[101] "Place Names in Bucks County" – George MacReynolds – Bucks County Historical Society. 1942.

[102] "The History of Bucks County, Pennsylvania from the Discovery of the Delaware to the present time " W. W. H. DAVIS, A. M., Democrat Book and Job Office Print. Doylestown, PA 1876

[103] Bucks County Tax Records – 1693-1778, compiled by Terry McNealy & Frances Waite. Bucks Co. Genealogical Society, PO Box 1092, Doylestown, PA 18901

revolution, prompted him to draw his will. It would seem that Dawson lived another six years, as the LWT was probated on December 7, 1782.[104]

It should be noted that Quakers make no oaths; therefore, their Last Will & Testaments do not contain the customary, "In the Name of God, Amen" but rather use "Be it Remembered".

THOMAS DAWSON[105]
LAST WILL & TESTAMENT
BUCKS CO., PENNSYLVANIA
1 August 1776
#1744

Be it remembered that I, Thomas Dawson of Solebury Township in the County of Bucks & Province of Pennsylvania, Yeoman, being advanced in age, but of sound & disposing mind & Memory, Knowing the Uncertainty of Time & that it is appointed for all men once to die; have thought proper to make & publish this my last Will & Testament concerning such Estate as it hath pleased the Lord to bless me with in this Life, in manner & form following, viz

First I will that all my just Debts & funeral Expenses be fully paid & discharged and all the rest of my Estate I give devise and dispose of as follows:

I Give & bequeath to my Wife Agness Dawson my olde place or plantation which I now live on with all the use & Profits of the same during her natural Life. I also give & bequeath to my said Wife so many of my Household Goods as she shall see fit to Choose and one Horse & one Cow to be her Choice.

Item – I give & bequeath to my Sister Ann Brown, the Sum of five pounds a year, to be paid to her Yearly & every Year during her natural Life.

---

[104] ftp://ftp.rootsweb.com/pub/usgenweb/pa/bucks/wills/willabstbk4.txt
[105] Transcribed by Francie Lane – www.familysearch.org – Bucks Co., PA Probate Records – Will Book 4, p. 242 <414/578>

Item – *I give & bequeath to my Daughter Esther Blackfan the Sum of One hundred pounds and to the Daughters of my said Daughter Esther; namely Elizabeth Blackfan, Rachel Blackfan, Hannah Blackfan, Sarah Blackfan, and Agness Blackfan, to each one Hundred Pounds to be paid to them severally as they arrive to the age of twenty one years, and if either or any of them should die before they arrive at that age, I will that the Legacy or Legacies of such so dieing be equally Divided among the Survivors - - -*

Item – *I give & bequeath to my Grandson Jonathan Smith, the Son of my Daughter Sarah, deceased, when he shall arrive at the age of twenty one years, the Sum of one Hundred pounds, & if he should die before he arrive at that age, I will the said Hundred pounds be equally divided between my two Grandsons John Blackfan & Thomas Blackfan, Sons of my Daughter Esther aforesaid - - -*

Item – *And all the Residue & Remainder of my Estate of what Nature or kinde soever, both real & personal, together with the Land above bequeathed to my Wife at her Decease, and all my other Lands with all the Hereditaments & Appurtenances thereunto Belonging, I give devise & bequeath to my two Grandsons John Blackfan & Thomas Blackfan above named if they shall arrive to the Age of twenty one Years to be equally Divided between them, according to the equal value thereof, to hold to them their Heirs & Assigns forever in severally as Tenants in Common, Subject to the payment of so many of the herein before mentioned Legacies, as the personal Estate may not hold out to pay, to be paid Equally between them at the rate of not less than Fifty Pounds a Year apiece (if so much shall be wanting) from the time Thomas arrives to twenty one Years of Age till the whole be paid. And if either of my said Grandsons should die before he arrives at the said age of twenty one years, I Will that his share go to my Grandson William Blackfan, Junior, to be held by him his Heirs & Assigns forever upon the same conditions--*

And lastly I do hereby nominate constitute & appoint my Wife Agness Dawson & my Daughter Esther Blackfan my Executrixes and my Grandson John Blackfan my Executor of this my last Will & Testament & do hereby revoke & disannul all other & former Wills & Testaments by me at any time heretofore made or uttered whether by word or Writing, ratifying & confirming this & this only to be my last Will & Testament and none other or otherwise. In Witness whereof I have hereunto set my

Hand & Seal this first day of the Eighth month (called August) in the Year of our Lord One thousand seven hundred & seventy six ---

Signed Sealed published pronounced &
Declared by the said Thomas Dawson to be
His last Will & Testament in the Presence
Of us who have hereunto subscribed our   *Thomas Dawson*
Names as Witnesses in the Presence of the   *{Seal}*
Said Testator & at his Request ---
Thomas Ross
Thomas Whitson
Daniel Martin

On December 7, 1782, Thomas Ross, Thomas Whitson and Daniel Martin appeared to attest Thomas Dawson's Will. Letters Testamentary were granted to Esther Blackfan and John Blackfan as Co-Executors.

It should be noted that Daniel Martin was one of the witnesses to Thomas Dawson's Will, written on August 1, 1776. Daniel Martin was Agnes' nephew, the son of Thomas Martin of Bucks Co., PA.

Agnes [Martin] Dawson died in c1787 about the age of seventy five.

AGNESS DAWSON[106]
Last Will & Testament
Bucks County, Pennsylvania
February 21, 1785
Proved March 26, 1787
#2089

BE IT REMEMBERED ~~

    That I Agness Dawson of Solesbury Township in the County of

---

[106] Transcribed by Francie Lane – www.familysearch.org – Bucks Co., PA Probate Records – Will Book 5, p. 26 <32/319>

Bucks & Province of Pensylvania, Yeoman: Being weak in Body but of perfect & disposing Mind & memory and being desirous to settle my Worldly Affairs Do make my will in manner following Viz

  I will that all my just debts and Funeral Charges be fully paid by my Executors herein after Named: I do give and bequeath to Rachel Blackfan my Daughter Esther's Daughter my mare & my cow also one Walnut Table also one Walnut Chest & one Walnut Candle Stand also three Candle Sticks & also three of my best Iron pots and two Brass Cettles ones size is about two Galions and a half the other about three pints also one tea cettle and a half dozen best Chears also two Hetchels & one Coffee Mill Also one bake Iron & friing Pan also one Pot Racken & one pair of Tongs also one Tosting Iron and half a dozen plates marked Sy also one blew Table & one Watering pot and half a dozen puter plates marked Sy and all my Sider Ware and my rideing apron also all my tea Canisters and all of my hetcheld and un Hetcheld Flax. I do give and bequeath to John Blackfan my Daughter Esthers son my Clock also one Walnut chest and also one Bed that he lodgeth in all the Bed Cloas that belongeth to it also one Dough trof & one pair of Hand Irons Also one pair of tongs and one pair of Stilyerds also one pot Racken & one gun also half a douzen Chears & one Arm Chear. I do give & bequeath to Hannah Blackfan my Daughter Esther's Daughter one Walnut Tea Table also one puter Tea Pot & all my Chaney Also half a douzen Silver Tea Spoons also one Small Bras Cettle & one pair of Flax & Ton Sheats. I do give & Bequeath to Sarah Blackfan my Daughter Esther's Daughter my case of Drawers & Looking Glass also one Brass Cettle that holdeth about three Galions & one pair of Flax & Ton Sheats also Two puter Dishes marked Sy. I do give and bequeath to Agness Blackfan my Daughter Esther's Daughter my Bed and furniture & Bedsteads also one large bras Cettle and one Puter quart also three puter Basens & two puter Poringers also one pair of Flax & Ton Sheats & one little wheel. I do give to Elizabeth Fell my Daughter Esther's Daughter my Warming pan. I do give to Jonathan Smith Son of Edmund Smith & my Daughter Sarah Smith, dec'd the sum of ten pounds to be paid to him at the age of twenty one also a Worsted Coat & Jacket also one hat & one fine shirt also two corce shirts. I do give to my Sister Esther Mason one blew & Yallow Worsted double gound also one broad Cloath Cloak & one old Quilt also one gold Riding Apron also My black Silk hood & one Silk hankerchief also one camebrick hankerchief and one Short brown worsted Double gound also one Linnen hankerchief & one check apron. I do give all my other waring aparel to my Daughter Esther Blackfan and I do Nominate & Appoint my Grandson John Blackfan & my Granddaughter Rachel Blackfan to be my Executors.

Agness Dawson {Seal}

Signed Sealed Published & Declared
By the Above said Agness Dawson the Testator
For & her Last Will andTestament In the Presance
of Us who have Hearunto Signed Our Names
In her Presance & at her Request This 21 Day of the Second month
One thousand Seven Hundred & Eighty Five
    Samuel Kitchin
    David Stackhouse

On March 26, 1787, Samuel Kitchin and David Stackhouse appeared to attest Agnes' Last Will & Testament. Letters Testamentary were granted to John Blackfan, with notation that Rachel Blackfan had renounced as Executrix.

I found it odd that a good Quaker, such as Agnes would own and then bequeath a gun to her Quaker Grandson, John Blackfan. It would seem from Agnes' Will that Grandson John was living in her home.

Agnes' bequests were very interesting in showing her prized belongings, but because of her spelling, I will help translate a few items:

Cettles	Kettles
Chears	Chairs
Blew	Blue
Puter	Pewter
Sider ware	Cidar ware
Cloas	Clothes
Chaney	China
Gound	Gown

Dough trof	Trough
Stilyers	Stillyard (a weighing scale)
Basens	Basins
Poringers	Porrigers
Corce shirt	Coarse
Waring	Wearing apparel

Webster's defines "ton" as high-fashion, stylish, so "Flax & Ton Sheats", were probably very nice Linen Sheets. "Hetcheld" and "Unhetcheld" flax refers to the final processing of flax and the use of a tool called a "hetchel" (also known as a hackle or hatchel), which is a board with long sharp nails driven through. The flax fibers are combed through the hetchel to remove any straw and to untangle the fibers. When the hackling is complete, the flax fibers can be spun into yarn.

Thomas & Agnes [Martin] Dawson had three daughters:

Esther [Dawson] Blackfan was born about 1736, and named for Agnes' sister, Esther [Martin] Mason. Esther married William Blackfan, Jr., born May 28, 1732, the son of prominent Quaker William & Eleanor [Wood] Blackfan. Esther's marriage to William Blackfan, Jr. is recorded on page 85 of the Buckingham Monthly Meeting Book[107], [Bucks Co., PA] and dated April 19, 1758:

"Whereas William Blackfan, Junr. of Soleberry in the County of Bucks and Province of Pennsylvania & Esther Dawson of the Same Place and Province, Having declared their Intentions of Marriage with each other before Several Monthly Meetings of the People Called Quakers at Buckingham in the County & Province aforesd. According to the good Order Used Amongst them, and having Consent of Parents & Relations Concerned, theire Said Proposals of Marriage was Alowed of by the Said Meeting ..

> *Wiliam Blackfan Junor*
> *Esther Blackfan*
> *William Blackfan*
> *Elinor Blackfan*
> *Hugh Ely*

---

[107] From Jeanie Smith Zadach – PA Magazine of History & Biography, Vol. 27, No. 1, January, 1903, p. 111-112.

Phebe Ely

Jane Scarbrough	Thomas Ross	<u>Thomas Dawson</u>
Sarah Pickering Juneor	Benjamin Fell	Elizabeth Ely
Sarah Pickering	John Scarbrough	Rebekah Bye
Deborah Mitchel	William Preston	Hannah Blackfan
Jeane Paxson	Jno. Ross	Crispin Blackfan
Hannah Pickering	Joseph Paxson	Joseph Bye
John Scholfield	Ely Welden	<u>Rachel Dawson</u>
Saml. Eastburn	Sarah Hill	<u>Sarah Dawson</u>
Jos. Pickering	Joshua Ely	Hugh Ely Junr.
Henry Paxson	Wm. Hill	John Ely
Richard Roberts		

It's interesting to note that Esther's mother, Agnes Dawson, unlike the father of the bride, does not appear as being present and witnessing her daughter's marriage.

For background information, I will briefly outline the Blackfan family lineage as I understand it to be:

I. John Blackfan "of Steyning Co., Sussex, England"
  II. Edward Blackfan (1652-1690) "of England"
      m. Rebecca Crispin – 24 Oct 1688, d/o
          Capt. William & Rebecca Penn [Bradshaw] Crispin*
          * Cousin to William Penn
   III. William Blackfan, Sr., b. c1689, Essex, England
      m. Eleanor Wood –20 February 1720/1, Pennsbury, PA
    IV. William Blackfan, Jr., b. 28 May 1732
       m. Esther Dawson, daughter of Thomas & Agnes [Martin] Dawson
    IV. Hannah Blackfan
       m. Thomas Paxson (1726-1767), s/o
          Henry & Ann [Plumley] Paxson & widower of
            Sarah Harvey (1730-1762)

"The Blackfans are descendants of John Blackfan, of Stenning, county of Sussex, England, whose son Edward married Rebecca Crispin, of Kinsale, Ireland, second cousin of William Penn, in 1688. At this wedding were William Penn, his wife, son and daughter, whose names are on the marriage certificate, in possession of the Blackfan family of Solebury. Edward Blackfan concluded to come to America, but died before he could embark, about 1690. The widow, with her young son, arrived about 1700, and was appointed to take charge of the manor house at Pennsbury, at a salary of ten pounds a year, paid by the council. They lived there many years. In 1721 the son married Eleanor Wood, of Philadelphia, and in 1725 the mother was married to Nehemiah Allen of that city. About this time Edward Blackfan removed to a 500 acre tract in Solebury, surveyed to him in 1718, and confirmed in 1733. He had six children, the two eldest being born at Pennsbury. At his death, in 1771, at the age of eighty, his real estate was divided between his sons, Crispin and William, the former marrying Martha Davis, had nine children, and the latter, Esther Dawson, had the same number."[108]

The children of William & Esther [Dawson] Blackfan, Jr. were recorded on the back of the Marriage Certificate of William Blackfan, Jr. and Esther [Dawson] in the Buckingham Monthly Meeting[109]. All of the following births were in Bucks County, PA:

Elizabeth Blackfan Daughter of William Blackfan Juneor & Esther His Wife was Born the 23d Day of ye Second Month about Eight o'Clock Morn in Ye year of our Lord 1759.
* married Watson Fell – April 28, 1784, Buckingham MM
died: June 30, 1844, Bucks Co., PA

Rachel Blackfan Daughter of William Blackfan & Esther His Wife was Born the 29th Day of ye 8th Month about 5 o'Clock in the afternoon, in the year of our Lord 1760.
* married Edward Chapman – May 14, 1794, Buckingham MM

---

[108] "The History of Bucks County, Pennsylvania from the of the Delaware to the present time " W. W. H. DAVIS, A. M., Democrat Book and Job Office Print. Doylestown, PA 1876
[109] Genealogies of Pennsylvania Families from the PA Magazine of History and Biography, Genealogical Publishing Co., Baltimore - 1981

died: February 28, 1804, Wrightstown Twp, Bucks Co., PA

John Blackfan Son of William Blackfan & Esther His Wife was Born the 20th Day of 2d Month between 8 & 9 o'Clock in the afternoon, in ye year of our Lord 1762.
* married Martha Quinby – June 14, 1786, Buckingham MM

Hannah Blackfan Daughter of William Blackfan & Esther His Wife was Born ye 17th Day of 7th Month near 2 o'Clock in ye Morning, in ye year of our Lord 1764.
*married Samuel Smith – April 14, 1795 – Buckingham MM

Sarah Blackfan Daughter of William Blackfan & Esther His Wife was Born ye 26th Day of the 10th Month in the afternoon in the year of our Lord 1766.
*married Samuel Godrey – October 5, 1796 – Buckingham MM

Agnes Blackfan Daughter of William Blackfan & Esther His Wife was Born ye 10th Day of 8th Month near 2 o'Clock in ye Morning, in ye year of our Lord 1769.
*married John Scholfield – June 14, 1797, Buckingham MM
died: April 4, 1804, Bucks Co., PA

Thomas Blackfan born the 8th day of 2nd Mo 1771 in the afternoon.

William Blackfan was born the 15th day of the first month 1773. Deceased the 4th day of the 4th Month 1773.

William Blackfan was born the 23d of the 7th month 1774. Deceased the 9th d. of 8th month 1777.

Aaron Blackfan was born the 8th day of the 11th month 1776 Deceased the 29th day of 3d Month 1777.

Jesse Blackfan was born the 17th day of 2nd mo. 1779.

Agnes [Martin] & Thomas Dawson's middle child was: **Rachel Dawson**, who remained a spinster until her death in 1773. Rachel made her Will as a resident of Solsbury, Bucks Co., PA, on June 19, 1773, which was proved a month later on July 26, 1773[110]. Rachel's first bequest was made to her nephew Jonathan Smith, son of Edmund & her deceased sister Sarah [Dawson] Smith, giving him £60 at the age of 21. He was also bequeathed a set of bed curtains and a "half silk gown" which was in the care of Rachel, but had belonged to Jonathan's mother. Rachel provided that should Jonathan Smith die before reaching the age of 21, that his £60 inheritance would be divided equally between her nieces, the daughters of William & Esther [Dawson] Blackfan; namely, Rachel, Elizabeth, Hannah & Agnes Blackfan, when they reached the age of 18. If Jonathan Smith died before age 21, the bed curtains and silk gown was to be given to niece Rachel Blackfan. Rachel Dawson bequeathed to her "loving mother", Agness [Martin] Dawson her horse and saddle and all other personal effects otherwise not mentioned. Rachel named as her Executor and Executrix her "loving" father Thomas and mother Agnes Dawson. Rachel's Will was witnessed by Henry Paxson, Aaron Paxson and William Blackfan. Only Henry Paxson and William Blackfan appeared in court to attest Rachel's Will on July 26, 1773. Letters Testamentary were granted solely to father Thomas Dawson.

Thomas & Agnes [Martin] Dawson's youngest daughter was: **Sarah [Dawson] Smith**. Sarah married Edmund Smith of Bucks Co., and their marriage date is recorded in the Buckingham Monthly Meeting as the 22nd day of the 4th Month, 1767. Sarah [Dawson] Smith died prior to June, 1773, because she was shown as "deceased" in her sister Rachel's Will. Sarah and Edmund had one son, Jonathan Smith, born between 1767 and 1773.

---

[110] Transcribed & abstracted by Francie Lane – December 30, 2013. Familysearch.org – Bucks Co. Will Book 3, p. 332 <193/578>

CHAPTER EIGHT

ESTHER [MARTIN] MASON
(c1718 – c1791)

Esther Martin was born about 1718, in County Tyrone in what is now Northern Ireland, the daughter of Alexander and Martha [Coughran] Martin.

Col. James' narrative stated of Esther [Martin] Mason, *"My Aunt Esther married Francis Mason, a farmer who lived in the forks of the Delaware. They reared three or four strong athletic sons as any to be found anywhere."*

From Francis Mason's Will and that of Uncle Robert Martin, there were only 3 sons named: William, Henry and Thomas Mason, so either Col. James was mistaken or one son died young.

The ancestry of Francis Mason has not been determined. The sons of Francis & Esther were active in the Presbyterian churches, which gives the impression that Francis had been one of the Scots-Irish immigrants to America.

It may be worth noting that a John Mason was recorded as an adjoining neighbor to Ralph Crispin in 1684. Esther's sister, Agnes [Martin] Dawson's son-in-law was a Blackfan / Crispin descendant. According to an article in "Genealogies of PA Families" from the PA Magazine of History & Biography" – beginning on p. 222…..

Ralph Crispin, a resident of Ireland, living near Kinsale, Co., Cork, received a 1688 land grant from William Penn, himself, calling him his "Loveing Coszen". "The grant was a rectangle of 500 ac in what then was known as the upper part of Dublin twp, Philadelphia Co. on the line of the present Abington Twp, Montgomery Co. It was bounded on the N.E. by Dr. Nicholas More's Manor of Moreland, on the S.E., by JOHN

MASON's land, on the S.W. by the Susquehanna Road and on the N.W. by Wm. Stanley's land..." [111]

The 1738 Voter List for Hunterdon County, NJ[112] shows no "Mason" families. However, Francis Mason may not have qualified as a Freeman.

It is likely that Esther met and married Francis Mason while both were young residents of Hunterdon Co., NJ. The early marriage bonds held by the NJ Archives show no entry for Francis Mason. They may have met earlier in Bucks Co., PA, as a Mason family appears to have been among the early settlers:

"*Alexander Hunter And Presbyterian Followers...1730...Permanent Settlement...Neighborhood of Martin's Creek.*" "*Early settlers were Miller, Moore, Lockard, Lyle, Moody, MARTIN, Nelson, Buchman, Hutchinson, Ross, McFarren McCracken, Silleman, Crawford, Galbraith, Boyd .... and the familes of Copland, Gaston, Wilson, Boyd, Hutton, Morris, MASON, ...*"[113]."

By 1741, Francis Mason was shown as a resident of Amwell Township, although not a near neighbor to either of his brothers-in-law, Hugh or Thomas Martin.

From the "County of Hunterdon Freeholders Book 1741"[114]:

The King agst. Wm. Tenent

Trenton April 14: 48 they agreed before me which I have numberd as they were named. ~ Ro: H: Morris.

Jury struck April 15: 1742:

Amwell Township: (selected entries only)
Peter Midage <sic Middaugh>
Francis Mason

==

Hugh Martin
Thomas Martin

---

[111] From Josiah L. Mason, a descendant of Ester [Martin] Mason
[112] Hunterdon Co., NJ, Historical Society Newsletter – Winter, 1993 – p. 658-660
[113] "History of Northampton County" - William J. Heller - 1920
[114] The Genealogical Magazine of NJ – May 1962 – Volume 37, No. 2, p 49-56

Mr. Josiah Mason, a descendant of Esther, contacted the Hunterdon Co. [NJ] Historical Society in 1979, in search of early NJ records of Francis Mason. The Society's response stated in part:

"[Francis Mason] is listed as a witness to the will of Daniel Howell, Amwell Township, Hunterdon County, written 9 September 1733."

"He [Francis Mason] is listed as one of the persons taking an inventory of the goods of the late James Cumin, Bethlehem Township, Hunterdon County, on 26 May 1753."

We know that Francis Mason died in 1790, and wrote his Will in 1781. Assuming he was a few years older than Esther, we could safely say he was born by 1715. If he was born c1715, he would have written his Will at age 66, and died at age 75, which was considered a fairly long life. My point is that for Francis Mason to act as a witness to the Will of Daniel Howell in 1733, he would have been about 18 years old. Daniel Howell was quite a prominent resident of Hunterdon Co., and one would wonder why he would choose an unrelated 18 year old as his witness. Perhaps Howell's witness was Francis Mason, Sr.

It had been previously presumed that mother Martha [Coughran] Martin removed to Northampton Co., PA to live with Esther & Francis Mason, and that is where Martha died on May 11, 1753. It's difficult to interpret Col. James' exact meaning, when he wrote: *"My grandmother, Martha, went to live and died with my Aunt Mason, aged upwards of seventy years".*

It is a fact that Francis & Esther Mason lived in Northampton Co., PA in the latter half of the 18th Century, but we do not know when their move took place. We know that Martha Martin was buried in Lebanon, Hunterdon Co., NJ. I feel in view of the fact that Francis Mason participated in taking an inventory in Hunterdon Co. on May 26, 1753, that he was living there when his mother-in-law died at his home 15 days earlier.

From the probate records of Esther's brother Thomas Martin, we now can see that Thomas' estate received £60 from Francis Mason on April 11, 1763, in payment of two years' rent for "the Mill and place in The Jerseys". Therefore, it would seem that Francis Mason rented from his brother-in-law a home and mill in Hunterdon Co., NJ, for at least the years of 1761 and 1762. [See Chapter 5]

Northampton County, PA, was established in 1752, and at that time there were approximately 6,000 inhabitants. The Scotch-Irish were concentrated in the Mount Bethel Township, but only numbered about 600 people.[115]

The 1772 Tax List for Mt. Bethel Township – Northampton Co., PA[116], lists both Francis Mason and his son William as paying taxes:

Francis Mason, fa'r <farmer>	£ 4.0.0
William Mason, fa'r	3.4.0
Peter Middaugh, fa'r	9.0.0

Esther & Francis Mason took her brother Robert Martin into their home to live until his death in 1776. Robert had been living in the Northampton Township of Bucks County during 1764 while administering Rev. Henry Martin's probate. From Robert's LWT, he indicated that he lived for a time in his nephew William Mason's household, which was presumably in Northampton County. Robert Martin wrote his will on June 25, 1776, as a resident of Mount Bethel, Northampton Co., PA and died within 3 weeks. Robert left legacies to his favorite nieces and nephews among the children of Esther & Francis Mason; i.e.,[117]

Brother-in-law Francis Mason - £10 + 2 suits of apparel
Sister Esther Mason - £40 + bed and furniture
"Cousin" William Mason – Undisclosed amount of loan,
including principle & interest for past favors "when I

---

[115] "Some of the First Settlers of "The Forks of the Delaware" and their Descendants" being a translation from the German Record Books of the First Reformed Church of Easton, Penna. 1760 to 1852.
[116] "Proprietary, Supply & State Tax Lists of Northampton & Northumberland for Years of 1772 to 1787", W. S. Ray, State Printer of PA, 1897
[117] From Josiah L. Mason; transcribed by Francie Lane: Robert Martin - LWT - #693 – Northampton Co., PA – WD June 25, 1776 –WP July 16, 1776

lived at his house".

"Cousin" Henry Mason - £50 + saddle, bridle, new leather britches and hat.

"Cousin" Thomas Mason - £50 + Robert's riding horse and a hat.

"Cousin" Mary Mason - £30

"Cousin" Lidia Mason - £30

Robert Martin named as his Executors: *"my beloved sister" Esther Mason and "legatees" Henry & Thomas Mason, and declared his confidence in their integrity as follows "nothing doubting their fidelity in discharging the trust I do repose in them, And I do allow them two years to pay the above legacies in, but no longer and to reduct for their reward what the law allows them, that is ten pounds out of every hundred except the gratuity, and no more".*

Witnesses to Robert's LWT were "A. Mason; Mary Mason". Agnes Mason & Henry Mason presented the Will for probate on July 16, 1776. A. Mason presumably is Agnes Mason. Robert named his niece as "Cousin Mary Mason", which indicates that she did not marry Peter Middaugh until after 1776. Francis Mason's will of 1781 does not name a son Thomas, or daughter Lydia, so perhaps those two children died between 1776 and 1781.

The 1780 Tax List for Northampton Co., PA's Mt. Bethel Township lists taxpayers, their occupations and assessed property values:

Francis Mason – Farmer: $1,012

Peter Middagh, Sr. – Farmer: $1,880

Esther was named as an heir in her sister Agnes [Martin] Dawson's[118] LWT, written February 21, 1785, and was bequeathed the following personal items: Blue & Yellow worsted double gown; one broadcloth cloak; one gold quilt; one gold riding apron; Agnes' black silk hood; one silk, one cambric and one linen handkerchiefs; one short brown worsted double gown; and one checked apron.

---

[118] Transcribed by Francie Lane – www.familysearch.org – Bucks Co., PA Probate Records – Will Book 5, p. 26 <32/319>

The Northampton Co. Tax Lists of 1785, 1786 and 1788 for Mt. Bethel Township do not list Francis Mason, but that's probably explainable due to his being elderly and past the taxable age. Son William Mason and son-in-law Peter Middaugh, Jr. are shown.

Francis Mason probably died in April, 1790.

FRANCIS MASON
Will Date: 8 July 1781
Will Proved: 23 April 1790
Northampton Co., PA
Will Book 2, page 85

In the Name of God, Amen. I, Francis Mason of Mountbethel in the County of Northampton and State of Pennsylvania, calling to mind the uncertainty of this Transatory Life and being of Sound Mind and Memory and perfect understanding do hereby publish this to be my Last Will and Testament, and as Touching Such worldly Estate as it hath Pleased Almighty God to favour me with, I do hereby Will, bequeath and dispose of in the following Manner, and

First, my express will is that all my just Debts and Funeral Charges be duly paid by my Executor hereinafter nominated & appointed, Recommending my immortal soul to the Infinite mercy of Almighty God who give its existence in hopes of a Glorius Resurrection through the merits of my Lord and Saviour Jesus Christ and my Body to the dust to be decently buried at the Discretion of my Executors.

And, next, I give unto my beloved Wife Esther Mason All my Stock of Cattle and Horses, Sheep and all my Farming utensils. And all my Household Furniture and movable Estate of every kind and Denomination Whatsoever to be at her own disposal and,

And also my Wife to have the full & Free use of a convenient room in the House at her own Election & Firewood to be provided and delivered at the door during her Widowhood, and also the Sum of Twenty Pounds a year to be paid to her Yearly & every year during her natural life or a decent & Comfortable Maintainance at her Own Option.

And I will unto my son William Mason, All my Lands & Tenements whereof I am now seized, however, Subject to the payment of the above Legacies and, to my daughter Mary, the Wife of Peter Middagh, the sum of Twenty Pounds – and to my son Henry Mason, the sum of Twenty Pounds, Current money of the State of Pennsylvania to be paid to Henry Mason at Ten Years next after my Decease, in full of his Birth Right and as the Words heirs and assigns was omitted where the Lands are herein before Willed to my son William it is my express Will to Will unto my son William Mason and to his heirs and assigns forever All my plantation & Tract of Land Situate in Mountbethel & County of Northampton & State of Pennsylvania, he or they Paying the money referred to his Mother & the Other Legacies herein mentioned,

And also to my daughter Martha White, the Wife of William White, the Sum of Ten Pounds like money as …

And I do hereby nominate, constitute and appoint my dearly beloved Wife Esther and my son William Mason, Executrix & Executor of this my last Will and Testament, hereby Revoking and making void and disannulling all and every other Will heretofore by me made, hereby Ratifying & confirming this to be my last Will and Testament and none other.

In Witness whereof I have hereunto set my Hand and Seal the Twenty Eighth day of July, One Thousand seven Hundred & Eighty One.

          Francis (his F mark) Mason

{Seal}
Sealed, Published and Declared by
Testator Francis Mason in the presence of
this request subscribed our names as witness thereto.

Sealed and pronounced
in the presence of us:

John Cunningham } Sworn 23 April 1790
Robert Galloway }
Alexander Sillyman }

On 23 April 1790, before John Arndt, Esquire, Register of Probate of Wills for Northampton Co., PA, personally came John Cunningham and Robert Galloway, two of the subscribing witnesses to the within written Last Will and Testament of Francis Mason, deceased, who being duly sworn on the Holy Evangelists did respectively depose and say that they were present and did see the said Testator sign his mark expressed to be the mark of Francis Mason, publish and declare the same as & for his Last Will and Testament; and that he the Testator was of sound Mind Memory and Understanding to the best of their knowledge and belief, and also that Alexander Sillyman, together with them, these deponents, subscribed his name as a witness to the same in the presence and at the request of the said Testator and in the presence of each other.

**Note: Alexander Sillyman's son Thomas Silleman married Mary [Middaugh], daughter of Garret Middaugh[119], brother-in-law of Mary [Mason] Middaugh.

No precise death dates or gravestones have been found for either Francis or Esther [Martin] Mason. They are probably buried in Lower Mt. Bethel Graveyard, Northampton Co., PA. Francis Mason died prior to the 1790 U.S. Census; if Esther survived Francis, she did not reside in her own home as "head of household". In fact, there is no "Mason" head of household to be found in Northampton County's 1790 census. It's very possible that Esther may have been one of the five females, living in the household of her daughter Mary [Mason] Middaugh during the 1790 census.

The 1790 U. S. Census for Lower Mount Bethel TWP, Northampton Co., PA – p. 258 <2/4>:[120]

Peter Middaugh -- 2 males, age 16 and up
2 males, age under 16
5 females of all ages

Because Esther was bequeathed a room in the home devised to son William, it's very likely Esther was living with her son

---

[119]Marianne (Arick) Senecal
[120] Ancestry.com – Film # M637_8

William Mason during the 1790 US Census. The problem is that either William Mason was omitted from the 1790 Census, or the census taker mistakenly wrote "William Neason", who is found residing amid the Middaughs, the Raes and Sillemans. William "Neason" had 5 females; 2 males 16 and up; 2 males under 16.

The children of Esther & Francis Mason were:

Thomas Mason, probably died between 1776-1781.

Lydia Mason, probably died between 1776 – 1781.

Henry Mason – other than the legacies left to him by his Uncle Robert Martin and through his father's LWT, written in 1781, nothing more is known.

Mary [Mason] Middaugh, married Peter Middaugh, who was christened 27 Nov 1748 in the Reformed Dutch Church, Readington, Hunterdon County, New Jersey. Peter and his brother Garret Middaugh moved from Hunterdon Co. to Lower Mount Bethel, Northampton Co., PA, presumably with their father, Peter Middaugh, Sr. Peter Middaugh, Jr. served in the Revolution as 1st Lieut. in Capt. Jayne's 4th Co. Peter lived adjoining Garret and they both were taxed as owning 115 acres, which would appear to be an equal division of their father's land. Peter, Jr. is first shown in the 1785 Northampton Co. Tax List, which verifies that he and Mary [Mason] were married by that date, because single men were listed and taxed separately. Peter died on November 28, 1829, in Lower Mount Bethel Twp, Northampton County, Pennsylvania, and is buried in Three Churches Cemetery, Lower Mt. Bethel, Northampton County, Pennsylvania[121]. Nothing more is known about Mary [Mason] Middaugh or their children.

Martha [Mason] White married William White, according to her father's Will. There were two William Whites residing in the 1800 U.S. census in Pennsylvania: (1) Easton Twp, Northampton Co., PA and (2) in Lower Makefield Twp, Bucks Co., PA. Additionally, there was a William Holmes White (1736-1792) of Roxbury, Morris Co., NJ, whose wife was purported to be Martha [Mason], b. c1740[122].

---

[121] Marianne (Arick) Senecal

[122] Ancestry.com

William Mason was born about 1741, according to his gravestone. Martha Mason, a descendant of William, advised me that he was married in c1763 to Mary [Van Dyke].

1785 Tax List – Northampton Co., PA - Mt. Bethel Twp[123]
    William Mason   200 ac 4 horses 4 cattle   £1.3.7
    Peter Middaugh, Jr. 115 ac 5   6   1.2.11
    Unmarried Men listed were: William Rea and Joseph Martin

1786 Federal Tax List – Northampton Co., PA - Mt. Bethel Twp
    William Mason   200 ac 4 horses 4 cattle   £1.0.0
    Peter Middaugh   115   4   5   .17.8
    Unmarried Men listed were: William Rea and Joseph Martin

1788 Tax List – Northampton Co., PA – Lower Mt. Bethel Twp
    William Mason   200 ac 4 horses 4 cattle   £0.18.6
    Peter Middaugh   115   5   4   .15.7
    Unmarried Men listed were: James Martin & Joseph Martin

William Mason died 1 February 1794, at Lower Mt. Bethel Twp., Northampton Co., PA. The Last Will & Testament of William Mason was written on January 25, 1794, and filed for probate in Northampton Co. on February 25, 1794[124]. Wife Mary, son Alexander Mason and Ephraim Simonton were named to serve as Co-Executors. William's LWT named his children: Alexander, Thomas, Jane [Mason] (Mrs. William) REA, Elizabeth [Mason] (Mrs. Joseph) MARTIN, Hannah, Mary, Hester & Martha Mason. The LWT was witnessed by James Edmiston, Isaac Covert, Jr. and William Hazlet.

    **Note: James Edmiston, b. 25 Feb 1769, Ireland; d. 27 April 1835; married Elizabeth Middaugh, b. 2 Feb 1772; d. 12 Feb 1837,

---

[123] "Proprietary, Supply & State Tax Lists of Northampton & Northumberland for Years of 1772 to 1787", W. S. Ray, State Printer of PA, 1897

[124] A Genealogical Index of Northampton Co., PA – 1752-1802, Closson Press, Apollo, PA - 1982

daughter of Garret Middaugh, brother of Peter Middaugh, who married William Mason's sister, Mary[125].

From the book, "The Old Grave-Yards of Northampton and Adjacent Counties in the State of Pennsylvania" by John Eyerman – Volume I, Easton, PA – June, 1899:

"One of the oldest grave-yards in Northampton Co., one of no little importance, containing, as it does the graves of many of the earliest Scotch-Irish settlers, is that of the Presbyterian congregation of Lower Mount Bethel township. This historic spot is situated near the village of Martin's Creek, about seven miles N. of Easton, and was undoubtedly in use prior to 1750, for "as early as 1738, services were held by the Rev. Gilbert Tennent, in a small Church adjoining the yard". In 1899, Mr. Eyerman described the graveyard as in a disgraceful condition. He wondered whether the stones would still be legible in another decade, so copied out those he could presently read – among those were:

    Plot #20 - MASON, William, d. 1 Feb 1794: aged 53 years
          #19 - MIDDAGH, Peter, d. 28 Oct. 1829: aged 82 years.

I will elaborate briefly on William Mason's daughter Elizabeth [Mason] Martin, who was born February 15, 1768, and married Col. Joseph Martin about 1789. Col. Joseph was born in then-Bucks Co., PA, c1749 (according to his gravestone transcription) or c1758, according to genealogy compiled by Hazel Michler from Galbraith family history (Two sisters of Col. Joseph Martin married Galbraith brothers). Col. Joseph was the son of James Martin (1708-1767) & wife Ann [Miller] of Martin's Creek, Northampton Co., PA. Unfortunately, after searching for many years, I've not been able to link the ancestry of James Martin of Martin's Creek, to our Martin ancestry. This James Martin might have had a relationship to Hunterdon Co. Sheriff David Martin, who was born 1698, Piscataway, NJ, but they were surely not father and son.

Joseph Martin served in the Revolutionary War under Capt. John Arndt of Easton, 1st Battalion of the Northampton Co. Militia,

---

[125] Marianne (Arick) Senecal

which was part of the Flying Camp of Ten Thousand Men. Joseph Martin "of Mt. Bethel Township" is listed as a 1st Lieutenant, as of July 9, 1776. Serving under him as Privates were Robert Lyle, Samuel McCracken, John McFarren and John Middagh[126].

Joseph was listed as wounded or missing in action after the Battle at Fort Washington on the 16th of November, 1776[127]. He was later promoted to militia Colonel.

Finding Joseph Martin as a 1st Lt. in 1776, gives more credence to his gravestone birth year of 1749. First Lieutenants were generally not selected from 18 year olds, but a 27 year old would be more likely to have been commissioned. Peter Middagh, for instance, was a 1st Lt. under Capt. Timothy Jayne's 4th Company in 1776, and Middagh was age 29, born in 1747.

The "Galbraith Genealogy" states that Joseph Martin was a miller as had been his father James. The first old stone mill at Martin's Creek was named in honor of his family.

Col. Joseph & Elizabeth [Mason] Martin had two sons – James Martin, born c1790; and William Martin, born July 22, 1792. Col. Joseph died in 1798, and is buried in the Presbyterian Cemetery, Northampton Co, PA. His gravestone read:

Col. Joseph Martin, died March 10, 1798, aged 49 years.

John P. Arndt and Joseph Rosencrans were appointed guardians of the young sons James & William Martin. Widow Elizabeth [Mason] Martin then married Jacob Rosencrans in September, 1800, and moved to Luzerne Co., PA. Jacob & Elizabeth later moved to Butler Co., OH.

Elizabeth [Mason] Martin Rosencrans died on January 22, 1818, undoubtedly near Hamilton, Butler Co., OH according to a letter Jacob Rosencrans wrote to his brother Levi, dated November 22, 1818. The letter also contained the information re his stepson William Martin: "I send by this packet a letter to William Martin who will spend the winter at Mount Bethel, where he is married,

---

[126] www.Footnote.com – PA State Archives, Series 5, Vol. VIII, Chapter: First Battalion Northampton Co. Militia, p. 21.
[127] www.Footnote.com – PA State Archives, Series 5, Vol. VIII, Chapter: First Battalion Northampton Co. Militia, p. 24.

direction to pay you on sister Poly note one hundred and ten dollars, money that I advanced for him when he left us here. The balance I shall make arrangement to pay the winter or spring following...."

The children of Elizabeth [Mason] Martin Rosencrans and Col. Joseph Martin were:

(1) James Martin, born c1790; died, unmarried, on April 28, 1813, at Cross Creek, Washington Co., PA, leaving a Will, and naming his brother William as co-executor, along with their maternal uncle, William Rea. A witness to the LWT was Thomas Mason, who from U.S. census records of Cross Creek appears to have been born c1780, and probably the son of William Mason, brother of Elizabeth [Mason] Martin.

(2) William Martin, born July 22, 1792, was living in Cincinnati, OH, in 1813, according to his brother's Will. Jacob Rosencrans wrote in 1818, that William had moved back to Mt. Bethel "for the winter", but he evidently remained there. The "Scholl genealogy" purports that William married (1) Mary Scholl on April 19, 1818; however, it also shows Mary died on April 18, 1810 – incredibly, eight years before her marriage. William married (2) Mary's sister Elizabeth Scholl. William Martin died August 18, 1838, at Martin's Creek, and is buried in the Presbyterian Cemetery, Northampton Co., PA.

For those readers who wish to pursue further research on the Mason family history, I would recommend you contact Mr. Josiah L. Mason, at the Law Offices of Mason, Mason & Kearns in Ashland, OH.

CHAPTER NINE

HENRY MARTIN
(1720 - 1764)

Henry Martin was born 1720, in Co. Tyrone, in the Kingdom of Ireland, the son of Alexander & Martha [Coughran] Martin. He came to America with his parents when no more than an infant. A short time later, because of the death of his father, Henry would have been deemed an "orphan" by law, but no orphans' court or guardianship records are known to exist. He and his mother moved across the Delaware River from Bucks Co., PA to live with his older brothers in what was then Amwell Township, Hunterdon Co., NJ.

Henry's nephew, Col. James Martin, wrote of him, *"He was well proportioned and handsome featured. He was to go frequently to preach in Philadelphia, where the ladies used to call him the handsome minister"*. *"I forgot to say that my Uncle Henry, after he came to my father's, signified he wished to have some college education, that he might study divinity and fit himself for the University. Not having funds of his own, my father and his other brothers, Thomas and Robert, contributed each their share, and sent him to Newark College. He learned very well and was soon prepared to take Holy Orders. He got a congregation in Harvey's, Pennsylvania, and was doing very well. Previous to this, he was the cause of father's sending my brother, Alexander, to the same college, which was before it was moved to Princeton...."*

From a book on the alumni of Princeton University[128]:

"Henry Martin, A.B., A.M., 1754, Presbyterian clergyman, was licensed by the Presbytery of New York and supplied churches at Maidenhead (now Lawrenceville) and Hopewell, New Jersey, in 1752. Martin was called to churches in Newtown and Salisbury,** Bucks County, Pennsylvania, in May 1753. He was ordained and installed as pastor at both places by the Presbytery of Abingdon on April 9, 1754.

---

[128] "Princetonians: A Biographical Dictionary" – James McLachlan, Princeton University Press, 1976.

Within a few years Martin gave up his pastorate at Salisbury** because of declining numbers. He remained at Newtown until his death on April 11, 1764. He married Elizabeth Slack."

**Note: I feel the Princeton biographical notes should read "Solebury" rather than Salisbury. Solebury is in Bucks County, and was the residence of Henry's sister, Agnes [Martin] Dawson.

From Col. James, *"But to account more of my Uncle Henry. He married a respectable and much beloved lady about two years afterwards."*

About 1754, Rev. Henry Martin married Elizabeth Slack, the daughter of Abraham Slack, a prominent member of the Newtown Presbyterian Church[129]. Elizabeth Slack was born in 1728; Henry was eight years her senior. The Slack <aka Schleght> family had immigrated to the American Colonies from Holland, as did the Wynkoop family.

Apparently, Henry married Elizabeth the year after Henry's mother's death. Martha [Coughran] Martin died May 11, 1753, across the Delaware River in Hunterdon Co., NJ.

The first instance I've found of Rev. Henry in Presbyterian Church records comes from minutes of the Philadelphia Presbytery's Synod meeting at Maidenhead, Hunterdon Co., NJ, on May 18, 1757, which records Henry Martin present as a Minister of Abington Presbytery - along with Samuel Finley, who founded the Nottingham Academy.[130]

Minutes recorded for the Synod meeting held at Princeton on July 29, 1757, state *"A supplication was brought in from Itico, Enno, and the Haw fields in North Carolina, for supplies, and for a candidate to be sent among them in order for settlement. As several of our members are to be absent from their respective congregations this summer, on public affairs, which this Synod approve of, the Synod took into consideration how to supply said congregations. And for supplies for Mr. Beatty's congregation, the Synod does appoint Mr. Thane the last Sabbath in June,*

---

[129] History of the Sycamore St. Presbyterian Church by Elinor Slack Campbell – p. 24
[130] "Records of the Presbyterian Church in the United States of America: Embracing the Minutes of the: Presbytery of Philadelphia from 1706 to 1716; Synod of Philadelphia from 1717 to 1758; Synod of New York from 1745 to 1758; Synod of Philadelphia and New York from 1758 to 1788" by the Presbyterian Board of Publication, James Russell, Publishing Agent, 1841, pages 277, 283, 285, 297, 306, 313, 316.

and the first in July; Mr. Lawrence the second and third Sabbaths of July; Mr. Hunter the last in July and first in August; Mr. Rogers the third and fourth Sabbaths in August; Mr. Ramsey the second, third, and fourth Sabbaths of September; Mr. Thane the first and second Sabbaths of October; that Mr. Marten and Mr. Chesnutt each supply two Sabbaths at the times wherein none is provided.*

It would seem from the above schedule that Rev. Henry was to preach at the Enno and Hawfields, North Carolina settlements on either the second week of August or the first week of September – those being the only times unassigned.

May 22, 1758, May 21, 1760, and May 20, 1761 Synod Minutes show Henry Martin as a Minister present from the Philadelphia Presbytery.

May 19, 1762, Synod meeting in Philadelphia shows Minister Henry Martin present. May 20, 1762: " [Ministers to supply Neshaminy] …. Mr. Martin the first Sabbath of July." On May 26, 1762, at "9 ante meridiem: Mr. Martin and Mr. Anthony Tate, his elder, have been absent the two preceding days, and yet are.

It would be usual to provide the Minister with a home in the church manse, but it's unlikely that the grounds of the Newtown manse were sufficient to raise produce and the number of animals Henry owned. Clearly, from the 1761 tax list and the data in his probated Inventory, Rev. Henry owned private land in Northampton Township, which adjoins Newtown Twp. Rev. Henry's Inventory of his Estate in 1764 lists a house & furniture; 5 horses; 16 head of cattle; 21 sheep; 5 pigs; geese, turkeys & Dunghill fowl (domestic barnyard chickens.); and a field of wheat.

Bucks Co., PA Tax Records: Northampton (Township) – 1761[131]:
"A Duplicate of a Three-penny Tax levied on the Inhabitants and Freeholders of the Township of Northampton for the Relief of the Poor:

Hen: Martin	15£, 3sh, 9d
Hen: Winecoop	50£, 12sh, 6d

---

[131] Bucks Co., PA Tax Records – 1693-1778, compiled by Terry McNealy & Frances Waite. Bucks Co. Genealogical Society, PO Box 1092, Doylestown, PA 18901

Henry Martin and Henry Wynkoop appear to have neighboring property as the listing for Northampton Twp is not alphabetized.

The Surety Bond posted by Robert Martin for the administration of Rev. Henry's estate, clearly states that <u>both</u> Robert and Henry were residents of Northampton Township in Bucks Co. in April, 1764.

The History of the Newtown Presbyterian Church has been published, and contains some references to Rev. Henry and interesting history of the early church, for example:

The first Presbyterian Church at Newtown was erected of either frame or logs and erected in c1734 on one acre rented land, later deeded on December 1, 1744 to Trustees George Logan, Anthony Tate, and James Cummings: "Beginning at a stone set for a corner by the side of the great road leading from the Neshaminy Creek to Newtown. This site is, in 1993, partially under the Newtown Bypass, lying between St. Andrew Catholic Church and the Council Rock High School."

From "A Booklet prepared for the celebration of the 250th Anniversary of Newtown, Bucks County, Pennsylvania", published at Newtown in June, 1934...

[p. 36] *"The first regular pastor of the Presbyterian Congregation was Rev. Hugh Carlisle, who presided until 1838* <sic – meaning 1738>. *He was succeeded the following year by Rev. Hugh Campbell, who, however, occupied the pulpit for only a few months. The church then continued without any regular pastor for a dozen years, until Rev. Henry Martin, a Princeton graduate, was called in 1752, and he remained in charge until his death in 1764."* "*All the marriage records kept by the ministers prior to this date [1769] have been lost, and the baptism and death records earlier than 1771 have also become destroyed."*

From Elinor Slack Campbell's chapter "History of the Sycamore Street Presbyterian Church, p.24: *"It was during his [Rev. Henry Martin] pastorate that a manse and several acres of ground were donated to, or bought by, the Trustees. In 1761, because both the manse and the church were in dire need of repairs, the church, having little cash* on hand, followed the custom of the time and sponsored a lottery with a goal of £400 to at least partially cover the expenses."

"For three weeks every month, from 1754 until his death in 1764, the Rev. Martin ministered to the Newtown Congregation. The other week of each month, his pastorate was spent ministering to the Bensalem Presbyterian Congregation. "

[p.32]   "The oldest institution in Newtown in continuous organization is the Presbyterian church, founded in 1734, and active in the community for two centuries. The first church building was a wooden structure located on the townstead boundary a half mile west of Newtown, at what is now the southwest corner of Green Lane and Swamp Road. The old graveyard attached to the church is still there, and a few of the quaint marble tombstones, which mark the final resting place of the founders of the community, remain in a most sorrowful condition. Ninety years ago Dr. Phineas Jenks was much concerned about the dilapidated state of this sacred ground, and his lecture to the Newtown Lyceum on the subject was printed in the Newtown Journal and Workingmen's Advocate of February 27, 1844, over his pseudonym "Olden Time." He began by saying:

'In this spot, the mortal remains of many of the pioneers of the wilderness are deposited – those early adventurers who came to the country and settled in this neighborhood, when all around them was one unbroken forest, when the war cry of the Leni Lenape or the howl of the wolf and the panther nightly assailed their ears. Voluntary exiles from the land of their birth, they cheerfully endured all the hardships and privations attendant upon the settlement of a new country inhabited by uncivilized men.."

Dr. Jenks' remarks were, however, of no avail, and a quarter of a century later when Eleazer F. Church, editor of the Newtown Enterprise, visited the spot, the place was in worse condition. He wrote the following in his paper of May 21, 1868,...

'Many of the tombs of the "Rude forefathers of the hamlet" are there too, no doubt, leveled with the earth, and encroached upon by the plow. Even the graves of those who could afford a tombstone and an epitaph, are almost in the same condition, but a few of the stones are yet left. The storms and frosts have eaten into the marble – but a follower of "Old Mortality" can yet find out the names and trace the epitaphs. We rescue a few of them from the tooth of time, and the destruction of the elements:

....

2. Here lyeth the body of Thomas Martin, who departed this life, August 27, 1760, in the 52d year of his age.

.........."

"Since the above was written, the tombstone of Martin has been removed."
**Note Thomas Martin's grave is now located at the Sycamore Presbyterian Church Cemetery.

"Apparently, the Presbyterian Congregation has never taken any interest in their original church and graveyard property since they abandoned it in 1769, although this year marks their bi-centennial anniversary. At a congregational meeting held on October 16, 1913, it was resolved to dispose of this burdensome acre of ground, so on September 14th of the following year, the Trustees leased the same for 99 years to the adjoining property holder for the munificent sum of $100 cash. Several stipulations were inserted in the lease; one of them being "nor shall he [the lessee] at any time sell or dispose or permit to be sold or disposed to any person any vinous, spirituous or malt liquors on said premises."

"However, no clause keeps cattle and swine off this hallowed ground, or prevents the ignorant from throwing old tin cans on the sacred, although forgotten graves of many of the founders of Newtown. Today, in 1934, this place, like the Yardley Burying Ground belonging to stately Falls Meeting, is a shameful disgrace to the community at large."

[p. 37] "The Presbyterian Church as originally constructed had the entrance on the south side. The pulpit was in the center of the north side, and was reached by a high flight of steps; the pews had high backs; and the floor was of brick." "There are at present nine cemeteries in Newtown borough and township, but the only one which contains the remains of any Revolutionary soldiers is the Presbyterian Graveyard. Here are buried 22 Patriots, two of whom also saw service in the Indian War. All of these graves have recently been marked by Bucks County Chapter, DAR:

Revolutionary Soldiers Buried in Newtown Presbyterian Church: (selected entries only)

11. Abraham Slack; died August 30, 1802, aged 72 years
12. Cornelius Slack, Sr.; did October 10, 1810, aged 68 y – 5 m
13. James Slack; died Jan. 31, 1832, in his 76th year
15 Anthony Teate; died April 4, 1781; aged 71 (Indian War)

The first of Henry's siblings to die was his brother Thomas, intestate on August 27, 1760. Henry was present in Bucks Co., PA the following day, along with Thomas' widow Mary & brother Hugh Martin, to post bond to administer his estate, as evidenced by the following excerpt from the bond[132]:

"*Know all men by these presents that we, Mary Martin of Middletown in the County of Bucks, Widow, and the Reverend Henry Martin of the said County, Clerk, and Hugh Martin of Hunterdon County in the Province of West Jersey, Yeoman And Anthony Tate and John Slack all of the said County are held and firmly bound unto William Plumsted, Esqr. Register General for the Probate of Wills and Granting Letters of Administration in and for the Province of Pennsylvania in the full and just sum of Five Hundred Pounds lawfull money of the said Province..........*"

Although Thomas Martin was residing in Middletown, Bucks Co., PA at the time of his death, his body was brought for burial to Rev. Henry's churchyard at Newtown Presbyterian Church, about 6 miles distant.

A mere two months later, Rev. Henry's faith must have been greatly tested. His beloved young wife, Elizabeth [Slack] Martin died at the age of 32, on October 28, 1760. It's not known whether Elizabeth succumbed to an illness, or whether she may have died in childbirth. If the latter, surely the baby did not survive, because Henry had no children from their marriage of six years. However, Henry's Inventory after his death listed his ownership of a "cradle". Elizabeth was buried at her father's farm on Quarry Road in Lower Makefield Twp., Bucks Co.

Four and a half months later, on March 9, 1761, Henry's eldest brother, Hugh Martin died at age 63. In another nine months'

---

[132] Thomas Martin – 1761 – Probate Records, Bucks Co., PA

time, in December, 1761, Henry's half-brother, James Martin, died at about the age of 65.

If all these personal tragedies were not enough, Rev. Henry certainly did not have an easy time administering his brother Thomas' estate. In September, 1761, Henry felt obligated to object to Thomas' widow Mary continuing as the guardian of son Daniel. The court had earlier appointed Rev. Henry's neighbor, Henry Wynkoop, Esq. to serve as a co-guardian, but with the objection lodged, the court added a third co-guardian, Henry Krewson. By the next Orphans Court session, guardians Wynkoop & Krewson both complained of Mary's lifestyle and new husband and petitioned for her removal. All the while, Rev. Henry was serving as a co-administrator with Mary Martin Marple, which must have been stressful. Rev. Henry asked for delays in his accounting due to the difficulty in dealing with "backward people", and ultimately hired an attorney for assistance in collecting debts owed the estate.

According to Col. James' recollection, *"He [Rev. Henry] was in health when he went to bed, and lying long in the morning, his servant went to call him to breakfast, and found him dead. His wife had died some time before so he was alone when it happened."*

Rev. Henry Martin died in April, 1764, at the age of 44. The exact day of his death is given in his Princeton records[133] as April 11, 1764. An inventory of his estate was performed on April 16, 1764, and administration bond was dated April 18, 1764. Henry was buried beside his wife Elizabeth at his father-in-law Abraham Slack's farm on Quarry Road, Lower Makefield Twp., Bucks Co., PA.[134]

Minutes from the Philadelphia Synod's meeting at Elizabethtown on May 17, 1764, state: "The first Philadelphia Presbytery report that since our last, Mr. Henry Martin is deceased."[135]

---

[133] "Princetonians 1748-1768" by James McLachlan, Princeton University Press – 1976, p. 40

[134] Cemeteries with Connections to the Presbyterian Church of Newtown – Slack Cemetery – by Elinor Slack Campbell – p. 11 LoC – Catalogue Card #94-070943

[135] "Records of the Presbyterian Church in the United States of America: Embracing the Minutes of the: Presbytery of Philadelphia from 1706 to 1716; Synod of Philadelphia from 1717 to 1758; Synod of New York from 1745 to 1758; Synod of Philadelphia and New York

In 1764, Robert Martin was the sole surviving brother, and thus would legally be Henry's heir-at-law due to Henry having no children. British Common Law held that in the absence of a will, the estate of the deceased would pass first to children of the deceased. If the deceased had no children, then the next in line under Primogeniture would be the eldest brother of the deceased.

It is not known how John Hagerman fits into the relationship, except it should be noted to cross-reference him to the John "Hagaman" of Hunterdon Co., NJ. John Slack of Lower Makefield Twp., was undoubtedly Henry's brother-in-law. The witnesses to the following bond are Richard Gibbs and John Gregg, who both have records in common with Daniel Martin, son of Thomas, found in Chapter 5.

REV. HENRY MARTIN[136]
BUCKS COUNTY, PENNSYLVANIA
FILE #1143

Know all Men by these Presents that we Robert Martin of Northampton Township in the County of Bucks, Yeoman, Brother of the Reverend Henry Martin of the same place, Clerk, Deceased, John Hagerman of the same Township in the County of sd. Yeoman and John Slack of Lower Makefield Township in the same County, Yeoman and held and firmly Bound unto William Plumsted, Esq. Register General for the Probate of Wills and Granting Letters of Administration In and for the Province of Pennsylvania in the full and Just Sum of Eight Hundred Pounds Lawfull money of the said Province To be Paid to the said William Plumsted Esq. Or his Successors Register Generals of the Province aforesaid, To which Payment well and Truly to be made we Bind Our Selves Jointly and Severally Each and Every of us by himself for the whole and the Heirs Executors and Administrators of us and Every of us firmly

---

from 1758 to 1788" by the Presbyterian Board of Publication, James Russell, Publishing Agent, 1841, page 334.

[136] Transcribed by Francie Lane – Bucks Co., PA Probate Files.

by the sd Presents Sealed with Our Seals Dated the Eighteenth Day of Aprill Anno Domini 1764.

The Condition of this Obligation is such that if the above Bounden Robert Martin, Administrator of all and Singular the Goods Chattels and Credits of Henry Martin ~ Late of the said County of Bucks, Clerk, Deceased do make or cause to be made a True and perfect Inventory of all and singular the Goods Chattels and Credits of the said Deceased which have or shall come to the hands Possession or knowledge of him the said Robert Martin, or unto the hands and Possession of any other Person or Persons for him and the same so made do Exhibit or Cause to be Exhibited into the Registers in the said County of Bucks at or before the Eighteenth Day of May next Ensuing and the same Goods Chattels and Credits of the said Deceased at the Time of his Death or which at any Time after shall Come to the hands or Possessions of him the said Robert Martin ~ or into the hands and Possession of any other Person or Persons for him do well and Truly Administer according to Law and further do make or Cause to be made a True and Just Account of his Administration at or before the Eighteenth Day of April In the Year 1765, and all the Rest and Residue of the said Goods and Chattels Rights and Credits which shall be found Remaining upon the said Administrators Account (the same being First Examined and allowed of by the Orphans Court of the said County of Bucks) shall deliver and pay unto such person or Persons Respectively as the said Orphans Court by their Decree or Sentence shall Limit and appoint and if it shall hereafter appear that any Last Will and Testament was made by the said Deceased and the Executor or Executors therein named do Exhibit the same into the Register Office Requesting to have it allowed and Approv'd Accordingly if the said Robert Martin above Bounden being thereunto Required to Render and deliver up the said Letters of Administration (Approbation of such Testament being first had and made in the said Registers Office) Then the above Obligation to be Void or Else to be and Remain in full Force and Virtue.

Robert Martin
John Hegeman
John Slack

Sealed and Delivered

In the presence of Us
 Rich^d. Gibbs
 John Gregg

The Inventory shows that Rev. Henry's personal estate was wholely in Northampton Twp. and was comprised of five horses, 16 heads of cattle, 21 sheep, 5 pigs, geese, turkeys and chickens. Among his personal items were a silver watch & buckles, gold buttons; large & small looking glass; a library of books; a clock; 2 feather beds; 2 bedsteads; 3 tables and 10 chairs; plus the usual kitchen items and tools. However, it's probably unusual to see that a minister in early Pennsylvania was also a slave owner, having one Negro man, and that Henry had contracted for the use of a Negro boy for ten years. The value of Henry Martin's estate was over £320, which would rival that of his brother Hugh, father of six, and who was characterized as a prosperous farmer.

April 16th 1764

A True Inventory of the goods and chattles

of ye Revd. Mr. Henry Martin, Late of Northampton Deceased

	£	S	P
His Purse & Apparel, Gold Buttons, Silver Watch & Buckles	20	17	
His House and furniture Valued at	22	0	
Two Horses and two Mares and one Colt at	35	0	
Five Cows, five Heifers, five Steers and a Bull at	44	16	
Twelve Sheep and Nine Lambs at	6	10	
Three Sows and two Pigs at	3	0	
A field of Wheat at 10/0 Pr. Acre			
Five Geese, three Turkeys and some Dunghill fowls at	1	0	
A Waggon, Cart and Geers & Harrow with Sundrys at	11	0	
One Slay, Two Plows and Plowirons ~at ~	3	14	
A Quantity of Indian Corn at 2/3 pr. Bushel			
Two Dungforks, two pitchforks & Sundry Iron lumber at	1	13	
A Box & Trunk, One large Looking glass & one Small D^o at	4	2	6
A Box with his Library of Books Valued at	4	0	0

Item	£	s	d
One Clock, two feather Beds and furniture ~at ~	25	0	0
Four Pewter Dishes, two Tankards four Basons 20 Plates, 2 Porringers, 6 spoons	3	6	
The Earthen ware frying pan Trenchant & Gridiron at	1	14	
A Bake Iron and Tea Equipage and two Iron pots at	1	17	
Handirons, Shovel, Tongs, 2 Potracks and two Smoothing irons	1	8	
Three Hogsd & four Barls, five Tubs, a Churn and two Wheels at	1	7	9
Three Tables, ten chairs and a Settle	2	5	
The dried Bacon and Beef and a pair of Stilyards at	2	17	6
Nine Bushels of Wheat, some Buckwt. And five Bags at	2	4	
Three Casks, an old wheel and Basket and some Flax & wool at	1	8	
One Grindstone and Spade at	0	6	
Two Bedsteads & Cords, a Settle Bedstead Some Leather & Lumber	0	14	
Maulrings & wedges, four Axes & a hoe & sythe & Cradle at	1	7	
A Doughtrough, Cutting knife, and four lbs of Candles at		6	
an Old Saddle and five Bottles and a Gun and Sundrys	2	5	
A Negroe man And Ten Years of a Negroe Boy at	125	0	

Prises____ & affirm
John Hegeman

Bucks Co., PA Orphan's Court Records – September 9, 1765, p. 420

Petition of Robert Martin, Administrator of Henry Martin – File #385. Robert's petition was read in court, stating he had become the administrator of all Goods, Chattels, Rights & Claims of his brother Henry Martin, Deceased, and that the Justices "in your goodness please to appoint suitable persons to audit and settle ye accounts of the administration…" The Court so ordered and referred Robert's administration account records to be examined by John Woolston, Anthony Tate & David Twining, and make a report at the next Court.

From Elinor Slack Campbell's book, p. 9 "The Slack Cemetery", directions state it is "located off Lindenhurst Road, going toward the Grey Nun Academy, then less than 1 mile, at the top of a small rise, which causes a bend in the road. It is a small cemetery, about 30' x 100', encircled by a stone wall, partially covered with ground ivy, and shaded by a large cherry tree. The property remained in the possession of Slack descendants until 1966. The property was neglected for many years, until purchased by Moon's Nursery, owned by the Flowers family, who cleared away the overgrowth. After the grave of Rev. Henry & Elizabeth were uncovered, Jean Fabian Torongo prodded the Newtown Presbyterian Church in 1987 to purchase the site".

The resting place of Rev. Henry and Elizabeth [Slack] Martin is now beautifully maintained by the neighboring Moon's Nursery, for which we, the Martin descendants, must be sincerely grateful.

I am also extremely appreciative of Mr. Joe Ryan,[137] who was kind enough to drive from NJ over to the Slack Cemetery to photograph the two Martin graves for me:

Large marble slabs cover the graves of Rev. Henry Martin and his wife Elizabeth. As best I can decipher the weather-worn stone, the epitaph on the Rev. Henry's stone reads:

---

[137] www.gratefuljoe.com

'HERE LIETH THE BODY OF
THE REVEREND HENRY MARTEN
WHO DEPARTED THIS LIFE THE 11 OF
APRIL A.D. 1764 AGED 44 YEARS

WHEN PREACHERS DIE, WHAT RULE THE
PULPIT GAVE
OF LIVING ARE STILL PREACHED FROM THE
GRAVE
THO FAITH & LIFE WHICH VOID DEATH BE TAUGHT
NOW IN ONE GRAVE WITH HIM, SIR, BUT
____ _____ _____ BRING SAL(VATION

IN MEMORY
of
ELIZABETH MARTIN
WIFE OF
THE REV. HENRY MARTIN
WHO DEPARTED THIS LIFE
THE 28TH DAY OF OCTOBER 1760
IN THE 32D YEAR OF HER AGE
(Elizabeth's epitaph is totally illegible)

THE THIRD GENERATION

As unorthodox as it is, I am extending Volume One of the Martin Family History into the third generation, with the inclusion of Hugh & Jane Martin's third son, Rev. Thomas Martin, for the following reasons:

After reading Chapters 5 through 9, I feel the readers's focus may have strayed from the principle subject of this volume; i.e., Hugh Martin. Introducing the following chapter on Rev. Thomas Martin, brings one's attention back to Hugh, Jane [Hunter] Martin and their children.

Rev. Thomas' history provides an excellent transition to the third generation as the children of Hugh made their way to their ultimate destination – North Carolina. Rev. Thomas touched each of his siblings in a unique interaction; he briefly provided a home in Virginia for his widowed Mother and his younger siblings; he kept in contact with his brothers, who were residing in New Jersey and North Carolina; and established a personal relationship with the James Madison family in what would be the first of many extraordinary links of the Martin family to the history of America.

CHAPTER TEN

(Reverend) Thomas MARTIN
(1743 – 1770)

Rev. Thomas Martin, the third son of Hugh Martin and Jane Hunter, was born about 1743, in Annandale, Lebanon Township, Hunterdon Co., NJ. No record of his birth is available; however, in biographies of President James Madison, it has been reported that there was a nine-year difference in age between James Madison and his tutor, Rev. Thomas Martin. President James Madison was born March 16, 1751, which would place Thomas' birth about 1743.

Hugh Martin sent Thomas to the College of New Jersey at nearby Princeton. Both brothers James & Thomas were enrolled at Princeton at the time of Hugh's death in March, 1761. A provision of Hugh Martin's Will, written shortly before his death, stipulated that sons James and Thomas were to complete their college education through proceeds from the sale of Hugh's real estate unless it was James' choice to return home to work the plantation. James did return home, and as co-executor of his father's estate, James paid out as a special legacy at least £30 to or on behalf of his brother Thomas.

Thomas Martin is listed as a Princeton Graduate, having earned an AB Degree in 1762. Thomas was ordained a deacon in the Church of England in the Chapel Royal, St. James' Palace, London, England on June 14, 1767. Thomas' Ordination to the priesthood followed on June 24, 1767. The original Ordination certificate and License are still in the possession of the Robert I. Upshur family, who graciously photographed the documents for me. My transcription follows:

~ ~ ~ ~ ~ ~ ~ ~ ~ ~ ~ ~ ~ ~ ~ ~

"Be it known unto all men by these presents that We Richard by divine permission Bishop of London holding by the assistance of Almighty God a Special Ordination on Wednesday the Twenty fourth day of June in the Year of our Lord one thousand Seven hundred and Sixty Seven, being the feast of St. John the Baptist, in the Chapel belonging to our Palace in Fulham did admit our beloved in Christ **Thomas Martin ~ A.B. of New Jersey College** (of whose virtuous and pious Life and Conversation and competent Learning and Knowledge in the holy Scriptures We were well assured) into the holy Order of Priests according to the manner and form prescribed and used by the Church of England, and him the said Thomas Martin did then and there rightly and canonically, Ordain a Priest ~ He having first in Our presence and in due form of Law taken the Oaths appointed by Law to be taken for and instead of the Oath of Supremacy and he likewise having freely and voluntarily subscribed to the thirty nine Articles of Religion and to the three Articles contained in the thirty Sixth Canon ~

In Testimony whereof We have caused our Episcopal Seal to be hereunto affixed _ Dated the day and year above written and in the fourth Year of our Translation.

        Mark Holman Depy Regr.
  Ric: London {Seal}

~ ~ ~ ~ ~ ~ ~ ~ ~ ~ ~ ~ ~ ~ ~ ~ ~ ~

Richard by Divine Permission Bishop of London ~
To our beloved in Christ **Thomas Martin** Clerk A.B. ~ Greeting
We do by These Presents Give & Grant to You in whose Fidelity, Morals, Learning, sound Doctrine of Diligence, We do fully confide our License & Authority (to continue only during our pleasure) To perform the Office of a Minister or priest in the Province of Virginia in North America.

in Reading the Common Prayers and performing other Ecclesiastical Duties, belonging to the said Office according to the Form prescribed in the Book of Common Prayer, made and published by Authority of Parliament & the Canons & Constitutions in that behalf; lawfully established & promulged and not otherwise, or in any Other manner / You having first *before Us Subscribed the Articles & taken the Oaths which in this Case are Required by Law to be Subscribed and taken.*

In Witness whereof We have caused our Seal which We use in this Case to be hereto affixed: Dated the Twenty fourth ~ day of June ~ in the Year of our Lord 1767 and in the fourth Year of our Translation.

On July 8, 1767, Martin received the King's Bounty (money for passage to America) and set out from England to become the rector of the Anglican Brick Church, St. Thomas' Parish in Orange Co., Virginia. In Virginia, a license for St. Thomas' Parrish for 1768-1769 was issued for: Rev. Thomas Martin.

The Orange County families who were prominent members of the Old Brick Church were the Barbours, Bells, Burtons, Campbells, Caves, Chews, Conways, Daniels, Madisons, Moores, Ruckers, Shepherds, Taylors, Taliaferos and Whites.[138]

"Old Churches, Ministers, and Families of Virginia", relates that Rev. James Marye, Jr. served St. Thomas parish from the "close of the year 1761." Parishioner James Madison, Sr. made the following entry in his family record regarding his mother's death: *"Frances, wife of Ambrose Madison, departed this life October 25, 1761, and was interred the Sunday following (at Montpelier in Orange). Her funeral sermon was preached on Wednesday the 30th of December following, by the Rev. Mr. James Marye, Jr., on Revelations xiv.13".* The Rev. Marye was the first minister recorded as living at the glebe. **"The Rev. Thomas Martin succeeded Mr. Marye in 1767-68. He was a young man of merit. He came with his mother and sister to reside at the glebe; but his residence was of short duration. Death removed him from the scene of his labours and his usefulness not long after he entered upon the duties of the parish.** He was followed by the Rev. John Barnett. His name occurs officially in 1771."[139]

---

[138] "Old Churches, Ministers and Families of Virginia" by Bishop William Meade, originally published: Philadelphia – 1857; reprinted by Genealogical Publishing Co., Inc., Baltimore, MD - 1966

[139] "Old Churches, Ministers and Families of Virginia" by Bishop William Meade, originally published: Philadelphia – 1857; reprinted by Genealogical Publishing Co., Inc., Baltimore, MD - 1966

Rev. Thomas Martin witnessed the Will of Phil Eastin, along with James Madison, Sr. on June 12, 1768. The Orange Co., VA Will Book[140] records that on July 28, 1768, Philip Eastin's Will was "presented into Court by Elizabeth Eastin and Johnny Scott. Proved by the Rev. Thomas Martin, James Madison and James Marsden....."

Rev. Thomas was soon well acquainted with parishioner and vestryman James Madison, Sr. of the Montpelier plantation, who recognized Rev. Thomas to be a scholarly young man, and as a graduate of Princeton, was well qualified to tutor and prepare the Madison sons for college. James Madison, Jr., age 16, was withdrawn from Mr. Donald Robertson's Scotch School in King & Queen Co., VA, and returned home to be tutored, together with his siblings – Francis, age 14; Ambrose (12); and sister Nelly (7).

The Madison family "autobiography" states that the Reverend Mr. Martin lived with the Madison family at Montpelier. The living arrangement was probably due to the convenience of having a live-in tutor, but must have also been due to the parish glebe being in a state of disrepair.

From "Sarah [Madison] Macon's Family Bible" deposited in VA Historical Society & transcribed by Patricia P. Clark[141]: [Mrs. Sarah Macon was the sister of President James Madison. The following records the birth and baptism of her sister, Elizabeth]

"*Elizabeth Madison was Born February 19th 1768, half an hour after 12 [OClock &] was Baptized February 22nd, by the **Revd. Mr. Thomas Martin** & had [for] God-Fathers Majr. Zachariah Burnley & Capt. Ambrose Powell & for God-Mothers Miss Alice & Miss Milly Chew.*"

The sons of the Virginia Planter society were expected to attend the Anglican William & Mary College at Williamsburg. However, through the influence of Rev. Thomas, consideration was being weighed in favor of Princeton. Certainly, James, Jr. would not have chosen a college in opposition to his father's wishes, so it is interesting to speculate on the factors influencing the decision. Rev.

---

[140] "Orange County, VA – Will Book I" abstracted by John Frederick Dorman - 1958
[141] FTM VA Vitals cd

Thomas had enrolled at Princeton during the presidency of Dr. Samuel Davis, famed for his defense of the rights of non-conformists in VA. Rev. Thomas completed his education under the presidency of Samuel Finley, who himself, had been arrested, convicted and driven out of Connecticut for preaching without a license. Government persecution of "non-conformists" by the Virginia establishment was particularly high in 1760's Virginia. Baptist preachers had been stoned out of Culpepper County in 1765. Many Baptists were jailed and fined heavily. If President Madison's lifelong championship of religious rights had its origin in what he witnessed in his teens, it would have been a logical decision to attend Princeton, a college devoted to religious freedom.

From a biography of President James Madison[142], "Of the two Princeton graduates, [Gov. Alexander Martin & Rev. Thomas Martin] both Anglicans, who advised Madison to go there, the Elder Martin, made a public record as a defender of dissenters." Further, "Many Anglicans graduated at Princeton, but their background was one of hostility to church establishment."

James Madison acknowledged Alexander Martin as the one who helped bring about the final decision for Princeton. Alexander, eldest brother of Rev. Thomas, was also an alumnus of Princeton and currently serving as the Kings Attorney in the Salisbury, NC Superior Court. Alexander had resided in Rowan Co., NC for nine years, and set about in the early summer of 1769, to make the journey home to Hunterdon Co., NJ to visit his widowed Mother and younger sisters and brothers. Alexander stopped along the way through Virginia to see Rev. Thomas and was brought into the discussion of the future college for young James Madison. A Madison biography stated, *"Noted as Alexander Martin was in later years for moderation and persuasiveness, his mature counsel may have won the elder Madison to a course on which the others already were agreed."* James Madison, Sr. entrusted his son to the care of Alexander & Rev. Thomas Martin, and along with a Madison slave named Sawney, set out for Princeton, making their way through

---

[142] "James Madison - The Virginia Revolutionist", by Irving Brant, Bobbs-Merrill Company, Indianapolis, NY (1941)

Fredericksburg, Alexandria, Baltimore, Philadelphia, along stump-studded trails, woods, and crossing rivers on poled ferries. They arrived at Nassau Hall in late July, 1769. The senior Madison recorded in his journal that the summer was so dry, the tobacco leaves withered, destroying his crop; and a hurricane pummeled the entire East Coast.

On August 10, 1769, writing from "Nassau Hall", young James Madison penned a letter to Rev. Thomas, who was still visiting his Mother in nearby Lebanon, NJ:

~~~~~~~~~~~~~~~~~

"Rev. Sir ~ I am not a little affected at hearing of your misfortune, but cannot but hope the cure may be so far accomplished as to render your journey not inconvenient. Your kind advice and friendly cautions are a favor that shall be always gratefully remembered, and I must beg leave to assure you that my happiness, which you and your brother so ardently wish for, will be greatly augmented by both your enjoyments of the like blessing.

I have been as particular to my father as I thought necessary for this time, as I send him an account of the Institution, &c, &c, of the College wrote by Mr. Blair, the gentleman formerly elected president of this place. You will likewise find two pamphlets entitled Britannia's intercession for John Wilks, &c, which if you have not seen, perhaps may divert you.

I am perfectly pleased with my present situation; and the prospect before me of three years' confinement, however terrible it may sound, has nothing in it, but what will be greatly alleviated by the advantages I hope to derive from it.

The grammars, which Mr. Houston procured for you amount at 2/10 each to 17/. Your brothers account with Plumb to 6/7. and Sawneys expense 4/2 the whole 1..7..9. Inclosed you have 15/. the overplus of which you may let Sawney have to satisfy those who may have been at any trouble on his account.

The near approach of examination occasions a surprising application to study on all sides, and I think it very fortunate that I entered College immediately after my arrival, tho I believe there will not be the least danger of my getting an Irish hint as they call it, yet it will make my future studies somewhat easier, and I have by that means read over more than half Horace and made myself pretty well acquainted with Prosody, both which will be almost neglected the two succeeding years.

The very large packet of letters for Carolina I am afraid will be incommodious to your brother on so long a journey, *to whom I desire my compliments may be presented and conclude with my earnest request for a continuance of both your friendships, and sincere wishes for your recovery, and an agreeable journey to your whole company.*

I am, sir, your obliged friend and Hl Ser.

James Madison

P.S. **Sawney tells me that your mother and brothers are determined to accompany you to Virginia;** *my friendship and regard for you entitle them to my esteem, and assure them that with the greatest sincerity I wish, after a pleasant journey, they may find Virginia capable of giving them great happiness."*

~ ~ ~ ~ ~ ~ ~ ~ ~ ~ ~ ~ ~ ~ ~ ~

Madison's letter is so very fascinating for its clarification of our Martin family history. This is the first implication that Rev. Thomas is not well, but nonetheless is capable of traveling back to Montpelier. Rev. Thomas purchased grammar books to take back to VA for use in tutoring. Apparently there are students at Princeton who have friends or relations in North Carolina, and Alexander has been requested to hand-carry letters back home. There was a "Jersey Settlement" near Salisbury, established by former Hunterdon Co. residents, and it would be reasonable to assume some of their children were sent to Princeton for their higher education. It's interesting to note that Sawney, a Madison slave, was apparently entrusted to travel between the Martin home in Lebanon Twp. to Nassau Hall and back again, carrying expense money, books and the packet of letters. Of course, the greatest revelation is to find that a family council was undoubtedly held with the result that widow Jane [Hunter] Martin, her sons Robert and Samuel, and daughter Jane Martin (a few days shy of her tenth birthday) would be leaving their New Jersey home to take up residence with Rev. Thomas in Orange Co., VA. At this point in time, Col. James Martin had been married to Ruth [Rogers] for six years with 3 young children, and was considered the head of the household. It is also apparent from later correspondence that daughter Martha [Martin] and husband Samuel Rogers were also living at the Martin plantation in Lebanon. The splitting of the household may have been an attempt to relieve some stress and burden from Col. James, or may have been only a Mother's concern for her ailing, unmarried son, Rev. Thomas. The Martin entourage; i.e., Alexander, Rev. Thomas, their mother Jane, younger brothers Robert and Samuel and sister Jane, including Sawney, arrived back at Montpelier by the end of August. I believe that somewhere along the journey, it was decided that Robert would not remain in Orange Co., but would continue on with Alexander to North Carolina.

Upon arriving at Montpelier, Rev. Thomas lost no time and must have set in motion a proposal to the Vestry for repairs to the parish glebe for use as a home by Rev. Thomas and his family.

A letter, dated March 7, 1857, from J. Earnest, reported the following discovery of a long-lost page from the vestry book:

"Right Rev. and Dear Sir: Since I wrote you some days since, a few items of interest in relation to this parish have come to my hands. A single leaf, and, that somewhat mutilated, of the old vestry-book of St. Thomas parish, was found among the papers of one of my communicants who died last week, and has since been handed to me. From this I am able to ascertain who composed the vestry as far back as 1769. The record states: ~ 'At a vestry held for St. Thomas parish, at the glebe, on Friday, the 1st day of September, 1769, present, Rev. Thomas Martin, Eras.[mus] Taylor, James Madison, Alexander Waugh, Francis Moore, William Bell, Rowland Thomas, Thomas Bell, Richard Barbour, William Moore.' The object of their meeting was to take into consideration

the repairs necessary to be made to the house and other buildings connected with the glebe." [143]

How fortunate that this single page from the vestry book should pertain to the repair of the glebe. The following letter, in Rev. Thomas' handwriting to his brother James confirms that the repairs were, indeed, being undertaken as of June, 1770, stating, "……*my House at present is in Confusion. Men by the appointment of the Vestry are repairing it"*

~ ~ ~ ~ ~ ~ ~ ~ ~ ~ ~ ~ ~ ~ ~ ~

Dear James   *Virginia June 20. 1770*[144]

By Cousin James I am favoured with yours of May, informing me of a Son being added to your family since my Departure, his Name Hugh. I approve your choice in endeavouring to perpetuate the Memory of a Man, who was the only dear deceased Relation that we have ever had any Reason to regret – a kind Parent, a tender provident Father. I am rejoiced to hear of Samuel's seperation from you, it is for the Interest of you both, but I cannot be reconciled to his Bargain in the Land – it is a small Tract, and much broken, I recollect that the Field above the Barn is cold spungy Land, that the Back field is near worn out and very little woodland upon any of it – the only advantage attending it, is a good Meadow, but the value of Grass there, you know is very precarious, being often overflowed ~ Hay will not do is chin ... [a crease in the paper obliterates the following line] *... altogether. Uncle Robert writes to me for the Money paid to V. Martin, in answer to him I have desired him to transmit Kate to me in Virginia, and I will pay Expenses and his Demand upon sight – if that cannot be done, to endorse the Bill of Sale to you, or some other Person. You or they to veil her at publick Sale, thence to satisfy himself, for he complains heavily & bitterly about it ~ most certainly she might be sold for thirty Pounds by any other Man than our Uncle ~ he has it in his Power to make himself whole, and I have no Reason to lie out of the Use of that Money but no services were done ~ I am at present much indisposed, a slow Fever*

---

[143] "Old Churches, Ministers and Families of Virginia" by Bishop William Meade, originally published: Philadelphia – 1857; reprinted by Genealogical Publishing Co., Inc., Baltimore, MD - 1966

[144] Transcription by Francie Lane of original letter in the possession of Mr. Robert I. Upshur

(but no Ague) has attacked me these eight Days past, about eleven O'Clock in the fore-noon and lasts 'till four ~ I doubt not but you are ready to jest in your usual Manner, and affirm it Conceit, Laziness &c be it as it will, it is very troublesome ~ indeed I am as sickly and crazy as any aged Man, and in what Manner to account for it I know not ~ The rest of the Family are well – Sam and Jane go to school with me, Sam will make a tolerable Progress, if he will be confin'd ~ The Expenses of Housekeeping I find are very great – my furniture, stock, Provision &c have amounted to near two hundred Pounds, since I saw you, yet when all are properly placed, I can scarce observe where they are: my Salary and school amounts to three Hundred Pounds nearly this year, how long I shall continue my school is uncertain. Mother seems to be well satisfied ~ [3 lines have been purposely inked out]

I expect Brother Sauney and Robert with Uncle John Hunter here every Day. Robert in a Letter to me says, he has thrown off his Coat of Bashfulness, and will assure me of it when he visits me ~ **my House at present is in Confusion. Men by the appointment of the Vestry are repairing it** ~ I have not yet purchased any Lands or Negroes, but should I live, I will the next year strike at one or the other: I am happily situated could I enjoy my Health, a Lot of honest worthy men are in my Neighborhood: ~ if you will permit me to advise you, Let me observe to you that a Man is generally known by the Company he keeps ~ there is a Method to use those kindly whom you would not choose to make Companions of and keep those at a proper Distance ~ the Messrs. Grandines are Gentlemen worthy of any Man's Intimacy; of the Rest in your Neighborhood, judge as Nature hath taught you ~ Don't forget me to your wife ~ Remember me to John Anderson, Esqr. & family and believe me

Your affectionate Brother.
Thomas Martin

Mother has sent by Cousin James to the
Children 3 ½ yards of Linnen, 1 pair of
Pockets for each of the Girls, 1 Thread Case
to your wife, 1 Thread Case to Sally, 1 Handkerchief
and two Old Shirts ~ ~ ~

Remember me to Philip Fisher tell him I shall Drink his Health this Harvest out of his cidar piggon which he made me.

~ ~ ~ ~ ~ ~ ~ ~ ~ ~ ~ ~ ~ ~ ~ ~

The letter from Rev. Thomas is one of the truly magnificent Martin family treasures; it has survived over 243 years, and is currently in the possession of the Upshur family. The following are my interpretations and observations concerning some of the passages:

- ❖ Thomas' reference to "Cousin James" having hand delivered a letter from Col. James, and then is to hand carry back to New Jersey various presents from their mother Jane was at first puzzling. My original inclination was to presume "Cousin James" was 1st Cousin James Hunter, son of Alexander Hunter, because he was known to be so close to the Martin brothers. However, I am now of the opinion that "Cousin James" was more likely Hunterdon Co., NJ, resident, James Martin, Jr., son of half-uncle James Martin. At the time of this letter, 1st Cousin James Hunter, was a resident of Orange Co., North Carolina. If he had traveled back to New Jersey to visit Col. James Martin, then stopped in Orange Co., VA on his way back to NC, it would not have been extraordinary; however, it is not logical that he would have turned around to deliver Jane's presents back to NJ. Further, the chronology of historical events surrounding James Hunter should persuade one to believe that he would not have time to travel back and forth from NC to NJ to VA to NJ to NC during such troubling times. As a leader of the NC Regulator Movement, James Hunter courageously filed suit for extortion against the infamous County Clerk, Edmund Fanning, in March, 1770, at the Hillsborough (Orange Co., NC) Superior Court, with Judge Richard Henderson, presiding. [Note: Judge Richard Henderson would, eight years later, become the brother-in-law of Jane

Martin through her marriage to Thomas Henderson.] As a result of Hunter's actions on behalf of the Regulators, he was twice indicted in March, 1770, but both indictments were quashed due to technicalities. James Hunter presented yet another Regulators' petition to Judge Henderson in September, 1770, which culminated in the Regulators' Riot of Hillsborough.

❖ From Thomas' letter, it is quite evident that he and James both revered their father Hugh, but I find it odd reading Rev. Thomas' sentiments that their father, "was the only dear deceased relation that we have ever had any reason to regret". At this point in time, Rev. Thomas' had lost a number of close family members, and would have been well familiar with them; i.e., Grandmother Martha [Coughran] Martin, Half-Uncle James Martin, and Uncles Thomas and Rev. Henry Martin.

❖ Rev. Thomas complained about the disagreements and treatment he'd been receiving from Uncle Robert Martin, who served as Trustee over Hugh's estate. Hugh's slave Kate cited in his Will and Inventory of 1761, was still with the family in New Jersey.

❖ Thomas was relieved to hear that his brother-in-law Samuel Rogers separated from James, which seems to infer that Col. James and wife Ruth [Rogers] Martin had been sharing their home with Samuel and wife Martha [Martin] Rogers, causing friction between the two couples.

❖ This letter is the only existing proof of the whereabouts of the other family members in 1770. Jane [Hunter] Martin is residing with Rev. Thomas and thought to be well satisfied. Jane has kept busy preparing gifts for her three granddaughters. Col. James' daughter Sally, age 6, is given a thread case. Jane has made a pair of pockets for Sally,

Mary Ann (age 4) and Jane "Jenny", age 29 mos.), which probably refers to decoratively embroidered pockets, which Ruth could then attach to the girls' dresses. Jane brought son Samuel and young daughter Jane (age 10), with her to VA, and they were being taught by Rev. Thomas.

- ❖ Brother (Alexander), Sawney (the Madison family slave) and Robert (brother Robert Martin) were expected to arrive any day in Orange Co., VA. Of course, it was the previous year, August, 1769, when Alexander was last in VA and NJ. It's evident that Alexander took his younger brother Robert to live with him in NC, but it's also apparent that Sawney accompanied Alexander to NC in 1769, and is only now being returned to the Madison family.

- ❖ Uncle John Hunter had been residing in then-Rowan Co., NC for over ten years. He undoubtedly accompanied Alexander to visit with his widowed sister Jane, and may have planned to extend the trip in order to visit family and former neighbors in nearby Albemarle Co., VA. John's former plantation was located on Crooked Creek of the Slate River.

- ❖ Rev. Thomas was still suffering from ill health – as he had been the previous August, 1769.

Unfortunately, less than three months after writing his letter, Rev. Thomas Martin died at the age of 27.

Virginia Gazette – September 20, 1770, Page 3, column 1[145]:
"Some short time past died the Rev. THOMAS MARTIN, rector of St. Thomas's parish, Orange county. He was a man of many virtues, affable and generous, discharged his office in life so much to the general satisfaction of men, that his loss is truly regretted,

"Quis desiderio sit pudor aut modus Tam cari capitis?"

---

[145] Colonial Williamsburg Digital Library: http://research.history.org

[Translation from Latin: What limit can there be in our grief for a man so beloved? -Horace]

From the North Carolina Archives' Collection of Private Papers I discovered a letter written by Alexander Martin, dated September 21, 1770, while an attorney in Salisbury, Rowan Co., NC, addressed to James Madison, Sr., proposing to have brother Samuel Martin administer the estate of Rev. Thomas with the assistance of Mr. Madison:

~ ~ ~ ~ ~ ~ ~ ~ ~ ~ ~ ~ ~ ~ ~ ~

To: Col. James Maddison <sic>[146]
Salisbury Septemr. 21st 1770

Dear Sir:

I received your two obliging letters, the first informing me of my Brother's dangerous illness, the last of his Death by Brother Samuel. A circumstance truely melancholy to us! A Brother on whom the Hopes and Honour of our Family much depended to be cut of <sic: off> just opening the Dawn of Life, and beginning to be of real Service to Mankind, is a matter of such a Nature, the most rigid must sympathize with me and though perhaps they cannot grieve, must excuse those Tears that flow from a Brother's Eyes. ~ However the Will of Providence must be done: ~ sooner or later it will be the Lot of us all.

I should have been very desirous of immediately going to Orange to afford some Comfort to my grieving Mother, and settle my Brother's affairs, but our Superior Courts are now sitting which require my immediate attendance, to which follow a Number of County Courts that it we <sic: will> be almost impossible for me to go in until Spring, without greatly injuring my Business; besides I imagine there will not be any great Necessity, as Samuel informs me some of the neighbouring Clergy have undertook very kindly to preach in the parish until the expiration of the year of my Brother's salary. The Crop is on the ground that must be gathered and disposed of before my Mother's Removal which cannot be till Spring.

---

[146] Transcription by Francie Lane – September 7, 2007, of copy of letter from Alexander Martin, in possession of NC Archives – Private Papers of Aubrey Lee Brooks Collection 1758-1875. P.C.359.1

I have instructed Samuel to take out Letters of Administration and to consult your friendly Direction therein, in paying Debts, receiving Monies due, and ordering the Estate in general which cannot be much. And as Security will be necessary, I should be very much obliged to you, or some other Gentleman to be his Security for that Purpose, as it will be a meer <sic: mere> Matter of Form, and I will enter into any Bond required when I come in, by way of Indemnification. The Cattle must be sold, the Beds bought of Murray returned or sold as also the Chair, & other articles needless for us to keep. ~ I have desired him to get a State of the Acct. with Mitchell, and know how stands the last year's Salary, and the present &c.

These things I make free to acquaint you with, from the Friendship I believed subsisted between you and my deceased Brother, from the several kind Civilities, and Politeness shown to my self and our Family, and which we that survive would flatter ourselves with a Continuance of, so long as we to merit them.

Accept of my best wishes for yourself, Mrs. Maddison, and the Family, and believe me to be with much Esteem

> *Dear Sir,*
> > *your most obliged,*
> > > *most affectionate hum. Servant*
> > > > *Alex: Martin*

NB *My Duty to my Mother &*
    Love to my Sister ~

~ ~ ~ ~ ~ ~ ~ ~ ~ ~ ~ ~ ~ ~ ~ ~ ~

Alexander's references to beds purchased from Murray and needing an accounting from Mitchell, causes me to wonder whether Rev. Thomas purchased the beds and other furnishings on credit with the Philadelphia merchants, Randle Mitchell and John Murray, uncle of Agnes [Murray] Martin, who would later become the wife of Daniel Martin, Alexander's 1st cousin.

I searched through the Orange Co., VA Court Minutes for the period of 1770 to 1772, and found no reference to Rev. Thomas Martin's estate – neither an administration bond, nor reports of Inventory or Sale were submitted to the court, which is the very least you'd expect to find. Estates of other resident decedents of Orange Co. were recorded in the minutes, though. The only explanation I can give is that James Madison, Sr. was the presiding Justice of the Orange County Court at the time and he personally certified the clerk's minutes of each session, but I don't know why Judge Madison did not require Rev. Thomas' estate to go through the normal process. Presumably, Rev. Thomas Martin was buried in the Old Brick Church cemetery, but according to the following passage, his gravestone would not have survived the bitterness felt by some in the community toward the Anglican Churches in the aftermath of the American Revolution.

From "A History of Orange Co., VA" by W. W. Scott, written in 1907:

"The "Middle," or "Brick," church, stood on the hill near where the Pamunkey road crosses Church Run. It was built between 1750 and 1758 of durable materials, and as late as 1806 time had made little impression on it. One of the first effects of the " freedom of worship " and the practical confiscation of the glebes and church properties was, that the people's consciences became very " free " also to do as they pleased with the church belongings.

This church was actually and literally destroyed, the very bricks carried off and the altar pieces torn from the altar and attached to pieces of household furniture.

The ancient communion plate, a massive silver cup and paten, with the name of the parish engraved on it, came to be regarded as common property. Fortunately by the exercise of vigilance the plate was rescued, and is now in possession of St. Thomas Church at Orange.

Nor did the despoilers overlook the churchyard when the work of destruction began. Tombstones were broken down and carried off to be appropriated to unhallowed uses. The Rev. Mungo Marshall, of hallowed memory, rector from 1753 to 1758, was buried there, but his grave was left unmarked. Years afterward a connection of his bequeathed a sum of money upon condition that the legatee should not receive it until he had placed a tombstone over Mr. Marshall's grave, which condition was soon fulfilled. That slab was taken away and used first to grind paints upon, and afterwards in a tannery on which to dress hides! What an injury was done to the history of the County in the destruction of the many tombstones there for not a vestige remains of church or churchyard."[147]

---

[147] "A History of Orange Co., VA" by W. W. Scott. - Everrett Waddey Co., Richmond, VA, 1907

A

ALLEN, 111
   Jedidiah, 144
   Nehemiah, 153
   Rebecca [Crispin] Blackfan, 152
   Thomas L., 124, 125
ALLISON
   Francis, 40
ANDERSON
   John, Esq., 17, 20-23, 38, 56, 57, 78, 194
   Richard, 57
APGAR
   Family, 56
ARMITAGE
   Enoch, 78
ARNDT
   John, 163, 166, 167
AYER
   Alexander, 143

B

BARBOUR
   Family, 187
   Richard, 192
BARNS
   Jacob, 86, 94
BEAKES
   Samuel, 144
   Stephen, 144
BEARD, 35
BEATTY
   George, 17
BEE
   Thomas, 12
BELL
   Family, 187
   Thomas, 192
   William, 192
BENWARD, 35
BILES
   Benjamin, 42
BLACKFAN
   Aaron, **154**
   Crispin, 152
   Edward, 152, 153
   Eleanor [Wood], 151-153
   Esther [Dawson], **142, 145, 147, 148-155**
   Hannah, 147
   Jesse, **155**
   John, **147- 150, 152-154**
   Martha, 145
   Martha [Davis], 153
   Martha [Quinby], 154
   Rebecca [Crispin], 152
   Thomas, **144, 147, 151, 154**
   William, III, **154**
   William, Jr., **100, 145, 147, 151-155**
   William, Sr., 152
BLACKSHAW
   Randal, 144
BLAIR
   John, 100
BLAKEY, 111
   Samuel, 116
   William, 76
   William, Jr., 114-116, 120, 123, 141, 144
BONHAM
   Hezekiah, 78
BOON
   Mr., 12
BOSS

Henry, 29
John, 29
Joseph, 73, 75
Peter, 70
BOYD, 35, 157
BRAINERD
   David, Rev., 35, 36
   John, Rev., 36, 39
   Thomas, Rev., 35, 36
BRAY
   Andrew, 38, 39, 56
   John, 39, 56
BROACH
   Rachel [Martin], **44**
BROWN
   Ann [Dawson], 142, 146
   Elizabeth [Dawson], 142
   George, 143, 144
   Joseph, 142
   Mary [Ayer], 142, 143
   Thomas, Jr., 142
   Thomas, Sr., 142, 143
BUCHMAN, 35, 157
BUNNER
   Andrew, 109
BURCHAM
   James, 29, 30, 69-71
   John, 38
   Joseph, 29, 30, 69-71
BURGESS
   Richard, 143
BURNLEY
   Zachariah, Maj., 188
BURR
   Aaron, Rev., 39
BURTON
   Family, 187
BYE
   John, 144
   Joseph, 152
Rebekah, 152
Thomas, 144

C

CAMPBELL, 100
   Family, 187
   Hugh, Rev., 172
   James, Rev., 39, 140
CANBY
   Thomas, 144
CANE
   Walter, 77
CARLISLE
   Hugh (Rev.), 172
CARPENTER
   John, 77
CARTER
   James, 112
   Rebecca, 112
   William, 96, 100, 101, 112
CARVER
   William K., 129
CASEY
   Asa, 105
CASIER
   Mary, 24
CAULFIELD
   Alice, 4
CAVE
   Family, 187
CHAPMAN
   Edward, 153
   Isaac, 145
   Rachel [Blackfan], **147**, **149**, **150**, **153**
CHARLEMONT
   Lord, 4
CHEW
   Alice, 188

Family, 187
Milly, 188
CHILDS
　Anna [Martin], **126**
　Thomas, **126**
CLARK
　Charles, 42
CLEAYTON
　William, 42
COATE
　Jno., 37, 72
CONNOLY
　John, 96
CONWAY
　Family, 187
COPLAND, 35, 157
CORYELL
　John, 142, 145
Coryell's Ferry, 29, 142
COUGHRAN
　James, 2, 6
COVERT, 35
　Isaac, Jr., 165
COXE
　Daniel, 16, 37, 72
　Family, 56
　William, 16
CRAIG
　Thomas, 34, 35
　William, 34
CRAMER
　Matthias, 39, 121
　Theodore, 38, 39
CRAWFORD, 35, 157
CRISPIN
　Ralph, 156
　Rebecca Penn [Bradshaw], 152
　William, 152
CROASDALE
　Ezra, 144

William, 143
CUMIN
　James, 158
CUMMINGS
　James, 172
CUNNINGHAM
　John, 162, 163

D

DANIELS
　Family, 187
DAVIDS
　John, 98, 99
DAVIS
　David, 78
　Jonathan, 78
　Reese, 142
　Samuel, Dr., 189
DAWSON
　Agnes [Martin], **7, 10, 45, 104,
　　141, 146, 148- 153, 155**
　Catherine [Fox], 142
　John, 141-145
　Jonathan, 142
　Margaret, 142
　Rachel, **142, 152, 155**
　Thomas, 5, **45, 104, 141, 142,
　　144- 146, 148, 151, 152, 155**
DE BOW
　John, Rev., 138-140
DEAN
　John, 77
Delaware
　New Castle, 3, 6, 26, 33
DICKINSON
　Moses, 77
DIMSDALE
　John, 70, 71
　Robert, 70, 71

DONNOM
   James, 12
DOUGLAS
   Martha Denny [Martin], **44**
   Stephen A., Sen., **44**
DOUGLASS
   George, 93
DOYLE
   Patrick, 111
DRUMMOND
   Gavin, 14
   James, 14
   James, Earl, 14
   John, 15
   William, Gov., 14
DUNHAM
   Family, 56
DYER
   James, 100, 101
   John, 116
DYMOCK
   Gilbert, 143

E

EASTBURN
   Family, 143, 144
   Samuel, 142, 152
EASTIN
   Elizabeth, 188
   Philip, 188
EDMISTON
   Elizabeth [Middaugh], 165
   James, 165
ELLICOTT
   Nathaniel, 98, 100
ELY
   Elizabeth, 152
   Family, 143, 144
   Hugh, 151

   John, 152
   Joshua, 152
   Phoebe, 152
EMLEY
   John, 37, 72
EVERETT
   Samuel, 78

F

FANNING
   Edmund, 195
FELL
   Benjamin, 152
   Elizabeth [Blackfan], **149**, **153**,
   Family, 143
   Watson, 153
FENTON
   Joseph, Dr., 112
FIELD
   Ann, 76
   Benjamin, 29, 30, 69, 71, 75, 76, 123
   Edward, 76
   Elizabeth, 76
   Jennings, 76
   Mary, 76
   Sarah, 75
   Susana, 76
   Thomas, 76
FINLEY
   Samuel, Rev., 39, 40, 170, 189
FISHER
   Anna, 57
   Peter, 29, 69, 74
   Philip, 195
FLEMING
   Samuel, 77
FLUCK
   James, 86, 101

FORESMAN, 35
FRANKLIN
　Benjamin, 26
FRAZER
　David, 8, 24, 56
　Rachel [Anderson], 56
FULKERSON
　John, 7, 8, 56, 57
FURMAN
　Moore, 28, 92, 93, 94
　Samuel, 73

G

GALBRAITH, 35, 157, 166, 167
GALLOWAY
　Robert, 162
GALRAITH, 35
GARRISON
　John, 42
GASTON, 35, 157
GIBBS
　Richard, 82, 112, 135, 177, 179
GILLAM, 111
　Ann [Paxson], 128
　Simon, 128
GODREY
　Samuel, 154
　Sarah [Blackfan], **147, 149, 154,**
GRANDIN
　Family, 194
　John F., 16
GREGG
　Francis, 118
　John, 72, 101, 111, 135, 174, 177, 179
　Mahlon, 114-117, 123, 131
　Michael, 111
　Patrick, 98
GROWDON, 100

GWIN
　Mr., 12

H

HAGAMAN
　Abraham, 69-72
　J. M., 30, 69, 70
　Peter, 70
HAGEMAN
　Aaron, 112
　Anna, 112
　Deborah, 112
　Henry, 112
　John, 112
　Mary, 112
HAGEMAN-KROESEN
　Mary, 112
HAGERMAN
　John, 72, 133, 177
HAMILTON
　Andrew, Gov., 15, 30, 69, 71
HANNA
　James, 114
　John, Rev., 50, 51, 54
HAPENNY
　Mark, 111
HARDING
　Francis, 143
　Nathaniel, 143
HARLEY
　Rudolph, 28, 29
HART
　Edward, 78
HARTLEY
　Edward, 144
　Roger, 144
HARVEY
　Martha, 142
　Sarah, 152

HAYHURST
  James, 101
  William, 112
HAZLET
  William, 165
HEATH
  Robert, 143, 144
HEATON
  David, 128
  Joseph, **105, 106, 123, 125, 128**
  Patience [Murray], 105, 128
  Robert, 76, 90, 91
  Sarah [Mitchel], **105, 106, 126, 128, 129**
HECKLIN, 100
HEGEMAN
  John, 72, 135, 178, 180
HENDERSON, 35
  Alexander Martin, **45**
  Elizabeth [Williams], 45
  Jane [Martin], **44, 45, 49, 54, 55, 61, 63, 65, 67,** 191, 192, **194 - 197,** 199
  Nathaniel, **45**
  Richard, Judge, 195
  Samuel, Dr., **45**
  Samuel, Sr., 45
  Sarah [Martin], **191, 194, 196**
  Thomas, **44, 45, 67,** 196
  Thomas, Col., 45
HEYDEN
  John, 29
HICKS
  Isaac, 76
  James, 105
HILL
  Sarah, 152
  William, 152
HIXT
  David, 12

HOGELAND
  Derrick, 70, 73, 74
  John, 73
HOOTON
  Rachel, 48, 88
HOUSELL
  John, 29
HOUSHELL
  Johannes, 29
  John, 28
HOWELL
  Benjamin, 77
  Daniel, 76 - 78, 158
  Daniel, Jr., 77
  David, 77
  Elizabeth, 77
  Hannah, 77
  Hezekiah, 78
  John, 77
  Joseph, 77
  Joshua, 77
  Josiah, 77
  Mary, 77
  Mary [Reading], 78, 79
  Phoebe, 77
  Prudence, 77
HUGHES
  Mary [Rogers], **63**
HUNTER
  Alexander, **16,** 32 - 36, **157,** 195
  Andrew, Rev., 39
  Elizabeth [Steele], **33**
  George, 32
  Isabella [Curry], 32
  James, 32
  James, Col., **35, 195, 196**
  Janet, 32
  John, **32, 33, 66, 76, 194, 197**
  Karhol, 32
HUTCHINSON, 35, 157

Isaac, 78
HUTTON, 35, 157

J

JACKSON
  Ralph, 143, 144
JAMISON
  Henry, 91
JENKS
  Charles, 128
  Eliza E. [Murray], 106
  Eliza E. M., 106
  John, 111
  Joseph, 116, 119
  Michael H., 126 - 128
  Phineas, Dr., 106, 107, 173
  Thomas, 76
  William, 118
JOHNSON
  Benjamin, 94
JOHNSTON
  Mary Oakley, 25
  Philip, **24, 25**
  Rachel [Martin], **18, 19, 23 -25**
  Samuel, Judge, 24, 25, 42
JONES
  Will, 43

K

KEITH
  Isaac, 104
KENDRICK
  Jane [Henderson], **45**
KITCHIN
  Samuel, 150
KREWSON
  Henry, 90 - 92, 97, 176

L

LACY
  Mary [Henderson], **45**
  Theophilus, 62
LAMBERT
  Thomas, 77
LARGE
  Ebenezer, 70, 71, 74
LARUE
  Daniel, **116, 118**
  Mary Ann [Mitchel], **128, 129**
LAWRENCE
  Mr., 36
LEAMING
  Thomas, Jr., 108
LEWIS, 36
LLOYD
  Thomas, 102, 120
LOCKARD, 35, 157
LOGAN
  Family, 143
  George, 172
  James, 144
LOMAX
  Catherine, 28
  William, 28
LONGSHORE, 111
  Euclydus, 76, 116, 117
LOWE
  Cornelius, 38
LUCAS
  Nicolas, 70
LUNGHOME
  Jeremiah, 143
LUNMAN
  _?_ [Hunter], **33**
LYLE, 35, 157
  Robert, 167

M

MACON
  Sarah [Madison], 188
MADISON
  Ambrose, II., 188
  Ambrose, Sr., 187
  Elizabeth, 188
  Frances, 187
  Francis, 188
  James, Jr., President, 43, 65, 188-191
  James, Sr., 43, 65, 187 - 190, 192, 197, 198, 200
  Nelly, 188
MARPLE
  David, 90, 92 - 96, 103, 111
  Mary Martin, 76, 90 - 99, 111, 124, 176
MARSDEN
  James, 188
MARTIN
  Agnes [Murray], 104, 107 - 113, 119 - 124
  Alexander, 1, 3 - 8, 10, 11, 14, 26, 27, 63, 64, 69, 132, 141, 156, 169
  Alexander Strong, 43, 44
  Alexander, Gov., 11, 12, 40, 41, 43 - 45, 50, 51, 53, 54, 58, 60, 61, 67, 68, 136, 138, 189, 191, 192, 197-199
  Ann, 18, 23
  Ann [Miller], 166
  Anne [Drummond], 14, 15, 17, 19 - 21
  Charles Alexander, 113, 120, 123, 124, 131
  Daniel, 29, 30, 69 - 71, 76, 78, 79, 89 - 91, 97, 101 -104, 107 - 123, 148, 176, 199
  Daniel, Jr., 120, 123, 124, 130, 131
  David, 26 - 28, 37, 72, 166
  Elizabeth [Doty], 26
  Elizabeth [Mason], 165 - 168
  Elizabeth [Scholl], 168
  Elizabeth [Slack], 49, 170, 175, 181, 183
  Frances, 113, 120, 122 - 127, 130, 131
  George, 4, 5
  Henry, 28
  Henry, Rev., 7, 10, 46, 72, 75, 80, 81, 90, 95 - 97, 99 - 101, 109, 133 - 135, 159, 169, 170 - 172, 175 - 179, 180 - 183, 196
  Hugh, 3, 5, 6 - 10, 7, 10, 14, 16 - 18, 25 - 31, 37 - 42, 44- 64, 69 - 72, 74, 76, 80 - 82, 86 - 89, 96, 120, 121, 132, 133, 135, 136, 138, 141, 157, 169, 175, 179, 184, 185, 193, 196
  Hugh II, 193
  James, 166
  James (Mason), 167, 168
  James, Col., 1, 3, 5 - 8, 11, 18, 24, 30 - 32, 34, 35, 37 - 40, 43 - 45, 50, 51, 53 - 57, 60 - 64, 66, 72, 121, 132, 135, 136, 141, 142, 156, 158, 169, 170, 176, 185, 192, 193, 195, 196
  James, Jr., 15, 19 - 25, 50 - 52, 54, 193 - 195
  James, Sr., 5 - 7, 10, 11, 14 - 23, 25, 39, 49 74, 133, 176, 195, 196
  Jane "Jenny", 197

Jane [Hunter], **31 - 34, 37, 38, 40, 42, 44, 45, 49, 50, 54, 55, 60, 63, 65 - 68, 184, 185, 191, 192, 194 - 197, 199**
John, 1, 2, 4, 5
John, **44**
Joseph, 26
Joseph, Col., **163**
Martha "Patsy", **18, 19, 23, 25, 50, 51, 54**
Martha [?Denny], **44**
Martha [Coughran], **3, 6 - 10,** 26, 42, 56, 69, **132, 141, 156, 158, 169, 170, 196**
Martha [Loftin] Jones, **43**
Mary, d/o Daniel, **113, 119, 120, 122, 124, 125**
Mary "Polly", **18, 19, 23, 25**
Mary [Gillam], **128**
Mary [Scholl], 168
Mary Ann, **63, 197**
Mary, d/o Thomas, II, **126, 128**
Mrs. [Caldwell] Campbell, **44**
Paul, 5
Robert, **7, 10, 39, 50, 53, 54, 55, 72, 80, 82, 86,** 121, **132 - 139, 193, 196**
Robert, Jr., **44, 67, 68**
Robert, Sr., **44, 50, 57, 60 - 63, 136, 138, 191, 192, 194, 197**
Ruth [Rogers], **43, 44, 63, 64, 192, 196, 197**
Samuel, Col., **44, 50, 51, 53, 61, 62, 65, 194, 196 - 198**
Sarah [Trotter], 26
Thomas, **7, 10, 17, 29 - 31, 37, 38, 46 - 49, 69 - 76, 78 - 88, 103**
Thomas, II, **113, 120, 123, 124, 126, 128, 130, 131**
Thomas, Rev., **18, 43, 44, 55, 64 - 66, 135, 136, 184, 185, 187 - 193, 195 - 200**
V., 135, 136, 193
William, 1, 2, 5
William, **5, 6, 10-13, 64**
William (Mason), **167, 168**
William Murray, **104, 120, 124, 130**
William, Lt., **18, 19, 23, 24**
MARTINE
John, 5
Thomas, 4
MARYE
James, Jr, Rev., 187
MASON, 35
Agnes, **139, 160**
Alexander, **165**
Esther [Martin], **7, 10, 31, 77, 133, 136, 138, 139, 149, 151, 156 - 164**
Francis, 7, 38, 77, 78, 98, **137, 138, 156 - 164**
Hannah, **165**
Henry, **138, 139, 160, 162, 164**
Hester, **165**
John, 156
Josiah L., **168**
Lydia, **138, 160, 164**
Martha, **165**
Mary [Van Dyke], **136, 165**
Thomas, **138, 139, 156, 160, 164**
Thomas, II, **168**
William, **139, 159, 161, 162, 164 - 166, 168**
McCRACKEN, 157
Samuel, 167
McFARREN, 35, 157
John, 167
MEASE

John, 108, 109
MERRILL
  William, 78
MIDDAUGH
  Garret, 163, 164, 166
  John, 167
  Mary [Mason], **138**, **139**, **156**, **160**, **163**, **164**
  Peter, **38**, **157**, **159 - 167**
MILLER, 35, 157
MITCHEL
  Ann [Martin], **106, 113, 120, 123, 124, 126, 128-131**
  Augustine, **123**, **128**, **131**
MITCHELL, 195
  Deborah, 152
  John, 109
  Randle, 108, 109, 199
MOODY, 35, 157
MOON, 181
  James, 101
MOORE, 35, 157
  Family, 187
  Francis, 28, 192
  Jacob, 38
  John, 38, 78
  Sarah, 28
  William, 192
MORE
  Nicholas, Dr., 156
MORRILL
  Richard, 78
MORRIS, 35, 157
  Benjamin, 41
  J., 105
  William, 41, 42
MURRAY, 195
  Emily, 106
  Francis Heaton, **105, 106, 128**

Francis, Gen., 105 - 109, 116, 117, 128
George, 108
George W., 106
George W., Jr., 106
Jane, 108
John Dormer, 106
John Dormer, Jr., 105, 106
John, Maj., 105, 108, 109, 116, 118, 199
Riselma, 104, 123
Rosalina, 107
William, 108, 109
William, II., 107

N

NAGEL
  R. C., 129
NAPIER
  Sarah [Martin], **44**
NELSON, 35, 157
New Jersey
  Hunterdon Co., Amwell, 17, 28 - 31, 37, 38, 69, 72, 74, 77, 94, 110, 157, 158, 169
  Hunterdon Co., Annandale, 7, 8, 16, 30, 38, 39, 42, 56, 121, 185
  Hunterdon Co., Clinton, 57, 89
  Hunterdon Co., Hopewell, 31, 169
  Hunterdon Co., Kingwood Plantation, 24, 54
  Hunterdon Co., Lebanon, 8, 18, 19, 22, 25, 30, 38, 39, 46, 49, 52, 54, 57, 64, 87, 121, 158, 185, 190 - 192
  Hunterdon Co., Maidenhead, 39, 77, 78, 169, 170

Hunterdon Co., Raritan River, 11, 14 - 16, 31, 71
Hunterdon Co., Ringoes, 17, 28 - 30, 74, 79, 132
Mercer Co., Trenton, 17, 77
Morris Co., Muskonetcong River, 16, 74
Newark College, 39, 72, 169
Princeton University, 18, 24, 40, 41, 43, 45, 62 - 66, 103, 104, 121, 139
Sussex Co., Greenwich, 113

NEWTON
John, 12

North Carolina
Alamance Co., Hawfields Church, 139
Mecklenburg Co., Charlotte, 44
Orange Co., Eno River, 140
Rockingham Co., Danbury, 43, 66, 67
Rockingham Co., Jacobs Creek, 66
Rowan Co., Salisbury, 60, 65, 189, 191, 198
Stokes Co., 43, 60

Northern Ireland
Co. Antrim, 33, 109
Co. Tyrone, 1-6, 10, 11, 14, 26, 32, 41, 58, 69, 109, 132, 141, 156, 169

O

Ohio
Butler Co., 167

OSBORNE
Adlai, 44

OXLEY
Henry, 29, 30, 69, 71, 78

P

PARTRIDGE
Richard, 41

PAXSON
Aaron, 155
Ann [Plumley], 152
Hannah [Blackfan], 152
Henry, 143, 152, 153
Henry, Jr., 142
Jeane, 152
Joseph, 152
Joshua, 116, 117
Mahlon, 110
Thomas, 110, 152
William, 76, 99, 101, 110

PEACE
Josh, 37, 72

PELLAR
Isaac, 144

PENN
William, 15, 34, 143, 152, 153, 156

Pennsylvania
Bucks Co., Attleborough, 120 - 122, 130, 131
Bucks Co., Buckingham Twp., 102, 142 - 144, 151, 153 - 155
Bucks Co., Coryell's Ferry, 29, 142
Bucks Co., Gregg's Mill, 72
Bucks Co., Lower Makefield Twp., 133, 164, 175 - 177
Bucks Co., Middletown, 46, 75, 76, 79, 80, 90, 91, 95 - 97, 101, 102, 110, **111**, 113, 114, 120 - 122, 124 - 128, 130, 175
Bucks Co., Newtown, 72, 76, 79, 105 - 107, 109, 110, 112, 126, 129, 169, - 175, 181

Bucks Co., Northampton Twp., 112, 128, 133, 159, 171, 172, 177, 179
Bucks Co., Plumstead Twp., 142, 143
Bucks Co., Solebury Twp., 102, 104, 141 - 146, 153, 170
Chester Co., New London Academy, 40, 133
Chester Co., Nottingham Academy, 40, 133
Forks of the Delaware, 7, 26, 27, 34 - 36, 156
Harveys, 169
Luzerne Co., 167
Northampton Co., Allegheney Creek, 36
Northampton Co., Craig Settlement, 35
Northampton Co., Easton, 26, 27, 34, 36, 164, 166
Northampton Co., Hunter's Settlement, 26, 31, 34 - 37
Northampton Co., Martin's Creek, 26, 35, 36, 37, 78, 157, 166 - 168
Northampton Co., Mt. Bethel, 26, 35, 36, 159 - 161, 163 - 165, 167, 168
Philadelphia, 27, 39, 40, 57, 108, 109, 139, 169, 190, 199
PETERS
Philip, 28
PHILIPS
Theophilus, 42
PICKERING
Hannah, 152
Joseph, 152
Sarah, 152
PICKLE
Family, 56
PIKE
Joseph, 143, 144
POWELL
Ambrose, Capt., 188
PRESTON
William, 152
PRICE
James, 77
Rachael, 125
PROUT
Ebenezer, 77

R

REA
Jane [Mason], **165**
William, **165, 168**
READING
George, 73, 74
John, Gov., 16, 17, 42, 73 - 78
John, Jr., 73
Joseph, 94, 98
REEDER
Isaac, 78
REYARSON
Marten, 37, 72
RICHARDSON
Joseph, 116, 122, 125
Joshua, 110, 111
Mary [Paxson], 122
Samuel, 110
William, 110, 119, 120, 123, 130, 131
RIGBY
Matthew, 78
RIGHTINGHOUSES
William, 77
RINGO
Cornelius, 28, 42

Philip, 42
ROBERTS
   Nicholas, 78
   Richard, 152
ROCKEFELLER
   Peter, 29
RODENBOUGH
   Herbert, 56, 57
ROGERS
   Alexander, 16
   John, Rev., 39
   Martha [Martin], **17**, **44**, **49**, **50**, **63**, **64**, **192**, **196**
   Samuel, **24**, **39**, **44**, **51**, **54**, **63**, **64**, **196**
   Thomas, 17, 54, **63**, 64
   William, 17, 20, 64
ROSENCRANS
   Elizabeth [Mason] Martin, **163**, **164**
   Jacob, 164
   Joseph, 167
ROSS
   John, 152
   Thomas, 118, 148, 152
RUCKER
   Family, 187
RUCKMAN
   Samuel, 78
   Thomas, 139
RUNKLE
   Adam, 38, 39, 56
   Jacob, 39
RUNYON
   Peter, 98
RUTHERFORD
   Steven V., 39

S

SCALES
   Peter, 100
SCARBOROUGH
   Family, 143
   Jane, 152
   John, 144, 152
   William, 144
SCHOLFIELD
   Agnes [Blackfan], **147**, **149**, **154**, **155**
   John, **144**, **152**, **154**
SCOTT, 35, 157
   Johnny, 188
   Joshua, **126**
   Susannah [Martin], **126**, **128**
SCUDDER
   John, 24
SEVERNS
   Benjamin, 38
   John, 77
   Theophilus, 20, 21,22, 42, 47, 48, 51, 52,53, 87 - 89, 93 - 95
SHARP
   Asa, 121
   Jacob, 116
   Joanna [Hager], 121
   John, 121
   Maria [Cramer], 121
   Morris, Jr., 121
   Peter, Esq., 113, 114, 121
SILLEMAN, 35, 157, 164
   Alexander, 163
   Mary [Middaugh], 163
   Thomas, 163
SIMONTON
   Ephraim, 165
SLACK
   Abraham, 170, 175

Cornelius, Sr., 175
George Loman, 101
Henry, 96, 101
James, 175
John, 46, 75, 80, 82, 86, 133, 135, 175 - 178
Slaves
  (Howell), Jack
  (Madison) Sawney, 65, 189, 190, 191, 192, 197
  (Martin) Bett, 41, 50
  (Martin) Billy, 67
  (Martin) Bram, 41, 51, 53
  (Martin) Jack, 39, 41, 50, 52
  (Martin) John, 111
  (Martin) Kate, 41, 55, 135, 136, 193, 196
  (Martin) Kit, 41, 53, 55
  (Martin) Prince, 41, 51, 53, 67
  (Martin) Rachel, 52
  (Martin) There, 67
SLOAN
  James, 108
SMITH
  Benjamin, 37, 72
  Edmund, **149, 155**
  Hannah [Blackfan], **147, 149, 154**
  John, 78
  Jonathan, **147, 149, 152**
  Richard, 70, 71, 73, 74
  Samuel, 154
  Sarah [Dawson], **147, 149, 155**
  Timothy, 98
South Carolina
  Colleton Co., Pon Pon, 11, 12
SPEAKMAN
  Randal, 143
SPRINGS
  Fanny [Henderson], **45**

STACKHOUSE
  Benjamin, 98
  David, 150
  Joseph, 76, 98, 100
STANLEY
  William, 157
STAPLER
  Edward, 127
STARR
  Jacob, 86
STEWART
  Charles, 16, 20, 21, 24
  Charles, Col., 16, 20 - 25, 109
  Walter, Col., 105, 109
STOCKDALE
  Sarah [Field], 76
STOUT
  Samuel, 42

T

TALIAFERO
  Family, 187
TATE
  Adam, 38
  Anthony, 46, 75, 80, 82, 101, 135, 171, 172, 175, 180
TAYLOR
  Erasmus, 192
  Family, 187
  Joseph, 117
TENNENT
  Gilbert, Rev., 39, 166
THOMAS
  Rowland, 192
TOMLINSON
  Kinsey B., 127
  Richard, 116 - 118
  William, 118
TRACEY

Mary [Murray], 107
TWINING
   David, 135, 180
TYSON
   Ezekiel, 128

U

USHER
   Abraham, 108

V

VAN HORNE
   Abram, 37, 72
   Gabriel, 90, 91, 99, 101
Virginia
   Albemarle Co., Slate River, Crooked Creek, 197
   Bedford Co., 35
   Buckingham Co., 35
   Orange Co., 43, 44, 64, 66, 139, 187,188, 192, 195, 197-199, 200
   Orange Co., Montpelier, 43, 44, 64 - 66, 187, 188, 191, 192

W

WALKER
   Deborah [Mitchel], **126, 128, 129**
   Phineas, **126, 129**
   Robert, **128**
WALTON
   Jonathan, 1117, 125, 131
WARNER
   John, 76, 125
   William B., 129
WARREN
   Eliza [Martin], **126, 128**
   Joseph, **126**
WASHINGTON
   George, President, 23
WAUGH
   Alexander, 192
   Samuel, 104
WELDEN
   Ely, 152
WHITE
   Alexander, 121
   Francis, 143
   Martha [Mason], **162, 164**
   William, **162, 164**
WHITEHEAD
   John, 98
WHITSON
   Thomas, 148
WILDMAN
   Abigail, 76
   Elizabeth, 76
   Jacob, 76
   James, 116, 117
   John, 76, 100, 101, 116, 117
   Joseph, 75, 76
   Joseph, III, 76
   Joseph, Jr., 76
   Martin, 76
   Mary, 76
   Rachel, 76
   Rebecca, 76
   Sarah, 76
   Solomon, 76, 116, 118
   Thomas, 76
   William, 76
WILLEMAN
   John, 86
WILLSON
   John, 42
WOODWARD

Henry, 78
WOOLSEY
   George, 77
WOOLSTON
   John, 99, 101, 118, 135, 180
WORFORD
   Joseph, 75
WYNKOOP
   Family, 170
   Frances [Murray], 106, 109
   Francis, 106
   Gerardus, 118
   Henry, 89, 91, 92, 97, 103, 105 - 107, 109, 172, 176
   John, 106
   Jonathan, 105 - 107, 109, 110

Y

YEARLEY
   Ann., 78
YEATS
   Thomas, 76
YOUNG
   Jacob, 115
   Peter, 56